Economic Development And Environment Issues

P.A. Koli

Department of Economics
Shivaji University
Kolhapur (M.S.)

SERIALS PUBLICATIONS
New Delhi

First Published- 2005

ISBN: 81-86771-66-2

Published by

Head Office : **SERIALS PUBLICATIONS**
4, B.S.S. Hall, Khyber Pass Market,
Civil Lines, Delhi–110054 (India)
Phone: 23245225
Fax: 91-11-23272135
e-mail: serials@satyam.net.in

Branch Office : *4830/24, Prahlad Street, Ansari Road,*
Darya Ganj, New Delhi-110002 (India)

Printed at : R.K. Offset Process, Delhi-32

PRINTED IN INDIA

Acknowledgements

This book is based on the research findings as well as on the theory of environment. It gives me a great pleasure to express my deep sense of gratitude to those who helped me in writing this book. I am very much thankful to Dr. R. R. Doshi, former H.O.D., Department of Economics, Shivaji University, Kolhapur, who inspired me to teach the economics of environment at the Post Graduate Level and allowed me to participate in number of National Level Conferences in the field of environmental pollution and management.

I am highly grateful to Dr. N. C. Sahu, Department of Economics (Environment unit) Berhampur University, Berhampur (Orissa), Dr. Mrs. Rajlaxmi, University of Madras, Chennai, Dr. Manomoney K. Kamraj University, Madurai, Dr. H.P. Trivedi, Sardar Patel University, V. V. Nagar Gujrat and Dr. G. K. Kadekodi (Banglore). Dr. Ms. Kanchan Chopra and Dr. M. N. Murthy of Institute of Economic Growth (Delhi) all who gave me their valuable suggestions in revising the earlier draft of the book.

I am also thankful to my wife Dr. Pushpanjali Koli for her encouragement.

I would like to place on record my sincere thanks to M/s S. K. Jha, Director, Serial Publications, New Delhi who agreed to publish this book well in time and in its present format.

Dr. P.A. Koli

Contents

1

Economic Development and Loss of Biodiversity

"So long this earth is full of nature, wild life and plants, human race is going to flourish." Charak Samhita 5th cent A.D.

"Man does not have the right to destroy what he cannot create. The human race is not an allion species to exploit it." (1) Granth sahib.

The above quotations clearly mention that universe along with its creatures belong to the Lord, and no creature is superior to any other. Human beings should not be above nature, or no one species encroach over the rights and privileges of other species. In short, human civilization depends directly and indirectly upon Bio-diversity for their basic needs such as food, fodder, fuel, fibre, fertiliser, timber, liquor, rubber, leather, medicines and several raw materials. This diversity is the condition for the long term sustainability of the environment.

As many as 500 millions myriad of species of plants, animals and microorganisms inhabited this earth since life began over 3.5 million years ago. And many of them have disappeared from the face of the earth in the normal evolutionary process, some of them have left their descendent and surviving remnants. Today there are about

30 millions species occupying this planet. However, our ignorance in this area is vast. Due to the 'struggle for existence' and the fittest survived while the others disappeared.

Form ancient time, human societies have established certain norms of social behaviour for the purpose of ensuring their survival and protection against environment pollution. The threat and emergencies for which these norms were designed originally were purely natural such as floods and dangerous animals etc. However, they are not adequate in the present day as environmental risks caused today are partly or wholly by human action or reaction with the nature such as water pollution, air pollution on dangerous man-made products. Hence it needs additional protective norms. To cope with the emerging problems of environment, a wide range of administrative and legislative measures have been taken by several nations.

UNO and Bio-diversity Protection

The United Nations Conference on the Human Environment met at Stockholm from 5 to 16th June 1972, and it has considered the common principles to inspire and guide the people of the world in the preservation and enhancement of the human environment. In all 26 principles were accepted and out of them 2 principles were regarding the protection of Biodiversity viz.

1. Principle 2: To safeguard the flora and fauna.
2. Principle 4: To wisely manage the wildlife and its habitat.

Five years ago, the nations of the world met at Rio-de Janeiro for the Earth Summit, (1992) and they made the far reaching promises to save the world's environment. The world leaders labeled it as the *"last chance to save the earth."* The *Rio Principles. Agenda, 21, the Convention on Bio-diversity and climate changed demanded global actions.*[2] We have spend twelve years so far, but unfortunately nothing has been done in this respect. This is because, no nations have sufficient money to implement environmental programmes. Ever increasing population, the poverty and the profligable life style are the main hurdles in these programmes faced by the developing countries.

Definitions of Economics and Bio-diversity

The Science of Economics is in crisis and is now questioning its own philosophic assumptions and methods. The century old reign of positivist economics, which included famous models and their versions such as neo-classical, Keynesian and Marxian have the lost track. Man has used the natural resources in unplanned manner for getting luxury and comfort. Two hundred years back, Adam Smith defined 'Economics as a Science of Wealth', and Dr. Marshall said not only wealth but welfare of the community should be basis of economics. Thus, the fathers of economics were well aware of the preservation of wealth (animal and plants). Bio-diversity is a wealth on earth. These authors were very close to the present concept of Bio-diversity. But due to industrialization, the consumption of natural resources accelerated and hence, Prof. Robbins came to the conclusion that economics is nothing but the study of problem raised due to scarcity. Scarcity of what? Scarcity of resources. What is meant by resources? The resources mean all living and non living things on the earth.

Meaning and Economic Significance of Bio-diversity

Before we study the economic significance of bio-diversity, let us see the meaning of it. Bio-diversity refers to any living organism and its natural habitat. It includes all plants, animals and micro-organisms other than the cultivated plants and domesticated animals.[3]

The Bio-diversity has economic value, it balances the wild life population and maintains food chains and natural cycles. The conservation of living resources has three special objectives;

(i) To maintain essential ecological process and life supporting systems.

(ii) To preserve the diversity of species or the range of genetic material found in the world's organisms.

(iii) To ensure sustainable utilization of species and eco-systems which support millions of rural communities as well as major industries.

A forest is a special biotic community of immense value to the environment and living begins. Forests and woodlands provide a large number of products of economic importance such as timber, firewood, oils, etc. Forest animals provide meat, silk, honey, lac, ivory, hide and skin.

Forest protects the soil from rapid erosion, prevent quick run off water and sustain springs and streams through the year, control air pollution and provide shelter to a large number of animals. (4)

Environmental Economic Value of a Big Tree

Tree provides us timber, fuel wood, food, fodder fertiliser fibre and raw materials for industries. But apart from these, the trees play important role in environment conservation. Environmental economic value of a tree was first estimated by Prof. Das in 1981.

A fully grown medium sized tree of 50 years age releases about 11 ton of oxygen every year and its economic value is about Rs.5,000/- per year and Rs.2,50,000/- totally for fifty years. Trees help to purify the air and it keep pollution free atmosphere and its economic value per year is about Rs.10,000/- and Rs.5,00,000/- for fifty years. Trees help to check the soil erosion and conserve the valuable fertile soil. Economic value of this mechanism for one year is about Rs.5,000/- and Rs.2,50,000/-for fifty years. Trees help to regulate water cycle in the nature and also help to retain humidity in the atmosphere. Its economic value per year is about Rs.6,000/- and Rs.3,00,000/- for fifty years. Trees give shelter for birds, insects, mammals, other plants and several microorganisms. Its economic value per year is about Rs.5,000/- and Rs.2,50,000/- totally for fifty years. Tree provides fodder and food for animals. Its economic value per year is about Rs.1,000/- and Rs.50,000/- totally for fifty years. Environmental economic value of a single medium size tree of 50 years age is about Rs.32,000/- per year and Rs.16 lakhs totally for fifty years.

Medicinal Value of the Bio-diversity Conserved by the Indigeneous Community of World

Since ancient, time man has used the plants as a source of medicine. About 80% of the world's population relies on traditional forms of medicines largely plant based to meet health care needs. Use of plants for human and veterinary health care forms one of the oldest, richest and most diverse cultural traditions of India. India is a birth place for variety of alternative traditional medical systems. The important among them are Ayurveda, Siddha and Unani. All these systems of medicine depends on plants as a major source of medicine.

The invaluable role of the indigenous people in the conservation of the plant genetic resource is now beginning to be recognized. However, the economic benefits from the utilization of this materials seldom accrue to them. Those who have conserved bio-diversity tend to remain poor, while those who have converted such genetic diversity into commercial products through biological technology are rich. (5)

The indigenous culture has provided several "miracle plants" of immense food and medical value to the modern civilization. For example, a useless wild wheat plant grown by the indigenous community of Turkey was used to give disease resistance to commercial wheat varieties worth of 50 million annually to the US alone. The *rosy periwinkle* from the Madagascar tropical forest of the aborigines have provided the million dollar weapon to fight the childhood leukemia. The Pacific yew preserved by the indigenous communities of pacific islands gave the million dollar worth anti-cancer drug *"Taxol"* for the treatment of breast cancer. In 1990 the National Cancer Institute (NCI) of US recognized that the leaf extract *"Michellamine B"* from the plant Ancistrocladus Korupensis obtained from indigenous people of Cameroon forest in South Africa had the capacity to inhibit HIV causing AIDS. The NCL had already possess the 'patent' of this compound.

Development and Indian Bio-diversity

The tribals of India are also dwindling under the impact of industrial development and modernization. Large tribal population have been up rooted and displaced as *'ecological refugees.'* In Central India due to the construction of ambitious Tehri and Narmada Dams, under the Project Tiger Scheme indigenous people have been displaced from their original homes in India. (6) Thus; with the disappearance of the indigenous culture all over the world the bio-diversity which they conserved for centuries is also disappearing. Therefore, the knowledge of the indigenous people must also be covered under intellectuals property right, and the development activities should be always eco-friendly.

Equal Treatment to all Creatures

Man worships the animals, trees, stones, earth, water, winds, rain, sun, moon, river and ocean. He supposes that the God has created the earth and also he has created birds, animals, trees etc. and hence there is a need for cooperation and co-existence of flora and fauna. (7)

Deforestation: The Main Threat to Biodervisty

Now-a-days the main threat to the plant diversity is deforestation. Majority of megabiodiversity centres and Global Hot Spot regions are situated in developing countries. In these countries rate of deforestation is very high. Every year about 15 Lakhs hector of forest is denuded every year from India alone. World Watch Institute (WWI) put India in a dubious 10th position in maximum species loss countries. Due to high rate of deforestation about 7500 plant species are becoming rare, endangered or extinct every year from the earth. Today we are loosing at least one plant species per day from tropical forest alone. If present trend continues, about 25% higher plants will be lost in next few decades. By the year 2050 nearly 60,000 plant species (one in every four) will become extinct or endangered.

World wide loss of Biodiversity has forced the man to think seriously about his future which has resulted in establishment of many international organizations such as, International Union of Conservation of Nature and Natural Resources (UCN), World Resources Institute (WRI), Threatened Plant Committee (TPC) etc.

One can raise plantation, one can develop artificial forests but we cannot generate natural biodiversity. We cannot regenerate new biological species. So there is a need to save, protect and to conserve the plant diversity and their natural habitats, forests.

Whether Politics or Bio-diversity?

Now a days there is a threat to bio-diversity due to economic and political reasons. One can cite the example of Chilika Movement in Orissa. Chillika the largest water lagoon in Asia (1000 sq. Km.) is the home of migratory birds of 158 kinds of species, and it is an earning sources (fishing) of 192 villages. But under the name of economic development, the lake is leased to the Tatas, and the politicians are playing worst role against poor. (8) Hence, the question comes whether to save the bird, fish, fisherman or finance? In short, our urge to enhance the per capita income has caused the economic problems. The other causes can be summarized as under:

1. Pressure of population on land.
2. Industrialization and pollution.
3. Increasing rate of urbanisation and loss of agricultural land.
4. House/Building Industry and deforestation.
5. Transport Development, Railways, Roadways, Waterways.
6. Increasing demand for food and construction of big dams, canals.
7. Increasing Tourism development.

Conclusion

Thus, the cause of all economic and environment maladies is the ever increasing wants. Hence Mahatama Gandhi, said.

"We are not always aware of our real needs, and most of us multiply our wants and thus unconsciously make thieves of ourselves. He further said, "Nature can satisfy our need; but nor our greed". Therefore the Gandhian philosophy is yet much useful to protect the bio-diversity. (9) The eco-friendly farming, social forestry, development of waste lands, tree growers cooperatives and training and education to masses population control shall be some of the remedial measure for economic development with bio-diversity and this can kill the two birds in one stone. Of course, this requires action at all levels, individual, the community and the government.

REFERENCES

1. Sinha, R.C. and Singh, D. Globe Bio-diversity INA Shree Publishers, Jaipur 1997.
2. Narain, S. and Anil Agrawal. All Talk, No Action. The Hindu Survey of The Environment 1997, p. 7.
3. Trivedi, R.N. and Roy, M. Dimensions of Safe Environment. Anmol Publications Pvt. Ltd. New Delhi 1996, p. 118.
4. Ibid Trivedi, R.N. and Roy, M.
5. Swaminathan, M.S. "The Rights of Traditional People" Lecture at the IV International Congress of Ethorobiology, Lucknow 17-21 Nov 1994.
6. Sinha, R.K. and Singh, Dalbir. Global Biodiversity, INA Shree Publications Jaipur, 1997, pp. 156, 57.
7. Joshi, M.V.: Environmental Economics, Atlantic Publishes, New Delhi, 2001.
8. Sheth, Pravin: Environmentalism, Politics, Ecology and Development; Ravat Publications, Jaipur 1997, p. 250.
9. Sharma, Rashmi: Gandhian Economics, a Human approach, Deep and Deep Publications, New Delhi 1997, p. 21.

2

Deforestation: Measures to Conserve and Promote Forestry

Introduction

The term forest is derived from the Latin word FORIS, means outside the walls of a house or town, etymologically, forest is a vast fallow tract of terrain covered with trees and underwood. Forest includes tree lots, grasslands, fodder and fuel plantations, shelter belts, strips and avenue plantations, etc. (1)

Ecologically, forest is not the result of only trees and other plants by chance but it is a gradually developed community of complex organism with specific biological laws.

Significance of Forests in Economy

Forests of India are in a critical stage. Due to rapid growth of population and mass poverty, forests are deteriorating day by day. This rate of deforestation is 2 hector per minute and 1% of the total land surface is left bare every day. According to recent report, the rate of deforestation in the world has been estimated to be between 25-55 hectares per minute. Now actual figure of forest is hardly from 16% to 23% of the total land area of the country, against the prescribed forest of 33% to maintain a good ecological balance in the country. In prehistoric times, people had not started to clean forest to make rooms for their cities, farms and factories. About 60% of the earth land area was forested. Now Japan is the only country where 66% of area is covered by forest in Asia region. As a result of excess deterioration many problems like; (1) Soil erosion, (2) frequent flood and drought, (3) irregular rain fall, (4) extremity of climate, etc. become a common phenomena in a country. About 39.34% of the total crop areas are affected by water and wind erosion, and it leads to low agricultural production, low per capita income and hamper in the process of economic development of the country. Hence a systematic planning and management of forests is strongly needed to increase forest area.

The forest management practices of ancient times highlighted the environmental role of forests. The Kautilya's Arthashastra indicates that during those days great importance was given for the preservation of forests and wild life. Elephants were captured from the forest and used in the army. The Aryan civilization was cradled in forests and Rishis who evolved the Hindu philosophy, lived in forests. They meditated in peace and serenity of forests. Rishis had their ashrams in the midst of the forest.

The vast variety of flora and fauna which represent the remarkable biological diversity and genetic resources of the state can be saved along with forest development. Afforestation programmes need to be stepped up to outplace the rate of denudation and to prevent damage to fragile ecosystem. During the last two-three decade, forestry has become an important part of efforts to promote and support rural development. Increasing forest cover would create additional rural employment and fulfill the basic needs of the rural community such as fuel, fodder, fruit, fibre, timber, organic manure and other produce traditionally derived from forest besides protecting fragile and irreparable eco-system of the state. (2)

Income and Employment Linlkages of Forests in India

The value of forestry outputs has registered about 7.98% growth rates on nominal terms. Income from forestry sector measured in term of GDP was Rs. 32 billion in 1980-81, which registered an increase to Rs. 78 billion in 1990-91, but in real terms it increased to Rs. 29 billion. The compound growth rate of forestry GDP was 9% in nominal terms and (-) 1% in real terms. About 90% of value of output from forestry activities is being converted in to value added by this sector. (3)

It is estimated that the forestry sector directly generates employment to a tune of about 36 million persons per year. Comparable estimation from 1991 census for occupation-wise main workers in India were 186 million in agriculture and allied activities, 35.5 million in mining and manufacturing, and 57.2 million in service sector. Out of agricultural workers, 107.1 million were cultivators and the rest (79 million) were agricultural workers including those employed in forestry. Therefore, employment potential in forestry sector can be said to be quite significant in the Indian context. (4)

Forest as a Resource

Forest is considered as a resource, and this resource is a set of natural elements, which support human existence. The various uses and abuses are decreasing the quality of natural resources. The “resource” has become the “source” and it is used repeatedly by man for his needs. Today the scene is frightening. Forests are being denuded, lakes are filled up for development, villages are devastated, cities are overbuilt and the air we breath is polluted with increase in carbon dioxide, sulpherdioxide etc. factories, mining activities, vehicles we travel in and the house we live in are all contributing to the disaster. The post 1991 economic policies of the Government of India and invitation to foreign concerns to enter in industries in the form of "Joint Ventures" has led to further disaster. To avoid the above impending suicidal activity one and all should resolve and resort to;

1. Stop denudation of forest.
2. Help to conserve the forest.
3. Ensure proper pollution controls in industries, sewage handling, etc.
4. Check vehicular emissions of injurious gases.
5. Abide the rules and laws of environment.

It is the only earth we have to save, care and share is the slogan to be implemented, not by lip service, but by dedicated, and collective efforts. The Stockholm Conference on Human Environment (1972) sounded as a catalyst to focus the attention of mankind to the deteriorating quality of the environment, demographic expansion, over exploitation of natural resources and developmental projects with least concern for sustainability and conservation have greatly affected the quality of environment. Our industries had only thought of the luxury of human being and they never cared about the animal, bird, fly, etc.

Present Position of Forests in India

One of the most important factors in the environment is the quality of soil. How much of it is used for cultivation? How much is degraded? What is the forest cover? What is the current rate of deforestation? The last few decades, prior to the 1990s, have witnessed deforestation of millions of hectares, as State Governments were happy to divert forests for all kinds of development and commercial purposes. The thick forests are becoming thin and mixed forests are becoming single-species. Table 1, 2 and 3 gives statistics on some of these variables in India. Deforestation continues in most states, though few states have increased forest cover.

Table 1: Extent of Dense Forest, Open Forest and Mangrove in 1997 Assessment

State/UT	*Dense Forest*	*Open Forest*	*Mangrove*	*Total Forests*	*Per capita (ha)*
Andhra Pradesh	23,048	19,859	383	43,290	0.07
A.P.	54,155	14,447	-	68,602	7.93
Assam	15,548	8,276	-	23,824	0.11
Bihar	13,300	13,224	-	26,524	0.03
Delhi	16	10	-	26	NIL
Goa	995	252	5	1,252	0.11
Gujarat	6,337	5,520	991	12,578	0.03
Harayana	370	234	-	604	NIL
H.P.	9,560	2,961	-	12,521	0.24
J & K	11,020	9,420	-	20,440	0.26
Karnataka	24,854	7,546	3	32,403	0.07
Kerala	82,745	1,880	-	10,334	0.04
M.P.	23,622	48,450	-	1,31,195	0.20
Maharashtra	4,937	22,397	124	46,143	0.06
Manipur	4,044	12,481	-	17,418	0.95
Meghalaya	4,438	11,613	-	15,657	0.88
Mizoram	3,487	14,427	-	18,775	2.72
Nagaland	26,101	10,734	-	14,221	1.18
Orissa	511	20,629	211	46,941	0.15
Punjab	3,690	876	-	1,387	0.01
Rajasthan	2,423	9,663	-	13,353	0.03
Sikkim	8,676	706	-	3,129	0.77
Tamil Nadu	1,819	8,367	21	17,064	0.03
Tripura	22,958	3,727	-	5,546	0.20
U.P.	3,557	11,036	-	33,994	0.02
West Bengal	6,520	2,669	2,213	8,349	0.01
A & N Islands	6	127	966	7,613	2.71
Chandigarh		1	-	7	NIL
Dadra & Nagar	159				
Haveli	-	45	-	204	0.15
Daman & Diu	-	3	-	3	NIL
Lakshadweep*	-	-	-	-	NIL
Pondicherry	-	-	-	-	NIL
Total	**367,260**	**261,310**	**4,827**	**633,397**	**0.07**

Source: The Hindu Survey of the Environment 98.

Table 2: Geographic area, Recorded Forest Area and Actual Forest Cover of Various States/Uts (sq. km.)

States/UT	*Geographic*	*Recorded Forest*		*Forest Cover*	
		Area	*Per cent*	*Area*	*Per cent*
Andhra Pradesh	275,068	68,814	23.20	43,290	15.7
A.P.	83,742	51,540	61.54	68,602	81.9
Assam	78,438	30,708	39.15	23,824	30.4
Bihar	173,877	29,226	16.81	26,524	15.3
Delhi	1,483	42	2.83	26	1.7
Goa	3,702	1,424	38.46	1,252	33.8
Gujarat	196,024	19,393	9.89	12,578	6.4
Haryana	44,212	1,673	3.78	604	1.4
H.P.	55,673	35,407	63.60	12,521	22.5
J & K	222,235	20,182	9.08	20,440	9.2
Karnataka	191,791	38,724	20.19	32,403	16.9
Kerala	38,863	11,221	28.87	10,334	26.6
M.P.	443,446	154,497	34.84	131,195	29.6
Maharashtra	307,690	63,842	20.75	46,143	15.0
Manipur	22,327	15,154	67.87	17,418	78.0
Meghalaya	22,429	9,496	42.34	15,657	69.8
Mizoram	21,081	15,935	75.59	18,775	89.1
Nagaland	16,579	8,629	52.04	14,221	85.8
Orissa	155,707	57,184	36.73	46,941	30.1
Punjab	50,362	2,901	5.76	1,387	2.8
Rajasthan	342,239	31,700	9.26	13,353	3.9
Sikkim	7,096	2,650	37.34	3,129	44.1
Tamil Nadu	130,058	22,628	17.40	17,064	13.1
Tripura	10,486	6,292	60.01	5,546	52.9
U.P.	294,411	51,663	17.54	33,994	11.5
West Bengal	88,752	11,879	13.38	8,349	9.4
A & N Islands	8,249	7,171	86.93	7,613	92.3
Chandigarh	114	31	27.19	7	6.1
Dadra & Nagar Haveli	491	203	41.34	204	41.5
Daman & Diu	112	N.A.	N.A.	3	2.7
Lakshadweep*	32	N.A.	N.A.	Nil	Nil
Pondicherry	493	N.A.	N.A.	Nil	Nil
Total	**367,263**	**765,210**	**23.28**	**633,397**	**19.27**

Source: The Hindu Survey of the Environment 98.

Table 3: Comparative Account of Forest Cover of State/UT 1997 Assessment Change (sq. Km.)

State/UT	*1995 Assessment*		*1997 Assessment*		*Change*
	Data Period	*Forest Cover*	*Data Period*	*Forest Cover*	
1	*2*	*3*	*4*	*5*	*6*
Andhra Pradesh	Oct. 89 $	47,112	Oct. 93	43,290	-3,822
A.P.	Dec. 91-Nov. 92	68,621	Nov. 94 Nov. 95	68,602	-19
Assam	M-D. 91 N-D. 92	24,061	D. 93, Apr-Nov. 94	23,824	-237
Bihar	Nov-Dec. 92	25,561	Nov-Dev. 94	26,524	-37
Delhi	Oct-Nov. 92	26	Oct-Nov. 94	26	Nil
Goa	Jan. 92	1,247	Dec. 93-94	1,252	5
Gujarat	Oct-Nov. 92	12,320	Oct-Dec. 94	12,578	258
Haryana	Oct-Nov. 92	603	Oct-Nov. 92	604	1
H.P.	Oct. 92-Nov. 93	12,501	Nov. 94-Nov. 95	12,521	20
J & K	Oct-Nov. 92	20,433	Nov. 94-95	20,440	7
Karnataka	Dec. 91-Jan. 92	32,382	Dec. 93-Jan. 94	32,403	21
Kerala	Nov. 93 & 94	10,336	Dec. 95	10,334	-2
M.P.	Oct-Nov. 92	135,164	Oct-Nov. 94	131,195	-3,969
Maharashtra	Oct-Nov. 92	43,843	Oct-Nov. 93	46,143	2,300
Manipur	Nov. 91 & 92	17,558	Dec. 93-Feb. 94	17,418	-140

Table 3: Contd...

1	2	3	4	5	6
Meghalaya	Mar-Nov. 91	15,714	Dec. 93	15,657	-57
Mizoram	Feb. Apr. Nov. 92	18,576	Dec. 93-Oct. 94	18,775	199
Nagaland	Nov. 92	14,291	Dec. 93-Oct. 94	14,221	-70
Orissa	Nov. 91	47,107	Oct-Nov. 93	46,941	-166
Punjab	Oct-Nov. 92	1,342	Oct. 94-Jan. 95	1,387	45
Rajasthan	Oct. 92-Nov. 93	13,280	Nov-Dec. 94	13,353	73
Sikkim	Nov-Dec. 93	3,127	Sep. 94	3,129	2
Tamil Nadu	Feb-Apr. 92	17,045*	Mar. 94	17,064	19
Tripura	Feb. 92	5,538	Dec. 93	5,546	8
U.P.	Oct-Dec. 92	33,986	Oct-Dec. 94	33,994	8
West Bengal	Nov. 91	8,276	Oct-Dec. 93	8,439	73
A & N Islands	Jan. 93	7,615	Dec. 94	7,613	-2
Chandigarh	Oct-Nov. 92	7	Oct-Nov. 94	7	Nil
Dadra & Nagar Haveli	Oct-Nov. 92	204	Oct-Dec. 94	204	Nil
Daman & Diu	Oct-Nov. 92	3	Oct-Dec. 94	3	Nil
Lakshadweep*	-	-	-	-	-
Pondicherry	-	-	-	-	-
Total		**638,879***		**633,397**	**-5,482**

Note: *An area of 721 sq. km. of tea gardens earlier shown as forest cover has been excluded from the forest cover.

$ Corresponds to 1993 assessment.

Source: The Hindu Sruvey of the Environment 98.

Table one reveals the following things;

1. The Mangrove forests, which are salt tolerant exist only in 09 states, The highest area covered by this forest was in West Bengal, Gujarat and A and N, Island. Of course, its percentage to total forest was negligible i.e. 0.76. Efforts to increase area under this category of forest is possible only in 09 states. Such forests can save the land from sea water.
2. The area under dense forests, which is very significant from climate point of view is rather satisfactory. The area under this category falls 57.98% out of total forests, while open forest consists of 41.26% only. But for practical purpose, the forest in this category can be taken as degraded forest.
3. The per capita average availability of [all types] forest was highest in Arunachal Pradesh [7.93 hector], followed by Mizoram [2.72] A and N Islands [2.71], while lowest per capita availability of forest was in Andhra Pradesh [0.07] & Karnataka [07], West Bengal [0.01] and Punjab [0.01].

The data shows that Gujarat and Maharashtra's per capita availability of forest was very low i.e. 0.03 and 0.06 hectors respectively, which is lower than the area fixed by the national Forest Policy of 1988, which says that "The existing forests and forest lands should be fully protected and their productivity should be improved" has remained only in black & white. (5)

Table 2 shows the geographic area, recorded forest area and actual forest cover of various states/Union Territories. The all India data shows that out of the total geographic area 23.28 per cent area is recorded as forest;

however the actual forest cover is 19.27 per cent; which is less than the required percentage of 33.

If we look into the statewise position of forest, we found that maximum recorded forest was available in states like A and N. Islands, Mizoram, Manipur, H.P. Arunachal Pradesh, Tripura etc. All these states are in eastern part of India and minimum forest cover was found in Delhi, Haryana, Punjab, Rajasthan, J&K, Gujrat and West Bengal. Gujrat and Maharashtra was having the forest cover of 9.89 and 20.75 per cent respectively. Table also shows the actual statewise forest cover in assessment year 1997. The actual forest cover in all the states was less than the recorded forest. Thus, this shows that situation of forests in India is not satisfactory.

Comparative Account of Forest in India

Table 3 gives an account of comparative position of forests in the year 1995 and 1997. The table shows the change in forest cover in sq.km. It is happy thing that the forest in the states like Maharashtra, Gujarat, Mizoram, H.P., Karnataka, Punjab, Rajasthan, Tamil Nadu and West Bengal. Tripura and U.P. have shown an increasing trend to some extent in 1997; as compared with the year 1995 but thc forest cover in the States like Andhra Pradesh, Arunachal Pradesh, Assam, M.P., Orissa has shown decreasing trend. The all India figures show that forest area of 5482 sq.km. has been decreased in 1997 as compared with the year 1995. This shows that all our efforts of forestation and tree plantation have failed to achieve the target; on the other hand the rate of deforestation seems faster than the afforestation.

Looking to the Future

Having regard to the present state of forests in India and the big gap between the demand for and the supply of forest products, it is essential to involve the people of every block in the development of forest. Mass media will have to be harnessed to promote an awareness of the rate of trees plantation for human welfare. Universities and schools can play an important role in this direction. A division of Forestry Extension should be set up at the Forest Research Institute, Dehara Dun.

In addition to strengthening and expanding the on-going programmes in forestry research, education and development; the following four programmes should be made effective.

1. Tree for Every child Programme

This programme envisages the promotion of school forestry programmes based on the interest of the children themselves in the trees of their choice. Each school can be provided seedlings. The each child can plant and protect one or more trees in their homes, school premises and public places. The trees of horticultural, floricultural and fuel value can be planted.

2. Eco-Development Force

An eco-development Force consisting of ex-servicemen will be formed for the purpose of restoring damaged hill eco-systems through afforestation and soil conservation.

3. Eco-Development Camps

The students from different collages can undertake and extensive tree plantation work in suitable areas such as hills, deserts and coastal regions. The NSS and NCC camps can help in this respect.

4. Agro-Forestry Programmes

Forestry Departments and the Indian Council of Agricultural Research has jointly undertaken agro-forestry research in order to develop suitable systems of land management; which involve the integration of sericulture with horticulture, agriculture, animal husbandry.

The above programmes are being undertaken under the National Rural Employment Project, and this will help to arrest the degradation of forests, build the ecological infrastructure necessary for sustainable development. (6)

Can Environmental Movements Conserve Forests?

Environmental movements which are an organized social activities consciously can be directed towards sustainable use of natural resources. Such movements aims at halting environment degradation. The movements have expressed their descent protest or agitation by starting movement against anti-environmental situations that emerge during the process of development. They have influenced the process. However, they are not antidevelopment movements. Some of the notable movements may be worth to mention. They are Chipaco, Appiko, Teri Dam Vishnuprayag Dam (Valley of Flowers) Save Silent Valley. Anti Narmada Dam Movements, etc.

The leader of Chipco, Ms. Mirben, a close disciple of Gandhi has traced the links between deforestation and water crisis. The government has also accepted that the large scale erosion and floods were the unintended result of what was called, development deforestation, road building, dams, and mining in the mountain catchments. In western ghats, in the Uttar Kannada region of Karnataka, the Chipco Movement has inspired villagers to start Appiko Movement. Appiko became a replica of the Chipaco in the South. Here, the destruction of forest was caused by commercial interest for obtaining timber. Natural forests were felled by the contractors which lead to soil erosion and drying up perennial water resources. Therefore, people demanded ban on felling of green frees. The protest within forest continued for 38 days. In the beginning the government ignored the people's sentiments, but after the visit of the forest officers and experts, the people's demand was accepted. The same situation has emerged in other parts of Karnataka [Western Ghat] state.

Thus, one can conclude that the environmental Movements has succeeded in its objectives. Chip-Appiko can be said as the Gandhian way of mobilization of people for a sustainable society in which neither man nor nature exploit or destroy each other. As Vandana Shiva observes, "It marked the beginning of this civilisational response to the threat of human survival." (7)

Conclusion

The above discussion shows that the forests in India are in a critical stage. Due to rapid growth of population and mass poverty forests are deteriorating day by day. Though the forests were regarded as holy thing in the Aryan civilization, yet it was lost sight of in the regime of British period. The British as well as the Indian Kings also used the forest for game hunting. What remains has over the years been exploited to meet the timber and fuelwood requirement. (8) Afforestation programmes are not keeping space with the denudation and hence the eco-system has came in to danger. The position of forest is not satisfactory. The comparative study shows that few states are having the minimum required level of forest cover but majority of states are without the required level of forest. This shows that all over India our efforts of forestation and tree plantation have failed. Having regard to the present state of forest and the big gap between demand and the supply, it is essential to involve community (tribal and village) in the development of forest. The forest laws and forest officials can also play an important role. Because, *the will of the people and the power is essential*; otherwise there is the threat to human survival.

REFERENCES

1. Rajalakshmi, N. and Birundha, D. (1994). Quoted in Environomics, Allied Publisher Ltd. (Madras) p. 31.
2. Singh, L.R. (1997). Social Forestry and Forest Development Planning. Daya publishing House, Delhi p. V, VII.
3. Kadekodi, G.K. and Ravindranath, N.H. (ed) (1996). Environment and Development, Rawat Publication, Jaipur. p. 119.
4. Kadekodi, G.K. and Ravindranath, N.H. Ibid 123.
5. Trivedi, P.R. Sudarsham IC N. (1996). Forest Management. Discovery Pub. House, New Delhi, p. 221.
6. Desai, Vasant (1990). A Study of Rural Economics. Himalaya Publishing House, Bombay, pp. 85, 86.
7. Sheth, Pravin (1997). Environmentalism: Politics, Ecology and Development. Ravat Publication, Jaipur.
8. Das, Priya (1997). Forest conservation, The Hindu Survey of The Environment, Chennai, p. 189.

3

Industrialisation, Population and Environmental Issues

Introduction

In the modern age of science and technology the quality of our environment is deteriorating. Industrialization, urbanization, and the consequent depletion of natural resources are leading to an exhaustion of non-renewable capital assets. The deteriorating quality of the environment and the consequent imbalance and disruption in the ecological relationship has become a matter of an ever increasing concern throughout the world. One can agree at a certain minimum standard of living to the bulk of the humanity particularly in the third world countries which is below the poverty line but there does not seem to be any justification for limitless luxuries and fanciful goods. There is no definition of enough available in modern literature on economic growth.

The main driving forces behind the exponential growth are the People, Production, Power, Places and Pollutants. Population when unchecked, increases in a geometric ratio, while subsistence increases only in an arithmetic proportion. This was stated by Thomas Malthus in 1798. In consideration with space and time, the present situation of human growth is alarming in India. There is a correspondingly intensive and consistent demand on the utilization of the country's total available water, soil and space. In the present chapter, an attempt has been made to provide glimpses of some of the economic problems created due to increasing population and industrial development in Ichalkaranji city (Kolhapur District) of Maharashtra.

History of Ichalkaranji City

Ichalkarnji city which is known as 'Manchester of Maharashtra', once upon a time was a small traditional village just like other villages in the district. But the village began to develop when it came into the princely state under the 'Jhagirdari' of late Shri. Vankatrao Ghorapade in 1739. The village was converted in Municipal Council and its population was at 7000 only. The village was having handlooms and traditional agriculture. There were no cash crop such as sugar cane as we find today. Thus the village economy was based on barter system with all the castes. The annual average rainfall in this area is generally up to 700 m.m.

Textile Industry in Ichalkarnji City

As stated earlier, the main forces behind the growth of Ichalkarnji city was increasing rate of industrial development and population pressure. Table 1 provides an idea of the industries in the city.

Almost all the four industrial units require water. However, cotton processing and sizing units require more water. Each processing units require about 5000 liters of water daily. The used water is left loose in the sewerage which directly goes to the river water. The power looms not only create water pollution, but they are also subject to air and sound pollution. The peace of the city had gone long back due to the monotonous sound. It is pitiable that out of 100 processing units, not a single unit had its waste water treatment plant. Neither the government authorities

Table 1: Types of Industries in Ichalkarnji City in 2000

Sr. No.	*Type*	*Total No. of Units*	*Workers engaged*
1.	Spinning Mills (small and medium)	35	12,000
2.	Cotton Processing	100	4,000
3.	Sizing	152	4,000
4.	Power Looms	more than 1,00,000	55,000
	Total		**75,000**

nor the Municipal Council have taken a note of these harmful industries. Should have been each sizing unit its waste or the effluent treatment plants there would be no water borne diseases. At present the waste water generated by the above textile units is estimated as constituting 10-15 per cent of the total city waste water. In the summer season the river has often no water and hence all the waste water remains in the river waiting for rain water. This situation also causes water pollution to the villages whose drinking water schemes are based on the Panchaganga river.

The table also shows that out of the total population 23 per cent population consists of workers and their family members, hence the city is known as 'workers city'.

Population Pressure

Increasing urbanization is serving as an index of frustration and an indicator of the potential explosiveness in urban slums. One can conclude that any increment in urban population will lead to a further deterioration in the quality of urban life. The major findings of the Global Report 2000, submitted to the President of United States of America are:

"Serious stresses involving population resources and environment are clearly visible ahead. Despite greater material output, the third world's people will be poorer in many ways than they are today."(2). The table 2 gives the population increase in Ichalkarnji city through the years.

Table 2: Growth of population in Ichalkaranji city, from 1911 to 2001

Census year	*Total Population*	*Decadal growth*
1911	9,245	—
1921	10,240	10.76
1931	11,904	16.25
1941	18,271	53.48
1951	27,475	50.37
1961	50,954	85.45
1971	86,872	70.49
1981	1,61,636	86.06
1991	2,14,835	32.91
2001	2,57,600	19.90

Source: Census Handbooks of Kolhapur District.

The above table shows the decadal growth in population during the last 95 years. The population of city has doubled during 30 years (1911 to 1941) and again in 1971 to 1987. If we consider the growth in population from 1991 to 2001, this shows that population has increased by 19.90 per cent. Thus, the population growth in the city was alarming from 1941 to 1981. After that due to slackness in textile industry, few workers have left the city. The growth rate was high due to the growth in small scale industries. The city was not only having the textile industries, but also engineering industries. The city is very close to Karnataka state and hence many landless laboures rushed to the city as a job seekers.

The city population is not only increasing but the share of unproductive population is also more. The Municipal Election (1996) data shows that the share of working population above the age of 18 years (voters) was 46.48 per cent. The increasing and unproductive population puts the pressure on housing, roads and transport, drinking water and sanitation, there by increasing the cost of development. The increasing population has also led to the formation of slum areas. The city is having 22 slums areas wherein about 15000 population (4.61%) is residing. The city is also not getting safe water. The foregoing discussion gives the water condition of the city.

Table 3: Pollutants in the water at different places in Panchganga River; 1998

Sr.No.	*Parameters*	*Values*	
		Waliwade (Kolhapur)	*Ichalkaranji*
1.	PH	7.19	7.30
2.	Cloride	32.00	60.00
3.	Amonia	0.12	00.27
4.	Nitrate	0.35	1.28
5.	Permanent Hardness	—	0.80
6.	Solids	200	320
7.	Iron	0.3	0.3
8.	Florida	0.2	0.2

Note: Nitrates and Florida causes serious injuries to health.

The distance between the village Waliwade and Ichalkarnji is about 25 kms., and the river Panchaganga flows from Waliwade to Ichalkarnji and hence all the parameters found in water at Waliwade seems less. The normal PH value of drinking water should be 7.7; however, it was 7.30 at Ichalkarnji from where the city lifts its drinking water. All the other minerals were present in excess. This shows that the quality of drinking water of the city is not hygienic as a result of this the city is facing the frequent water borne diseases.

Water Pollution and Epidmics Diseases in Ichalkarnji City

As the quality of drinking water of Ichalkarnji city is deteriorating; the city is facing the problems of epidemics acute health problems. This situation also leads to a chronic gastroenteritis illness symptoms in very large number of individuals. Millions of man-hours are estimated to be lost due to these diseases. The table 4 reveals the disease wise patients suffered and deaths during the year 1990 to 1996.

The table 4 shows every year the city had faced the problem of water borne diseases. The average annual patients of gastro (475) dysentery (320) were more, and some years there were deaths also. Jaundice is also one of the common epidemics which has affected the citizens. If we think from the expenditure side of such disease it will be seen that patient has to take rest for months together as well as Municipal Council and the patient himself has to bear the cost of medicine and health care. This is sheer waste. The Municipal council is spending about Rs. 25 lakhs per year on such expenditure. Apart from the Municipal hospitals there are about 15 indoor private hospitals where the patients take treatment.

The socio-economic impact of the disease is huge, because diseases like typhoid survivors take several months to recover and resume work. The WHO Report, 1996 says that "Almost half the world's population suffers from diseases associated with insufficient or contaminated

Table 4: Distribution of Patients As Per Different Water Borne Diseases from 1990 to 1996

Year	*Diseases*							
	Jaundice		*Gastro*		*Dysentery*		*Typhoid*	
	AFF	*D*	*AFF*	*D*	*AFF*	*D*	*AFF*	*D*
1990	54	01	369	0	97	0	179	01
1991	36	01	294	0	131	0	220	01
1992	51	00	1203	3	905	1	162	01
1993	32	00	1090	0	663	0	83	01
1994	30	01	43	1	264	0	135	01
1995	27	00	42	1	84	0	48	01
1996	39	00	290	0	98	0	167	01
Total	269	03	3331	05	2292	01	994	07
%	3.93	—	48.73	—	32.80	—	14.54	—
Average per year Number patient	38	—	475	—	320	—	42	—

Note: AFF = Affected Number.
D = Death Number.

water and is at risk from water – borne and food borne diseases. Their vital importance as a public health problem is often overlooked, because their true incidence is difficult to evaluate and severity of their health and economic consequence is often not fully understood."(3)

The above table shows that the annual cost of sanitation of the city for the year 1996 was Rs. 3,18,82,000/-. This shows that average per head annual cost of sanitation comes about Rs.95. Yet 80% of the people surveyed were dissatisfied about the performance of the sanitary department. (4) Such costs are met through the

Table 5: Annual Cost of Sanitation on Employees and Vehicles in 1996-97

Sr. No.	*Particulars (Posts / vehicles)*	*No. of Employees*	*Per Head Monthly Salary Rs.*	*Annual Cost Rs.*
1.	Chief sanitary inspector	01	7000	84,000
2.	Sanitary Inspectors	10	6000	7,20,000
3.	Malaria Inspector	01	6000	72,000
4.	Sweepers/Workers	700	3500	29,40,000
5.	Vehicles (owned)	16	200	11,68,000
6.	Vehicles (Hired)	06	200	4,38,000
	Total	—	—	**3,18,82,000**

different sources of revenues collected by the Municipal Council. As mentioned earlier, the city was producing daily Rs. 2.5 Crores worth of textiles and Rs. 0.5 Crores of other products. We can roughly estimate that the citizens were earning annually about (Rs.3cr. X 312 days = 936) Rs. 936 Crores. Though we cannot measure the exact cost of development of the city yet one can roughly estimate that about 34.06 per cent of the total annual incomc of the city is being spent on single item like sanitation.

Cost of Safe Water for Ichalkarnji City

At present the guidelines for safe (quality) drinking water have been given by two agencies Indian Council of Medical Research and the Indian Standards Institution (ISI). The latter agency has given a variety of standards for allowable levels of water quality variable for different types to water uses and waste water disposal practices.

National Standards and Minimum Cost of Pollution Control

With regards to industries, the Central Board for Prevention and Control of Water Pollution, has set up

Minimum National Standards (MINAS). These standards are evolved keeping in view the technological competence of the country and economic sustainability of the industry. The annual cost of control, termed as annual burden, is correlated with the annual turnover of the industry to ascertain the MINAS. For most industries, the annual burden (capital, operations, maintenance and repair costs) of pollution control never exceeds one per cent of annual turnover and for fertilizer and textiles require two per cent, distilleries five per cent. It is generally agreed that the pollution from most of industries may be contained to the desired level of 3 per cent of annual turnover which is put towards burden for water pollution control. (5)

But unfortunately no industrial units (except cooperative units) in Ichalkarnji have made an expenditure on abatement of pollution. Therefore, the Municipal Council has been compelled to bare the cost of safe water. The table 6 gives the costs so far made by the council on drinking water and drainage work.

The above table indicates that due to increasing population and industrial units, the demand for water has gone up and hence civic authority has forced to make increasing expenditure. The table shows that total as well as per head cost incurred by the Municipality on water and sanitation has increased. The per head annual average cost on water in 1966 was Rs. 20.31, which has jumped upto Rs. 555/- in 1997 showing an increase of 27 times excess than before. The same trend can be seen in case of drainage expenditure.

Conclusion

Cleanliness of the water is not the only issue; the importance of an adequate water supply for household hygine cannot be overemphasized. Washing hands after defecation and before preparing food is fundamental to controll diseases. But even if this principle is understood

Table 6: Cost of Drinking Water and Drainage in Ichalkaranji City (from 1924 to 1997)

Item	*Year*	*Rs. Spent*	*Total Amount*	*Population*	*Per Head* Cost Rs.
WATER	1924	N.A.	24 H.P.	10,240	N.A.
	1924	Engine oil cost		20,000	N.A.
		N.A.	20 H.P.		
	1956	Motor		50,954	27.34
	1966			86,872	20.31
	1975	Pump		88,000	306.67
	1994	13.93 lakhs.		2,14,835	628.39
	1997	17.64 lakhs.		3,25,000	554.77
		269.87 lakhs.			
		1350.00 lakhs.			
		1803.00 lakhs.			
DRAINAGE	1981	15.05 lakhs		1,61,636	9.31
	1994	22.06 lakhs.		N.A.	N.A.
	1997	1321.00 lakhs.		3,25,000	406.46

fully, hand washing is impossible without sufficient water. Thus improving the quality of drinking water, ensuring proper sewage disposal and providing more water for both personal and domestic hygine are the keys to the prevention or control of major scourges such as diarrhoeal diseases, cholera, typhoid, guined-worm diseases, giardiasis and jaundice. The estimates, relating to the developing world for 1995, indicate that about 25 per cent of the population do not have access to safe water and over 66 per cent lack adequate water and sanitation. (6) This is due to lack of adequate finance available with the government and local government and increasing population. For example, the Ichalkarnji city is earning per day about Rs. 3 crores from production. People have also got employment in the industries. But are citizens happy? No they are not paying fees for sanitation and water charges regularly. Though, their health condition has remained unsatisfactory on account of poor drinking water and ill sanitation. In short, only money income can not be a source of livelihood; but it is the safe environment, and one can not purchase it. Hence, we can conclude by saying. "A clean environment is a means of livelihood rather than an end."

REFERENCES

1. Sengupta, Smita – Environment and Development. (edt) by Singh Onkar, Nag. etc; Concept Publishing Company, New Delhi 1993.
2. Global Report To The President Of United States – Washington. DC. U.S.Government, 1980 p. 1.
3. WHO Report – 1996 p. 215.
4. Chougle, Anita –Project Report presented to Shivaji University, Kolhapur. 1998 p. 41.
5. Nandeshwar S.A.Abhasi, and Others – Environmental Pollution as a Consequence of Urban Development. Opcitsing Onkar nag. etc., p. 307.
6. WHO World Health Report 1996 – appeared in The Hindu Survey of the Environment 1997 p. 221.
7. Note: The data was collected from the office Record of Ichalkaranji Municipal Council Ichalkaranji through its various section by Shri. Prasad, Rande. M.A. student Eco. Of Environment, Shivaji University in 1998.

4

Co-operative Sugar Industry and Environment Protection

Introduction

India ranks second in the group of 84 countries producing sugar from sugarcane followed by Brazil. In the industrial scenario of the country, agro-based industries are assuming a predominant position. Among the agro based industries Sugar Industry ranks second in importance after textile industry. In last four decades the number of sugar factories increased from 139 to 393, an increase by 282%. The average crushing capacity per day also increased from 882 to 2,325 tonnes which shows an increase by 263%. The growth in the sugar factories was supported by increase in production of sugarcane which in turn depends on growth in area under sugarcane and yield of sugarcane per hectare. The area under sugarcane went up from 17 lakh hectares to 36 lakh hectares, while the yield per hectare improved from 30.9 tonnes to 64 tonnes. The production of sugarcane increased from 52 million tonnes to 231 million tonnes leading to an increase in the annual production of sugar from 11 lakh tonnes to 106.99 lakh tonnes. The production of sugarcane increased by 964 per cent. It is the result of diversion of cane for sugar production from gur production. (1)

Role of Co-operative Sector

Co-operative sugar factories constitute a distinct and important sector of the co-operative movement. In 2000-01, there were 436 sugar factories in the country of which 281 (nearly 65 per cent) were in co-operative sector. The co-operative sugar factories were crushing the sugarcane of more than 12 lakhs canegrower members. During 2000-01 they produced about 10,499 million tonnes of sugar which accounted for about 56 per cent of the total production in the country. The industry (private and co-operative sector) employs about 1.75 crores persons directly and indirectly, thus, playing a pivotal role in both the agricultural and industrial development. (2)

Progress of Co-operative Sugar Industry in Maharashtra

After independence Maharashtra emerged as a leading state in the sugar production. At the national level the area under cane increased from 28.35 lakh hectares to 36.18 lakh hectares showing 27.5 per cent increase in area while in Maharashtra, the area increased from 1.71 lakh hectares to 4.04 lakh hectares showing an increase by 136 per cent during the period 1965 to 1993. As a result the share of Maharashtra in total area under cane increased from 8.85 per cent to 13.38 per cent during the same period. The share of Maharashtra in sugar production also increased from 23 per cent to 31.7 per cent during the period 1965 to 1993. Eventhough Maharashtra claims only 11.17 per cent area under cane, it contributed 1/3 of total sugar production indicating the greater efficiency in sugar production.

Progress of Sugar Co-operatives in Maharashtra

Table No. 1 shows the increasing trend of growth of sugar factories in co-operative sector from the year 1950-51 to 2001-02.

During the last 3 decades the growth trend of sugar co-operatives is remarkable. As on 31st March, 2002 the

Table 1: Progress of Sugar Co-operatives in Maharashtra during the period 1950-51 to 2001-02

Year	*No. of Factories*		*Total Factories in Products*
	Co-operative	*Private*	
1950-51	01	13	14
1960-61	14	13	27
1970-71	30	11	41
1980-81	67	10	77
1990-91	93	11	104
1993-94	94	11	105
1994-95	109	11	120
2001-02	139	11	150

Source: Godava, Marathi Journal.

number of sugar co-operatives in production went upto 139. Due to the government policy the number of private sector factories are also emerging. The sugar co-operatives in Maharashtra are acting as an instrument of rural development.

Co-operative Sugar Factories and Rural Development

It is widely recognised that the co-operative sugar factories in Maharashtra have made significant contribution to the socio-economic development of the area around them. They have emerged as rural growth centres and have acted as powerful stimulants to the economic development of their command areas. They have undertaken several growth oriented activities and welfare schemes which benefit not only their members, but the society at large.

Sugar industry being an agro-based industry, is closely linked with agriculture; and any progress in agricultural production essentially depends on the quantum and availability of irrigation facilities. Almost all the sugar co-operatives in Maharashtra have put efforts for increasing the irrigation potential in their command areas through lifts, canals, construction and deepening of wells etc.. Co-operative sugar factories in Satara, Sangli, Solapur and Kolhapur districts where there is no significant canal irrigation, have undertaken several lift irrigation schemes for benefit of the farmers.

The sugar co-operative in Maharashtra have also contributed significantly for creation of basic infrastructure facilities in their command areas. For example, most of the factories have developed and maintained a network of roads in their areas for the speedy transport of sugarcane.

The factories have undertaken several schemes to encourage the farmers to go for use of improved varieties of seeds, supply of chemical fertilizers, subsidy for cane (seed), plantation, soil testing, technical guidance, research, etc. The factories extend their guarantee for crop loan advanced by village credit societies and recover the loans from the sugarcane bills of the farmers. The factories have also provided direct and indirect employment on seasonal and permanent basis. Each sugar factory on an average provides jobs of about 5000 persons on seasonal basis and to about 1000 persons on permanent basis. They have also contributed to the creation of employment opportunities by initiating several ancillaries such as dairy, poultry, repair work of bullock carts, tractors, trucks etc. Most of the sugar co-operatives have taken by-product such as paper, distilleries, chemical plants, cattle feed etc. Some of factories (Panchganga) have also accepted social responsibility by cultivating the tiny plots of backward class members (89 acres) charging only 8 per cent supervision cost and remaining amount is paid to the respective farmers. Such type of farming is practicised in six village of Bastwad, Manjarewadi, Kanwad and Dattawad etc. of Kolhapur district. This has been done with a view to make the Backward Classes free from money lenders. (3)

Different factories have undertaken different activities depending on the local needs and resources. Some of the factories have introduced 'earn and learn schemes'. Many of them have organizing community marriages also which shows the change in outlook of the rural people.

Sugar Factories and Environmental Degradation

Activities of sugar factories result into various type of wastes which ultimately lead to environmental degradation. All types of solid wastes (pressmud, sludge, bagasse, molasses, paper waste etc.) and liquid waste (waste water, waste oil, waste grease, waste chemicals) make the water and air pollution.

Some factories are not taking proper care of waste so they are making environmental pollution. But there are some sugar co-operatives who are taking proper steps to protect the environment. Out of such sugar factories, we can take the example of Tatyasaheb Kore Warana Co-operative Sugar Factory, Warananagar, Dist. Kolhapur. An in depth study of 'Warana Sugar Factory' will give the various steps taken by the factory to protect the environmental degradation.

Sugar Factory and Environmental Protection: A Case Study of Tatyasaheb Kore Warana Sugar Co-operative Ltd., Dist. Kolhapur

About Warana Sugar Co-operative Factory

Shri Tatyasaheb Kore Warana Sugar Co-operative Factory Ltd. was established on 27th September, 1955. It's registration number is G-271 and industrial licence number is L-25L-215-69 LC. It is briefly called as 'Warana sugar factory'.

During the year 1998-99 (i.e. 30-10-1998 to 6-5-1999) 12,37,475 M. tonnes sugarcane was crushed and 14,40,000 sugar bags (weight per bag is 100 Kg.) were produced in all crushing days.

Steps Taken by Warana Sugar factory in Environmental Protection

The Warana sugar factory is leading in the environment protection efforts. Though the activities of sugar factories degrade the environment, the Warana sugar factory has already taken the steps to protect the environment. The following steps were taken by the Warana sugar co-operative factory:

Steps:
1. Bio-earth compost
2. Horticulture and nursery
3. Distillery plant
4. Soil testing
5. Waste water treatment
6. Paper industry etc.

We can discuss in depth the environmental protection efforts of the Warana sugar factory.

Bio-earth Compost

Bio-earth compost project is an important step taken by the Warana sugar factory. Different effluents of the sugar factory and drawbacks into the effluent treatment plant causes ecological imbalance. Organic compounds and nutrients that are taken by sugarcane and other crops from the soil are destroyed. Bio-earth composting is unique method to complete the nature cycles, by recycling all organic matter back to the soil.

Following is the mechanical devices and equipment's involved into the process of bio-earth composting.

1. Aerotiller: Natural decomposition of solid wastes takes a long time. With Aerotiller, the decomposition is accelerated due to mechanical mixing and forced aeration of the solid wastes. Following are the features of aerotiller.

   (a) Compost processing capacity is 1000 to 1500 MT Per Hr.

   (b) Horse power of machine is 300 H.P.

   (c) Cost of aerotiller is Rs. 70 Lakhs.

2. JCB Machines: JCB machines are used for mechanical handling for formation of windrows and trimming, loading of compost. Capacity of this machine is to handle 50 MT/Hr. H.P. of the machine is 70 H.P. and cost is 11.00 (eleven) lakhs.

Financial Requirement

Following is the financial requirement of the bio-earth composting:

1.	Capital expenditure		Rs. in Lacs	
	(a)	Land development 25 Acres x Rs. 10,000 per acre	2.50	
	(b)	Technical know-how	12.50	15.00
2.	Civil work			
	(a)	Storage Tank	23.50	
	(b)	Office cum workshop	2.00	
	(c)	Fencing/ tree plantation	5.50	
	(d)	Water supply	0.50	
	(e)	Roads	1.70	
	(f)	Spentwash pipeline	3.50	36.70

3.	Mechanical/ Electrical		
	(a) Aerotiller	58.70	
	(b) Spraying system	12.00	
	(c) Pay leader	11.00	
	(d) Pumping units	1.00	
	(e) Electrification (Rs. 17,200/- per acre, for 25 Acre)	4.30	97.00
4.	Lab Equipments	1.30	1.30
		Total	150.00

Process Details:

A composting cycle is of 15 weeks which is as follows:

- 1st Week : Collection/ Hauling of materials, formation windrows and trimming.

- 2nd Week : Ist pass of Aerotiller to reduce the moisture content of PM to 50%. Inoculation of culture - Fabearth micro - 110 to stimulate the microbial activity and stops the development of odour.

- 3rd to 12th Week : IInd pass of Aerotiller. Maintenance of moisture between 50% to 60% temperature rises from 40 degree to 70 degree at the peak of composting process.

- 13th and 14th Week : Curing, Aging and Drying spentwash application is stopped at the end of 12th week and compost is allowed to cure. Water is applied during the 13th week. Until moisture stabilizes at 20 to 30%.

15th Week : Disposal of Bioearth to End user Farmer.

Example:

Material Balance: Sugar Factory

(i)	Crushing capacity	4000 TCD
(ii)	Days of operation	180 days
(iii)	Total crushing	720000 MT

(iv)	Pressmud produced (PM) (3.5%)	25200 MT
(v)	Molasses produced (4%)	30000 MT
(vi)	Moisture content of PM	70%

Distillery

(i)	Capacity	25000 Lit/Day
(ii)	SW produced per day	200 Cum/day
(iii)	Working days	300 days
(iv)	Spent wash produced	60000 Cum.
(v)	Solid content of SW	15%
(vi)	Ratio of PM: SW	1:2.22

Following culture is required for bio-earth.

(i)	Rate of culture application	0.5 of PM

Material Balance

Annual Raw Material MT	Solid contents	Total solids
PM 27,000 M.T.	30%	8100
SW 40,000 M.T. (Consumed)	15%	6000
	Total solids	14100
	(-) Gasses evolved	4425
	(CO_2; CH^+ etc.) 20%	2820
		11280
	With 30% Moisture	16114
	i.e. Annual compost produced	16000 MT

Production Cost

(A) Capital cost Total Rs. in Lacs

		Rs. in Lacs	
(i)	Civil works	36.70	
(ii)	Plant and machinery	97.00	
(iii)	Land development and know-how	15.00	
(iv)	Laboratory equipments	1.30	
		150.00	150.00

(B) Recurring expenditure	Rs.in Lacs	Total
1. Labour (a) 150 x 50 x 22	1.65	
(b) 100 x 20 x 16	0.32	
	1.97	
2. Culture 16600 Kg x 180	29.88	
3. Electricity H.P. Hrs. Days Rs./ KWH		
15 x 8 x 150 x 2.2	= 00.26	
4. *(i)* Diesel Aerotiller 40 x 6 x 150	= 02.55	
(ii) JCB machine 13 x 12 x 270 x 7.07	= 02.98	
5. Land rent 27 x 10000	02.70	
6. Interest 150 x 18%	27.00	
7. Depreciation 97 x 15%	14.55	
Civil 36.70 x 10	3.67	
8. Cost of pressmud 2,70,000 x 6	1.62	87.18

Benefits accruing to the compost users can be calculated as follows:

Thus 'Bio-earth' with a nutrient value of Rs. 3,117/- per ton is available to the farmers at substantially subsidized price, which is made through the waste from sugar factory.

Application of Compost

Bio-earth compost is applied on land as organic fertilizer. Rate of application is 4.00 MT per hectare or as directed by Agronomist.

Benefits

1. Restores the process of fertility. High micro-organic life carried by Bio-earth Humus resuscitates the badly depleted micro-organic population of the soil.
2. Protect the nutrients elements of the chemical fertilizers by absorbing same instead of being leached out. Thus, recycling of solid waste maintain the ecological balance.

Table 2: Net Worth of Compost Considering Market Value of Nutrient Contain

Sr. No.	*Particulars of Nutrient*		*% age in Compost*	*Nutrient Kg/ton of compost*	*Market rate per Kg. (Rs.)*	*Value per ton of compost*
1.	Nitrogen	N	3.13	31.03	7.21	225.67
2.	Phosphorous	P	1.67	16.70	17.26	288.42
3.	Potassium	K	3.83	38.30	6.33	242.43
4.	Sulphur	S	2.25	22.50	10.58	238.05
5.	Magnesium	M	0.77	7.70	18.48	142.29
6.	Calcium	Ca	2.96	29.60	20.00	592.00
7.	Sodium	Na	0.13	1.30	70.00	26.00
			ppm.			
8.	Iron	Fe	19500	19.50	13.20	257.40
9.	Aluminium	A	12000	12.00	20.00	240.00
10.	Manganese	Mn	417	0.417	3.30	1.37
11.	Copper	Cu	180	0.180	20.00	3.60
12.	Zinc	Ze	143	0.143	9.90	1.41
13.	Boron		47	0.047	10.00	0.47
14.	Humic Acid		8.68	86.80	10.00	868.00
						3117.00

Source: Annual Report of the Tatyasaheb Kore Warana Sugar Co-operative Sugar Factory, Warananagar (1998-99).

3. Nitrogen fixing bacteria in Bio-earth taps atmospheric nitrogen and supply it to the plant.
4. Hasten decomposition of residual poisons from toxic chemical elements coming from herbicides, insecticides as well as chemical fertilizer.
5. Improved nutrient and water holding capacity for sandy soil, hence better nutrition and crop stand.

Soil Testing

There is laboratory with the Warana sugar factory to test the soil of its farmer members. Every year about 850-900 samples of soil were tested and guidance was given to members regarding the use of fertilizers. This soil testing is good from crop productivity and control of soil pollution point of view. An application of organic fertilizers is useful in maintaining the ecological balance.

Horticulture and Nursery

There is well maintained "Warana Nursery" in the premises of Warana sugar factory, producing different plants of flowers, fruits and different type of trees which are protecting the environment as well as increasing the yield of farmers.

During the period 1998-99, following horticultural plants were produced and distributed among the member farmers by the Warana factory.

	Type of plant/ tree	No. of plants distributed
(i)	Coconut	8469
(ii)	Chikkoo	1138
(iii)	Mango (Hapus)	7236
(iv)	Guva	2065
(v)	Pomegranate	700

Source: Annual report of Warana Sugar Co-op.Factory for the year 1998-99.

Addition to above plants, 94,126 plants of Nilgiri, Suru and Tickwood were provided to member farmers to plant in their farms. Farmer members have also taken the advantages of 'State Government Horticulture Grants' to develop the horticulture farming. In addition to this the Warana Co-operative Sugar Factory has planted different trees of fruits, show and flower plants in the office premises. This plantation also helps to control the pollution.

Economics of Horticulture and Nursery

In order to know the 'Economics of Horticulture and Nursery', the average yield of per plant of different types are taken into account. The yield is highly variable factor depending upon cultivator and age of the plant, climatic condition, incidence of pests and disease and above all, on the upkeep of the plantation.

Table 3: Crude estimation of yield from planted trees by farmer members and distributed by 'The Warana Factory'

Sr. No.	*Name of the grafted and planted tree (plant)*	*Average life of the plant*	*Annual average fruits per plant*	*Market rate per fruit (assumed) (Rs.)*	*Annual yield per plant approximately (Rs.)*
1.	Coconut	80 Yrs.	50	5.00	250.00
2.	Chikkoo	25 Yrs.	2000	1.00	2000.00
3.	Pomegranate	25 Yrs.	125	3.00	375.00
4.	Guva	35 Yrs.	125	1.00	1250.00
5.	Mango (Hapus)	20 Yrs.	2050	10.00	20500.00

Note: All the estimations are crude in nature.

Source: Bose T.K. and Mitra S.K. (edited), (1990) Fruits tropical and subtropical, NAYA PROKASH Publication, Calcutta, India. and

Patil and Karale - Maharashtra til Falzade (1993), Continental Prakashan, Pune.

Crude (rough) estimation of the yield of the plantation is made in the year 1998-99 on the basis of average life of the plant, average annual fruits, market rate at present and annual average yield or revenue approximately.

Distillery Project

During the year 1998-99, in all 180 days distillery plant was in operation. By using 20881.18 M.T. molasses, the total of alcohol 51,81,184 Litres was produced by the Warana factory. The per tonne recovery rate was 288.1 Lit. in the reported period.

Waste Water Treatment

The Warana sugar factory provided full-fledged combined effluent treatment plants for three industrial units viz. sugar, paper and distillery plants. The details of effluent treatment plants are as follows:

(A) Sugar Mill Effluent

Primary treatment plant is provided in factory premises. It consists of following things:

1. 'V' Notch for measurement of flow.
2. Screens to remove coarse solids.
3. Oil and grease chamber.

After primary treatment the sugar effluent is taken to ETP for further treatment. At effluent treatment plant secondary oil and grease removal arrangement is provided. After removing oil and grease traces here sugar mill effluent is pumped into buffer tank of black liquor seal tank No. 1 for PH correction and dilution.

(B) Paper and Pulp Mill Effluent

In pulp mill all flows are segregated. Black liquor seal tank No. 1 effluent after clarification is stored into lagoon.

From storage lagoon effluent is taken to buffer tank where sugar effluent is added to black liquor seal No. 1 effluent to correct PH and dilution.

Chlorination, Hypo and Alkali Extract

This scheme is having very low BOD and large quantity after correction of PH and primary clarification the effluent is taken to dilution and disinfection to dilution tank.

Paper Machine Effluent

After primary clarification white water is taken to dilution of tank.

(C) Distillery Effluent

Spentwash from distillery after cooling tank is taken to buffer tank. Here effluent from seal tank No. 2 is added to buffer tank for correction of PH and the effluent is then taken to Bio-paq reactor. Here with the help of bacteria methane gas is generated. The generated gas is collected to common gas holder. Superenanant from Bio-paq reactor is taken to aeration tank. Part of primary digested spentwash is taken to bio-earth composting process and remaining spentwash is taken to aeration tank having 130 HP. aerators. Overflow from aeration tank is taken to secondary clarifire.

Tertiary Treatment

In territory treatment all effluent from all streams is collected and diluted with spray pond overflow, condensed water and fresh water. The treated water from dilution tank is used for crop.

The Warana sugar factory has provided air pollution control equipments for control of air pollution as follows:

(i) Warana factory has five boilers fly ash arrestors (Scrubber type).

(ii) The factory has four Sulphur Burners of continuos type. Hence, there is no possibility of ejection of Sulphur dioxide gas.

(iii) In sugar house dust catchers are provided at various places to collect sugar dust.

Paper Industry

The Warana Co-operatives sugar factory is using its own bagasse (waste) for the production of paper. The capacity of the plant is 20 tonnes daily. Annual working days in the year 1999-2000 were 161 only.

The Warana paper industry produced 3,174.9 tonne paper in the year 1999-2000. Total cost of paper produced in the year 1999-2000 was Rs. 1050.42 lakh and total revenue after the sale of the paper produced was 756.80 lakh. The Warana factory has incurred loss of Rs.293.62 lakhs. But plants like Bioearth and distillery are in profit. Though the paper plant is in loss.

The Warana co-operative sugar factory is protecting environment by implementing the recycling of waste such as molasses, sludge, pressmud, bagasse, paper industry waste, etc. which are used for the purpose of recycling. The recycling of waste is protecting the environment from pollution.

Conclusions

1. The Tatyasaheb Kore Warana Sugar Factory has played important role in environment protection and rural development.

2. Bio-earth compost project is very useful in maintaining ecological balance.

3. Recycling efforts (viz. distillery project, wastewater treatment Bioearth) are making both economic and environmental protection benefits.

4. 'Horticulture and Nursery' is also income yielding and environmental protecting one.

In short, co-operative sugar factories can play very positive role in the environmental protection. The Model of Warana factory regarding 'recycling of waste, horticulture and nursery' can be replicated in other parts of the county.

REFERENCES

1. Souvenir, 54th Annual Conference of Indian Agricultural Society of Agricultural Economics, held on 26, 27 and 28th November, 1994 at Department of Economics, Shivaji University, Kolhapur.
2. Koli, P. A., Co-operative Sugar Factories and Rural Development: A Case Study of Maharashtra (1998), India's Rural Co-operatives, edited by Gursharan Singh Kainth, p. 321.
3. Ibid., p. 322.
4 Annual Reports of The Tatyasaheb Kore Warana Co-operative Sugar Factory.

5

Environmental Conditions of Women Sweepers

Introduction

There has been heated debate in the feminist movement that the women should be considered equal to men. Many argues that women and men are more or less a blank slate on which gender identity is inscribed in the process of a lifetime of learning experience. Evidence suggests that the degree of inequality is closely related to the level of income and also the strategy of development of the government. These factors include the distribution of productive assets, the distribution of educational opportunities, the employment and the general policy of Government. If we look into the socio-economic position of SC/ST women; it shows the dismal picture.

The Problem

This study is an attempt to highlight the present position of Backward Class Women even after 57 years of independence. The study gives the scope for expanding the capabilities of the dalit women, whether they have obtained dignity and self respect? Can they read, write and communicate and develop their minds and provide qualitative life to children? Can they escape from avoidable habits and illness? Can they live long life like other upper castes? This is essential because, the ultimate objective of economic development is human development.

The present study will provide answers to many of the above questions. Considering the level of income, nature of job and the education of children of female workers under study, we found that still the Dalit Women are worse hit.

Research Methodology

For the purpose of this study the female workers in sanitary department of the Kolhapur Municipal Corporation (KMC) were selected. Out of the total (858) female sweepers, 44 (5.12%) female sweepers were randomly selected. The sample was from all the sub-sections of the sanitary wards. These sweepers were engaged in sweeping and cleaning of roads, hospitals, schools, public buildings and drainages, etc. Only female workers (sweepers) were interviewed. For this purpose a questionnaire containing 20 points with sub-points was served. The interview was conducted at both places i.e. work-sight and at the homes of the female workers. Many workers were hesitating to give the information feeling that they would be removed from their jobs if they talked anything against their work-situation.

Main Hypothesis of the Study

For the present study, the following hypothesis was considered.

"The Female workers engaged in sweeping work of sanitary Department of KMC mainly belong to SC/ST categories and their socio-economic and environmental conditions are bad."

About the Sample City

Unlike other cities, the Kolhapur City is old and is known for its Kolhapur footwear and jaggary. It is also famous for the grain market and for jewellery. The Mahalaxmi Temple is known as South Kashi of this area. However, the city in recent years has grown faster in respect to population, trade and small-scale industries and educational facilities. Table 1 will show the growth of population during the last six decades.

Table 1: Growth of Population of Kolhapur City from 1941 to 2011

Sr. No.	*Year*	*Population*	*Net Increase*	*% Growth Over Decade*
01.	1941	93,032	26,304	39.42
02.	1951	1,36,835	43,803	47.08
03.	1961	1,87,442	50,607	39.98
04.	1971	2,59,050	71,008	38.20
05.	1981	3,88,575	1,29,525	50.00
06.	1991	6,02,291	2,13,716	55.00
07.	2001	9,63,665	3,61,375	60.00
08.	2011*	15,90,048	6,26,383	65.00

Source: Census Reports * Estimated Population.

The above table shows that the population of Kolhapur City is growing fast i.e. more than 50 per cent in a decade; and the same trends seems to be continued. Thus, population has created the problem of environment pollution. This will put heavy burden on water supply and sanitation. Due to increasing population, the demand for houses has been increased. The 15-20 years back, the city was having independent house type constructions, but now it has given rise to flat type houses. This has created the major problem of cleaning the city. Table 2 shows the demand and supply for houses from 1961 to 2011.

It was revealed that every year about 3250 new

Table 2: Demand and supply of Houses from 1961 to 2011

Year	*Population*	*Total Need for Houses*	*Total Supply of Houses*	*Net Deficit of Houses %*
1961	1,87,443	37,488	37,488	0
1971	2,79,050	51,811	49,219	5
1981	3,88,575	77,715	69,944	10
1991	6,02,201	1,20,458	96,366	20
2001	9,63,665	192,733	1,34,913	30
2011	15,90,048	3,18,010	1,90,806	40

Source: The Kolhapur Architecture Association, Kolhapur.

housing permits have been allowed by the Kolhapur Municipal Corporation. The data shows that decade after decade the net deficit of houses is increasing. If we consider one house for five persons, then the city will grow in its size than at present. By the end of 2011 about 40% of the population will be without houses or they will be in a congested houses. As a result of this the number of slum area is rapidly increasing. Twenty years back, Kolhapur city was having only 02 slum areas, now the city is having about 60 registered slum areas, where in the corporation has provided minimum facilities. Thus, due to increasing population and new construction work, the roads are becoming dirty and unmanageable to the sanitary department.

Profile of Health and Sanitary Department of Kolhapur Municipal Corporation as on Jan. 1999.

The Kolhapur Municipal Corporation (KMC) is 25 years old of its life span spread into 72 wards with 72 councilors. The profile of the Health and Sanitary Department can be seen from Table 3.

Table 3: Profile of KMC Health & Sanitary Department

Sr.No.	*Particulars*	*Number*
1.	Total workers/sweepers	1,144
	(a) Female	858 (75%)
	(b) Male	418
	(c) Vacant posts	68
2.	Vehicles Engaged	18
3.	Area of Operational Work	
	1. Hospitals (Big)	02
	Hospitals (Small)	31
	2. Gardens	49
	3. College	01
	4. Primary Schools	66

Analysis of the Data

Primary Information

As mentioned earlier, the hypothesis of this study is that the Female workers engaged in the sweeping work are belonging mainly to SC/St category; as this job is considered to be of lower status. This hypothesis (Table 4) was proved to be correct.

The data revealed that the large number of workers (72.73%) among the sample were only from Scheduled Caste and Scavenger (18.18%) and remaining from other castes. The workers from the Dominated caste i.e. Maratha were only 2.27 per cent; though their share in the district population was 72 per cent as per the Census 2001. This shows that cleaning and sanitary work is done only by SC people.

Table 4: Distribution of Female Sweepers on the Basis of Caste

Sr. No.	*Caste*	*Percentage*
01.	S.C.Mahar	59.09
	Mung	13.64 = 72.73
02.	Stone Cutters	2.73
03.	Bhangis/Scavengers	18.18
04.	Muslims	4.55
05.	Maratha	2.27
06.	Other	Nil
	Total	**100.00**

Educational Level of Workers

The data (Table 4A) shows that 66 per cent of the workers were illiterate; and only 9.08 per cent have studied upto SSC and SHC; while others studied upto 7th standard school. As illiteracy rate is high, among the sweeper the incidence of poverty is also very high.

Table 4A: Education, Age, Where about and Tenur

Sr. No.	*Particulars*	*1*	*2*	*3*	*4*	*5*	*6*
1.	Education	Nil	<-4	<-7	<SSC	<HSC	
	Number	29	7	4	3	1	44
	Percentage	65.91	15.91	9.10	6.81	2.27	100
2.	Age	<-35	<-40	<-45	<-50	<-50	
	Number	11	4	9	12	8	44
	Percentage	25.00	9.10	20.45	27.27	18.18	100
3.	Village or	KOP	VILL				
	Kolhapur	21	23	-	-	-	44
	Percentage	47.72	52.28	-	-	-	100
4	Permanent	P35	TO9				
	Temporary	79.55	20.45	-	-	-	100

Age at Work

The age of workers is important factor because the sweeping work is to be performed in the open air. They have to work in all the seasons, in severe winter as well as in heavy rainfall. It was found that most of the workers (Table 4A) were below 50 years of age, the age in which one can take hard work. Only 18.18 per cent of them were above the age limit of 50 and more. It was observed that the women after the age of 50 have to face lot of physical pains while they sweep.

Where about of Workers

Every family in Indian villages asks themselves the question; To migrate or to stay? The poor agricultural labour ask this question to escape from poverty and unemployment. Small farmers ask the same question to escape from their possible proletarianisation in view of the increasing pressure of capital and market. This assumption was also found to be true (Table 4A) as 52.28 per cent of the workers were migrated from villages while remaining 47.72 per cent were from the Kolhapur City. It was found that many of the workers have now settled in certain habitats known as 'Workers habitat' such as *Vare Vasahat, Sadar Bazar, Mahar Wada, Bhanji Wada, Ganji Mal,* etc. These areas are known for their slum and unhygienic conditions. It was found that the sons, daughters in law or daughters of the retiring workers were recruited as temporary workers. If a lady has no son in such case her son-in-law also has a chance to get job in Sanitary Department. Thus, it has become the traditional work of the same caste and same family.

Employment, Wages and Non Waged Advantages

Out of total respondents about 80 per cent of them were permanent in their job; while rest of them were casual. Of course, there was job security to all. Without serious allegation or unnoticed absence, no worker was removed. They were also the members of the union which is strong in its actions. The temporary workers have the chance of being permanent and the permanent have the chance of promotion as 'Mukadam' i.e. head sweeper.

The total monthly salary average of the sample women was Rs. 3000/-, however, a few workers were getting upto Rs. 4000/-. But the temporary sweepers get Rs. 90/- per day. Apart from salary, permanent workers were entitled to get 12 days casual leave, 30 days privilege leave and 14 days additional leave and bonus. Therefore, once, a lady gets the job, she hardly leaves, though the working condition is worst, i.e. always in dust and dirt. Out of the sample workers 79.55 were permanent and others were temporary.

Deviation of Monthly Income

Data (Table 5) reveals that the respondents have spent their monthly income on various items such as house rent, grossory, health, cloth and education purposes. The break-up of income was as follows.

Table 5: Break-up of Monthly Income

Sr. No.	*Items*	*% age share in Monthly Income*
01.	House Rent	19.54
02.	Grossory	52.73
03.	Cloth	20.00
04.	Education	7.73
05.	Health	00.00
06.	Savings	Nil
	Total	100.00

It has seen that most of the income is being spent on the food items, followed by cloths and house-rent. While the negligible amount was spent on education. It was found that most of the children of the workers were studying in Municipal Primary Schools and hence there was no fees. The B.C. students use to get a pair of uniforms and a set of Text Books and note-books, hence the cost of education to the workers was not a botheration. The same thing was found in case of health expenditure, as KMC provides free medical aid to workers and their family members. It was found that no worker has cultivated the habit of saving except the monthly subscription of his cooperative credit society and Provident Fund.

Indebtedness

It can be seen from the table that almost all the respondents were in debt. Every worker has to work for 08 hours and hence they spend money on tea and eatables outside the home. As a result of this they are forced to take less money at home. Many workers take money from private money lenders and these money-lenders recover it on the day of monthly salary by charging exorbitant rate of interest i.e. 40 to 60 per cent per year.

Working Hours

The workers spend more time on the job i.e. from 6 am to 10 am and again from 2 pm to 6 pm. Hence, they have no time to look after their children's health and food also; while they never think of their school performance. The work-place is always uncertain. Thus, they are being forced not to take greater responsibility in both parenting and providing for their children. Physical and mental burden is more on the working women. Many studies (Yadav-Pani) have proved this fact.

About the Size of the Family

The study reveals that the size of family is some what big, i.e. having more children. This might be due to low education and caste. Many gender and poverty studies (Maya Kumar 1997) have shown the positive co-relation between the caste and number of children. The (Table 6) shows that still 54.55 per cent of the women workers were having more than 03 children. In this situation the target of 2 or single child seems difficult.

Table 6: Number of Children in Family

No.of Total Children	0	1 to 2	3	4 to 5	6 to 7	Total
No.of Workers	01	06	13	15	09	44
% in Total	2.27	13.64	29.55	34.09	20.46	100

The level of education of the worker's children was (Table 6A) another indication of future prospects of this caste; but it was not satisfactory. Hardly 15.91 per cent of the workers were having the educational level of their children upto HSC and above. This shows that remaining workers' children would again take up low status job. While replying the question as '*What are your future plans for your sons?* Only 40.91 per cent replied that their sons would like to join the good services and 54.55 per cent were indecisive and 2.27 per cent preferred business. This shows the expectation from the future generation of SC sweeper is low.

Table 6A: Level of Education of Children

Edn. Stand	*No School going*	*1st-4th*	*5th-10th*	*HSC-Grad*	*Total*
No.of Workers	03	Nil	34	07	44
% in Total	6.82	Nil	77.27	15.41	100

Environmental Conditions of Sample Workers

With a view to find out the environmental conditions of the female workers, an enquiry was made (Table 7) regarding the nature of work, sanitation, physical and mental strains, housing space and minimum needs available in their houses. The facilities provided by the KMC were also studied. Because the quality of life is a function of several factors, such as income, health, housing, sanitation, social dignity, energy, security of life and the environment. Some of the environmental aspects have been summarised.

1. The KMC has provided the houses to only 10 per cent of the workers, and 30 per cent of them are provided vacant plots on minimum rent, while 60 per cent are living in rented houses. These plots are in a slum area, where there is air pollution. All the house constructed by the workers are *Kaccha Houses*.

2. About 2/3 of workers were staying in a narrow rooms either rented or owned. Out of total sample workers, 86.36 per cent workers were living in 100 to 200 ft. houses.

3. No proper bathroom facilities were available to 70 per cent of the workers. No toilet facilities were available in their residence.

4. The KMC provides two uniforms i.e. sarees, blouse and a pair of footwear in a year only to permanent workers. But since last year, they have not got the footwears.

5. The nature of the work was monotonous, as each has to work for eight hours per day in dust and dirt i.e. drainage work.

6. All the workers have reported that they have one or the other occupational diseases like Ashtama, T.B. body ailment, cancer, etc. This was revealed by the retired workers. But the KMC serves free medical facilities; hence there was no complaints.

A few workers, said, that it is *better to be alive rather than to die of starvation.*

Table 7: Details about Workers House Rent Paid, Size etc.

Sr. No.	*Particulars*	*1*	*2*	*3*	*4*	*5*
1.	Nature of Municipal Help	Quarters	Vacant Space	Rented	-	
	Number	4	13	27	-	44
	Percentage	10	30	60	-	100
2.	House Catg.	Temp.	Perm.	No. Res.	-	
	Number	27	13	4	-	44
	Percentage	61.36	29.55	9.09	-	100
3.	House Size	100	200	300	400	
	Sq. Ft.	12	26	4	3	44
		27.27	59.09	9.09	4.55	100

Why only Scheduled Castes in Sweeping Work?

As this caste has no sufficient property to fetch sufficient income to support their families, as well as there are no; other jobs available wherein the illiterate women could be employed. Due to increasing cost in agriculture; the demand for labour in rural area is restricted; and the same is true in cities also. It was made clear by the Municipal Sanitary Officer that the city is having certain areas from where the workers for sweeping come and they are the known places for B.C. Colonies.

Main Conclusions

1. The Sanitary job is done only by the B.C. Community people.
2. The workers were having low status job.

3. No job prestige and promotion avenues.
4. No asset has been built by the workers.
5. No chances of better education and services to the sons/daughters of workers.
6. Lack of savings habits among the workers.
7. The quarrels and absenteesiam was common among the workers.
8. All the workers were in a clutches of money lenders.
9. Health and environment conditions of sweepers is worst.

Suggestions

Here we are giving some main suggestions. Establishment of self-help Group (SHC) a mini voluntary agency for self help at the micro level would be useful solution for the economic development of the women. SHG has got great potential in creating awareness on day to day affairs of women, promoting savings habit, developing self and community assets, increasing income and educational level, improving social power etc. HSG – Bank linkage can improve their credit worthiness and repaying capacity. This will help to educate worthiness and repaying capacity. This will help to educate the children and improve health and sanitation, etc., through women's organisation. SHG concept generates self confidence, self security and self reliance. The issue of poverty of female workers can be solved by the female social workers and buy the female corporators. At the same time there is a need for the emergence of the leaders among the Backward Class Community to come forward and educate the B.C. workers. It has been rightly said by Dr. Babasaheb Ambedkar, 'educate, agitate and then get'. This holds true till today.

REFERENCES

1. *Bhatt, Ela, Structural Reforms*: View from the other side. NEP and women. Indian Association for Women's Studies. (1993). New Delhi.
2. Mittal, L.N.: *Women the Worse Hit*. Social Welfare, January, 1998.
3. Mukhopadhyay, Lipi. *Women: The Search for Identity*, Social Welfare, January, 1998.
4. Yadav, N. Kashyap and Rani. *Working Women and their Constraints*. Journal of Social Research, Delhi. Jan-March 1998.
5. Shapa, Vijaya and Gadakari A. *Environment, Development and Quality of Life*. OEC Seminar, on Environment, Department of Sociology. Shivaji University, Kothyam (Feb. 1998).
6. To Migrate or to Stay? EPW, Dec. 5th, 1998.
7. Maya-Unnithan-Kumar. Identity, Gender and Poverty. Berghahn Books, Oxford, 1997.

6

Implication of Technological Changes in Agriculture

Today farmers in India are found to be in a depressed and in angry mood. The depression is resulted partly from growing rural-urban disparities and partly from declining trends in profitability of agriculture in almost all the states, the rates of decline being higher in the more developed states (1) The farmers are also angry under the impression that the Government under the direction of World Trade Organization (WTO) had withdrawn various forms of farm subsides protection which may affect their future prospects adversely. While the reasons for relatively greater decline in agricultural profitability is in developed States which are the main beneficiaries of green revolution. Due to the adaptation of new technology, the yields and income levels of farmers are low.

The problem of low productivity has become a serious problem to small and marginal farm holders. About 78 per cent of the total operational holdings in the country are owned by small farmers which comes about 32 per cent of the total area. Given the recent trends and sectrol patterns of population growth and labour absorption, it is obvious that the proportion of small and marginal farmers in the country would continue to grow. Of course, it is of no use merely saying that our farmers are non-viable and non-sustainable. The primary question is why the farmers are becoming non-viable, and what alternative we should provide them? Is the present technology anti environment? What would be the role of bio-technology and bio-fertilizer in this regard? Is there need for farmers' education? All these questions need to be studied from scientific point of view.

Significance of Land and Extent of Land Sallinity in India

The per capita availability of land in our country is 0.48 hect., as against 4.14 hect. in U.S.A. and 8.43 hect. in CIS (Former USSR). Man-land ratio in relation to urban land is only 0.27 ha., and it is likely to reduce further in the coming years. India is already densely populated and putting heavy pressure on the environment, infrastructure and basic services. The percentage of permanent pasture land to total land is only 3.7. There would be chronic shortage of cultivatable land, again rapid industrialization is damaging the environment.

The total cultivatable land area in India is about 304 million ha., and according to an estimate made by the Ministry of Agriculture as much as 175 million ha. (57.37%) of land is suffering from environmental degradation. The land suffering from salinity and water logging is 11.5 million ha. i.e. 3.77% of the total cultivable land. This problem is arising out of: Wind, Water erosion, Water logging, Salinity.

Alkalinity represent the mis-management of soil resources and disregard of ecological principals. (2) The degradation of this order has a serious economic and ecological implications for a country like India which has a predominantly rural population and an agricultural economy. For example; nutrient loss caused by erosion on account of NPK alone, represents a loss of Rs.700 crores per annum.

Some Observation about Over Irrigation and Fertilizers

The water logging is a serious problem in newly irrigated areas of Rajasthan deserts. Similarly, the adverse effects of changes in traditional cropping in the States of Punjab, Bihar, West Bengal, Madhya Pradesh, Gujrath and Maharashtra are quite conspicuous. The State of Tamil Nadu and coastal districts of Andhra Pradesh are not an exception to the fast decling fertility of soils. In certain areas over irrigation is leading to water logging, while in other areas, the chemical properties are getting transformed resulting into saline and alkaline formations. Dr.Swaminathan said, 'If electricity is free in Punjab, then why not people should use more/excess water for agriculture? And the result is land salinity'. He has further stated that the over application of chemical fertilizers and excessive use of irrigation is destroying the micro-organism of the soil which are vital for maintaining the fertility of the soil. At the same time the changes in the cropping pattern though giving more agricultural returns is injurious for the health of the soil, creating ecologically adverse conditions which may render the fertile plains unproductive, infertile and barren, if remedial steps are not taken. (3) He has warned that in future the food growing zones such as Punjab and Hariyana will loose their significance while the state like M.P. will be on the map of food growing states.

Objective of the Study

Keeping in view the above mentioned facts, the present study was undertaken with the following objectives:

1. To analyse the present practices of agriculture production with special reference to excess use of water and fertilizers.
2. To analyse the anti-environment practices followed by the farmers.

3. To suggest appropriate policy measures to avoid land salinity.

Hypothesis

The growth in fertilizer consumption and excess use of water substantially damages the environmental quality i.e. low crop production.

Methodology

This paper is based on the data collected in four villages in Kolhapur, Sangli and Solapur districts of Western Maharashtra. The data was collected during the year 1998-99. All the farmers were having irrigated land; and they were suffering from land salinity. In all 67 farmers (Table1) were selected randomly.

Table 1: Village-wise selection of sample farmers affected by land salinity

Sr. No.	*Name of village*	*District*	*No. Sample farmer*
1	Shirol	Kolhapur	12 [17.62]
2	Ichalkaranji	Kolhapur	20 [30.00]
3	Bhilwadi	Sangli	20 [30.00]
4	Sangam	Solapur	15 [22.38]
	Total		**67 [100.00]**

Note: Figures in the brackets show the percentages.

Results and Discussion

The following discussion will highlight the educational level, average land size of the sample farmers. The types of fertilizers used, the mode of irrigation and the cropping pattern of the sample farmers was analysed. At the same time the economic loss of farmers due to land degradation was also studied. The remedial measure are also sought out.

Educational Level of Sample Farmers

It was observed from the Table No.2 that out of the total (67) farmers, 83.39 per cent of the farmers were educated and remaining 16.41 per cent of them were uneducated. It means majority of the farmers were able to read and understand the newspapers, radio and T.V. news about agricultural production; yet their land was subject to degradation.

Table 2: Level of Education of sample farmers

	Level	*Shirol*	*Ichalkarnji*	*Bhilwadi*	*Sangam*	*Total*	*%*
1.	Illitreate	Nil	2	1	7	11	16.14
2.	Up to 7th Std.	8	7	10	6	31	46.27
3.	Up to 12th	2	9	5	2	18	25.37
4.	Graduate	2	2	4	0	8	11.95
	Total	**12**	**20**	**20**	**15**	**67**	**100**

An examination of Table No.3 shows the village-wise total cultivable land belonging to sample farmers as well as land under salinity. The table also gives the percentage of salinity of each village. It was seen that about 24.95 per cent of the total cultivable land was out of use due to salinity. On an average each farmer is having 8.47 acres of land out of which he has lost about 2.11 acres. The main causes behind the salinity expressed by the sample farmers were as follows:

1. Due to black soil and use of excess water.
2. Due to use of excess/unmeasured dose of fertilizers.
3. Lack of soil testing before the use of fertilizers.
4. Over irrigation and water logging; out of the total farmers, 73% farmers responded for this reason.

5. Lack of proper crop planning i.e. monoculture/ single crop like sugarcane, banana, etc. It was found that 91% of the farmers were cultivating sugar cane, which requires water all the year.

Table 3: Extent of Land Salinity in Sample Villages

(Land in Areas)

Sr.No.	*Name of village*	*A*	*B*	*C*	*D*
1	Shirol	65.25	18.03	28.04	2.33
2	Ichalkaranji	135.95	39.08	28.43	1.42
3	Bhilwadi	215.77	63.07	29.23	1.46
4	Sangam	146.75	21.50	14.65	0.97
		567.72	141.68	24.95	2.11

Average land size of farmer –8.47.

A = Total Cultivatable land of sample farmers.

B = Out of total, saline land.

C = Percentage of saline land.

D = Average per farmer saline land.

The traditional cropping patterns evolved on the basis of empirical experience by the farmers has been completely transformed. The rotation of crops followed by the enriching crops has been given up. This is a clear testimony to the fact that year after year the natural fertility of arable land is declining at a faster rate. In short, land is being polluted by the human and by excess fertilizers and water.

Consumption of Fertilizers by the Sample Farmers

Table No. 4 reveals the consumption of different types of chemical fertilizers by the sample farmers in a village Bhilawadi in Sangli district. It was observed that every farmer has utilised the fertilizers. The main brands were

Urea (20:20:20), Suphla, Potash Urea (DAP), Sulphate and Super Phospet. The fertilizers were used for the crops such as sugarcane, banana, soyabean, wheat etc.

Table 4: Gross Consumption of fertilizers by sample farmers (1996-97)

Sr.No.	*Particulars*	*Quantity*
1.	Total land under cultivation	85.67 Acres
2.	Total fertilizers used in above land (206 bags each of 50 kgs)	10300 Kgs
3.	Per acre average use	120.22 Kgs

It was seen that on an average each farmer has used 120.22 Kgs. of fertilizers; which is too much from the environment point of view. The All India Data shows that about 50 Kgs. of chemical fertilizer is used per acre. But the case study shows it is two and half times excess than the national average. As we know that fertilizer consumption has jumped since the introduction of HYV. It has gone up from a mere one Kg/ha. in the early 50's to 99 Kgs./ha. today. While the world average use is 87.3 kg. per hect. Therefore, here is need for shift in our thinking, a careful policy formulation and designing an appropriate institutional framework to safeguard the agricultural land.

Farmer's Attitude Towards Scientific Cultivation

Table 5 reveals the attitude of farmers towards the soil testing, use for mass-media in agriculture and government assistance. It is assumed that if proper guidance in agricultural production is availed by the farmer, there would be no environmental problems. The perusal of table gives the idea that only 13.43 per cent of the sample farmers were testing their soil before the use of fertilizers. Though the educational level of the farmers was satisfactory.

Table 5: No. of Farmers Availing Extension Facilities

Sr. No.	*Name of village*	*ST*	*TV*	*GA*
1.	Shirol (12)	2	10	Nil
2.	Ichalkaranji (20)	3	12	2
3.	Bhilwadi (20)	1	16	Nil
4.	Sangam (15)	3	2	Nil
	Total (67)	**9**	**40**	**2**
	Percentage	**13.43**	**59.70**	**3.00**

ST = Soil Testing.

TV = TV/News paper on Agriculture.

GA = Government Assistance.

Note: Figures in the brackets show the number of sample farmers.

The awareness of reading the newspapers and watching the T.V. was satisfactory. However, very few (93%) farmers have contacted the Zilla Parishad and Block Level Agricultural Officer for modern and scientific farm practices.

Economic Loss of Farmers Due to Land Salinity

It is difficult to ascertain the loss of farmers affected due to land salinity. Because, the farmers are not keeping the accounts of crop production. However, an effort was made to ascertain the economic loss considering that the farmers were taking a single crop i.e. sugarcane. The following table shows the loss of 15 farmers in one sample village i.e. Sangam. The per acre sugarcane production is considered 35 tonnes.

The data shows that in Sangam village, about 21.5 acres of land of 15 sample farmers had gone out of order and the village had lost Rs. 18,76,975 since six years with an average loss of Rs. 1,25,125 per farmer.

Table 6: Economic Loss of Farmers Affected due to Land Salinity in Sample Village During Last Six Years

Sr.No.	A	B	C	D	E
1.	3	3	315	750	2,36,250
2.	1	4	140	-	1,05,000
3.	1.5	5	262.5	-	1,05,000
4.	0.5	1	17.5	-	13,125
5.	2	2	140	-	1,05,000
6.	1	6	210	-	1,57,500
7.	1.5	4	210	-	1,57,500
8.	0.5	1	17.5	-	13,125
9.	2	3	210	-	1,57,500
10.	0.5	2	35	-	26,500
11.	3	4	420	-	3,15,000
12.	1.5	4	210	-	1,57,500
13.	1	5	70	-	52,500
14.	2	3	210	-	1,57,500
15.	0.5	2	35	-	26,250
Total	21.5		2502.5		18,76,875
Average loss per farmer (Rs)					**1,25,125**

A = Total Barren Land (Acres).

B = Since How long Barren (Years).

C = Approximate Loss of sugar cane Production (Tonnes).

D = Per Tonne Price (Rs).

E = Total loss Rs.

Conclusions

The following conclusions were drawn from the study.

1. Most of the farmers (75%) who were affected by the problem of land salinity were small and marginal category and each farmer had lost 2.11 acres of land in salinity.

2. About 83% of the sample farmers were educated, and out of them 37.32% farmers' educational level was more than 12th standard, yet they lacked the scientific approach to agriculture.

3. It was found that 100% farmers were using the chemical fertilizers and the average per acre use was more than 120 Kg., which was higher then the present national average of 50 Kgs.

4. Out of total sample farmers 80% farmers were cultivating sugarcane crop each year.

5. It is striking to note that hardly 13.43% of the sample farmers have tested their soil before the use of fertilizers and water.

6. A case study of Sangam village shows that due to land degradation, the each sample farmer had lost an income of Rs. 1,25,125 during the last six years.

Future Course of Action: Some Suggestions:

With a view to avoiding the further loss of agriculture; we can give the following suggestions.

The minimum education of farmers for safe agricultural practices is essential. There is an urgent need to enlighten them about modern and efficient water management practices and advantages of crop rotation.

REFERENCES

1. Haque, T. Economics of Agriculture, NDRI, Mimeograph, 1992, Hyderabad.

2. Varshaney, C.K. and Sardesai, D.R. (Ed.), Environmental challenges, Wiley Eastern Limited, New Delhi (1993), pp. 11, 12.

3. Husain, Majid: Ecological Crisis and Changing Cropping Pattern in India (Ed.), Environment and Development Cnundrum, Discovery Publishing House, New Delhi (1992), p. 146.

4. Subramaniyan, G. Fertilizer Demand in India, Classical Publishing Co., New Delhi (1994), p.13.
5. Varsheney and Sardesai, op.cit., p. 42.
6. Rao, B., Ranade, S. and Gadgil, J. Environmental aspects of Land Disposal of Organic Wastes; Environmental Challenges (Ed.) Wiley Eastern ltd., (1993), p. 44.
7. Trivedi, H.P. and Patel, N.M. Use of fertilizers in Indian Agriculture; Artha-Vikas, Vol. XXVII (1992-94). Department of Economics, S.P. University, V.V.Nagar, Gujrat, p. 20.
8. Nadkarni, M.V. (1996). Agricultural and Environment (Edt.) by Rathore M.S. Environment and Development, Rawat Publications, Jaipur. p. 55.
9. Referred the M.A. Project reports (Shivaji University) of 'Economics of Environment' submitted by Mr. Mane, G.R., Mithari, M.L., Wavare, A.K. and Mahadik, T.J.
10. Dr. M.S. Swaminathan, Director, M.S. Swaminathan Foundation, Chennai, Valedictory Address delivered at National Seminar on Environment cost of Economic Development, held on 16-17 April 1998.

7

Misuse of Common Property Resources in Rural Area

India has a unique environmental heritage with its geographic, climatic and biological diversity. The country represents almost all types of habitats of the world and land has lot of water bodies and an extremely rich variety of plants and animals. However, development based on intensive utilization of natural resources and polluting and energy intensive industrial technology, along-with pressure of population and poverty have taken a heavy toll of these environmental assets over the years. All economic activities have adversely affected on natural and environmental resources. Moreover, economic activities today affect the stock of natural resources available for the future. Environmental degradation imposes high costs on the economy, which results in output and human capital losses.

Major Environmental Concerns

A country's environmental problems vary with its stage of development, structure of its economy, production technologies in use and its environmental policies. While some problems may be associated with the lack of economic development e.g. inadequate sanitation, and clean drinking water, while others are exacerbated by the growth of economic activity. i.e. air and water pollution. Poverty presents special problems for a densely populated country with limited resources.

Major Environmental Problems

The major environmental problems can be summarized as under:

Soil Degradation

Out of the total geographical area of 329 million hectors 177 million [53.84%] hectors is considered degraded.

Table 1: Soil Erosion and Land Degradation

Sr. No.	*Particulars*	*Million Hectors*
1.	Total Geographical area	328.7
2.	Area Subject to Water and wind erosion *Area Degraded through Special Problems*	143.3
A.	Water logged area	8.5
B.	Alkali Soil	3.6
C.	Acid Soil	4.5
D.	Saline Soil (Coastal Area)	5.5
E.	Ravines and Gullies	4.0
F.	Area Subject to shifting cultivation	4.9
G.	Reverine and Torrents	2.7
	Total A to G =	33.7
	Grand Total	**177.0**

Deforestation

Forest are a renewable resources and contribute substantially to the economic development by providing goods and services to forest dwellers, people at large and forest based industries, besides generating substantial volume of employment. Forest also play a vital role in enhancing the quality of environment by influencing the ecological balance and life support system. The withdrawal of forest products, including fuel wood, timber, etc are much beyond the carrying capacity of our forests.

Presently, the recorded, forest area is 76.52 million hector which works out to 23.3% of the total geographical area and actual forest cover is 63.3 million hectors, which constitutes only 19.3% of the total land area. As against the National Forest Policy (1998) stipulation of a target of 33% of forest area.

Table 2: Forest covers estimates 1981-1995

Period	*Total Forest cover million hector*	*% of geographical area*	*% of area under Dense Forest*	*% of area under Open Forest*
1981-83	64.08	19.5	—	—
1989-91	63.94	19.5	60.2	39.1
1991-93	63.89	19.4	60.2	39.0
1993-95	63.34	19.3	58.0	41.3

The Forest cover is the sum of dense forest plus open forest, plus mangroves forest which is not shown. Since 1950 to 1980 annual rate of diversion of forest land for non forest purpose was 0.15 million hectors. Forest Conservation (Act 1980) is enacted; but it has failed to reduce of diversion of forest area for non-forest purposes. Presently, 16000 hectors area is diverted to non-forest per year.

Bio-Diversity

With only 2.4 per cent of the total land area of the world, the known bio-diversity of India contributes 8% cent of the biological diversity. India is one of the 12th mega bio-diversity centres in the world. In terms of number of mammalian species, the country ranks 10th in the world and in terms of the endemic species of higher vetebrates, it ranks 11th. It stands 7th in the world for the number species, contributed to agriculture and animal husbandry.

The bio-diversity in forest, grasslands, wetlands and mountains, deserts and marine ecosystems is subject to many pressures. One of the major causes of the loss of biological diversity has been the depletion of vegetative cover in order to expand agriculture. According to estimates, over 1500 plants species are endangered and about 79 mammals, 44 birds, 15 repties, 3 amphibians and several insects are listed as endangered. There are some protected areas consisting of 85 National Parks, 448 wildlife sanctuaries, 10 Biosphere reserves and specific programmes for management and conservation of fragile ecosystems. Approximately, 4.2 % total geographical area of the country has been so earmarked for extensive in situ conservation of habitats and ecosystems. Besides ex-situ conservation is also undertaken through 70 botanic gardens, 275 wildlife preservation in the form of 200, park; aquaria etc.

The loss of forest cover and loss of biodiversity prevails even in villages., The citizens, who are living on the natural resources are not environment conscious and they are destroying the environment. Day by day, the situation is becoming worst. This can be seen by our case study of a village.

Misutilisation of Common Properly Resources: A Case Study of Alave Village

With a view to getting an idea of participation of villagers in the conservation of Common Property Resources (CPR), an in-depth study was made. For this purpose a village named ALAVE in Kolhapur District was selected. This village is situated about 30 km, in westside away from Kolhapur. The village is in hilly area, and hence the rainfall is upto 50 to 60 inches. The soil is fertile, due to good rainfall the village is having large number of trees in the private farms as well at public places.

Geographical Situation

The total geographical area of the village is 287 sq. Mtrs with its 1500 population. The main crops taken by the farmers are sugar cane and paddy and the farmers are in habit of using chemical fertilizers. Except the dairy animal other animal such as bullock, goats have become rare. The village has a high hill, on which few tree are grown. At the same time village has all the natural gifts such as natural landscape, peacock, natural beauty, river, etc.

The Problem

The villagers are using the common properly of the village recklessly and in unplanned manner. The utilization of resources is made in uncontrolled manner. We can describe it as under;

1. Depletion of High Hill

The village has a hill, which is about 100 meters high and about ½ kilometer long. This hill has added the natural beauty of the village. In rainy season, the villagers graze their animals free of cost. The hill has good quality of grass. But due to increasing population, since 1995 onwards, the villagers are digging hill and taking the rock for filling of roads and their house sites. It is also used for the farm bunding. Similarly, the farmers, who have used their land for a single crop, since long, have lost the fertility of their soil. Therefore farmers dig the upper part of the hill and take the fertile soil for their farms. The hill has been injured at 5-6 places and hence, the natural beauty of the original hill has been destroyed. Another loss is of trees and shrubs on the hill. The Village Panchayat has planted the trees; but these trees have also came in danger. Earlier people use to take hard soil/ rock by the bullock cart, but now, they are utilising it by lorry. Therefore, the rate of extraction is high. A small survey was conducted of this activity. It was found that during 2002-2003, about 270 trolleys hard soil was taken by 26 households, which would have been worth of Rs. 81000/-. Considering the so far uncontrolled utilization of hill the total loss goes to Rs. 2.10 lakhs but nothing has been paid by anybody to any authority; though the Village Panchayat is the Public Vigilance Authority to care for such property. In another word, the Village Grampanchyat has lost its income, which could have been used for public utility such as repairs of roads, cleaning of water stream, repair of village temples etc.

2. Miss-use of Public Common Places, for Individual Benefit

The village has primary school, credit cooperative society, dairy cooperative and village Panchayat. The village has an open area of about 300 acres; but this is used for private and unwise purposes, such as:

1. Dumping of Dung.
2. For preparation of Dung Cakes.
3. For storage of Grass and farmyard manure.

3. Unplanned use of River Water

The river flows very close (200 mtrs) to the village. People use the river water for agricultural purpose and for domestic need alongwith their daily washing and cleaning buffaloes. Due to use of detergent soap the river water has polluted.

4. *Uncontrolled Fishing*

The fishing activities are generally taken in rainy season. But due to summer, water level goes down and hence all the fish stock in the river is caught by the villagers.

5. *Over Use of Irrigation Water*

Farmers are using the river water for agriculture, but they utilise the water in uncontrolled manner. Due to over irrigation, the soil has lost its fertility and hence loss to the farmers' income. Therefore farmers are becoming poorer and poorer. About 10% of the total cultivable land has become saline.

6. *Cutting of Forest Trees for Firewood*

Due to uncontrolled forest activites, the trees are cut off by the villager. Though there are strong provision in forest conservation act yet the village authority has never penalized to any villager for cutting of trees. So far about 300 ucalyptus trees have been cut off.

7. *Brick Making Activities*

The village pot makers as well even upper caste people have now undertaken the digging of soil from Gram Panchyat land for brick making. Every year, 70000 to 80000 bricks are made for which no soil cost is paid. But these bricks give the total income of more than Rs. 100000/- of brick production; a net profit of Rs. 50000/- is earned by the people who are engaged in the activity. The brick industry makes a permanent loss of fertile soil.

These are some of the village activities, which are damaging the common properly resources/environment. This is not only true in case of Alave village, but is true in all villages in India. There is need for solution otherwise the life of future generation will; come in danger.

Need for Capacity Building

Capacity building refers to the efforts of people to improve their effectiveness. Though at present process have the inefficiencies in the operation yet one has to rebuild the capacity by making necessary changes. An effort to develop and utilize the skills of people and village institutions to follow the path of sustainable development. For this following things should be made.

1. To organize People's movement for green India for example, Vanrai in Pune and Ralegan Sidhi in Ahmednagar District has started the movement. Accordingly the villagers must agree to put in voluntary labour (Shamdaan).

2. No axe, no free grazing programme, gobar gas plants and latrines policy for every house may be accepted.

3. Every Primary as well as Secondary School should have one nursery. The Head master should be entrusted this work by giving them training. There are few examples in Maharashtra having done this work.

4. Women clubs in rural areas may be made well aware of causes of water pollution. The common water resources such as tanks, rivers etc. may be utilized so as to avoid pollution and water borne diseases.

5. Women clubs should also take part in health and family planning activities. The Block Development Officers are only looking at the disbursement of funds to the rural people,but they should also undertake these activities. The women's clubs should form the 'Bhumata Trust' which will care for local rural environment by organising 'Nature Clubs'.

6. The Center for Environment Education (CEE) a national institute supported by Ministry of Environment and Forest should promote wise use of common properly resources.

7. Atleast one farmer in one village can be promoted to establish Kisan Nursery. This has been done by BAIF in Pune District.

8. The village Grampanchyart has now been given autonomy to impose the local taxes as well it can make the rules in the Gram Sabha for the protection of bio-diversity and the common properly resources. This can be done through the Zilla-Parishad or by the grant-giving authority.

9. The rules regarding the extraction of village property may be framed by the body consisting of village heads including teacher, students, youth clubs etc.

10. Annually an ideal villages should be awarded which have kept the common properly in orderly manner.

REFERENCES

1. School of Health Sciences, University of Pune, Agenda 21 Handbook (1999).

2. IEG Resources Economic and Measurement of Environment Resources Value. Course mater Faculty Upgradation Programme in Environment Economic Delhi – 1999.

3. IGIDL Land and Forest Environmental Governance – 3.

4. University of Victoria Victoria BC The role of Environmental Degradation in Population displacement. Research Report 1998.

5. The Hindu Survey of the Environment 1997.

8

Pollution of Coastal Tourist Centres

This chapter deals with the analysis and interpretation of data, which was collected in the field survey (2003) in Sindhudurg District of Maharashtra. The data regarding the age, educational level, distance traveled, expenditure incurred on travel, etc. have been analysed. This data shows the income group of tourists. At the same time, awareness about the environment of the tourist has been shown. The following socio-economic factors have been studied.

Socio-Economics Characteristics of Tourists

With a view to knowing the age group of the tourist, an enquiry of 66 respondents was made. Table 1 shows the age of the tourists.

Table 1: Age of Sample Respondents i.e. Head of Tour

Sr. No.	*Particulars*	*Age group years*			*Total*
		18-35	*36-50*	*51-70*	
1.	No. of sample respondents	36	16	14	66
2.	% in total	54.55	24.24	21.21	100
3.	Lower & Higher age	-	-	-	17 years 81 years

Age

The data regarding the age of tourists shows that majority of the tourists were in the age group of 18 to 35 followed by age group between 36 to 50 years. Very few (21%) of the tourists were among the age group of 51 and above. The youngsters seemed to be more enthusiastic about the tours. There were very few persons above the age group of 70 years, and these were especially retired persons as they were getting 50% State Transport bus concession. This shows that the people who were active in their jobs and services found no time for touring purpose. It can also be concluded that one should go for environmental tour at the young age rather than above the age of 51 or after the retirement.

Education

The minimum and maximum education (Table 2) of the tourists was second year primary school and B.A., LL.B. respectively. But the majority of them (42.42%) were having education upto 10th standard, while 36.46% were graduates. It was found that none of tourist was illiterate. The literacy is the essential factor for going on tour. The knowledge of map reading seems to be the important

Table 2: Educational Level of Sample Respondents

Sr. No.	*Particulars*	*Level of education*				*Total*
		Upto 10th	*11 to 12th*	*Graduate*	*Professional*	
1.	No. of sample respondents	28	14	24	0	66
2.	% in total	42.42	21.12	36.46	0	100
3.	Lower and Higher education	-	-	-	-	2nd Std. B.A. LL.B

factor in touring. Of course, illiterate persons can also go for touring alongwith their literate relatives. As touring hobby is mainly among the well to do families, and such family members are able to get education easily, and hence there was no any illiterate respondents.

The Distance Traveled by the Tourists

As Sindhudurg district is the coastal area and it lies on the western side of Maharashtra, therefore, tourists have to spend lot of amount on travel.

Market Based Methods: The Travel Cost Approaches

Travel cost models are based on an extension of the theory of consumer demand in which special attention is paid to the value of time and the choice of site visits. They are used to value the benefits of recreational facilities in parks or the value of cultural sites that are visited by people from many different locations. The recreational value is known by the people who visit the sight, whether local, regional, national or international. If the visitors are visiting from long distance, then it is said the value of the site is more. The travel distance shows the cost of trip made by tourists.

Table 3 shows that majority of the tourists (63.64%) traveled within the distance of 200 kilometers, while 36% of them have traveled more than 300 kms., and one passenger had traveled from Bangalore i. e. more than 700 kms. More the distance traveled by the tourist more the significance of the tourist centre. This is clear from the table that the tourists centres in Sindhudurg district have not still attracted the people from the long distance. This will require the publicity and also there is a need to increase the publicity of the places.

Mode of Transport

The Sindhudurg district is having all the usual mode

Table 3: Distance Traveled from Home to Tourist Centre

Sr. No.	Particulars	*Distance (Kms)* Below 100	101 to 200	201 to 300	301 and more	Total
1.	No. of respondents	28	14	2	20	64
2.	% in total	42.42	21.12	6.16	30.30	100
3.	Minimum and Maximum distance	-	-	-	-	5 kms 727 kms

Note: 1. Passengers from nearby places also visit the places.

2. Maximum distance traveled by passenger was Bangalore.

3. Two passengers were not knowing the distance.

of transport i. e. road, rail and water transport. The district is not having the air transport facilities. The Konkan Railway has opened the era of tourism since last 5 years. There are as many 15 to 16 trains, passing through the Sindhudurg district; but most of them are express and hence there are limitations on the passengers to plan their journey to coastal centers. It was seen that 42.42% of the tourists had traveled by state transport buses, while 27.7% and 21.21% passengers had travelled by their hired private vehicle and their own cars, respectively. It was seen that hardly 9.1% of the sample passengers travelled by railways. Though rail transport is cheap and luxurious yet passengers prefer to travel by road ways only because very few trains stop in Sindhudurg district. The main railway stations in Sindhudurg districts are Sawantwadi, Kankawali and Kudal. With a view to develop tourism and attract more number of tourists the tourism development department should request the railway ministry to stop the trains at major tourist places.

Number of Persons and their Relationship with the Head in Tour

The number of persons in the tour shows the level of income of family. If we increase the number, one has to spend more amount on travel and other costs. It was seen that majority of the families (42.42%) were a couple i. e. wife and husband, and the equal number (42.42%) of families also travelled with 3 to 5 persons. Of course, they were wife, husband and children. While very small numbers (15.16%) of the tourists had accompanied by 6 to 9 persons. It was seen that out of 66 samples, 8 samples were friends and officers in a company. A few officers, when they go on official tour they visit tourist spots. When the children and young boys participate in the tour, their eating habits like eating ice-cream etc. results in environmental pollution.

Halt at Tourist Centres

It was assumed that the hault at tourist centres causes pollution. The night haults causes the generation of solid waste, water, noise as well as air pollution. Some persons prefer to live in an open space available at the tourist centre and prepare their food in the open air, using stove or firewood. Many times wood which is available in the open forest is used for cooking and fire in winter season. On few places, wine glass bottles were thrown here and there. Some places (Amboli) were littered with small pieces of glasses. An enquiry was made with sample tourists and it was found that out of total 21.21% tourists said that they will take night halts at the centre while as many as 78.79% of them said that they will either travel to next centre or go their homes. This shows that night haults made by tourists is responsible for environmental pollution of the tourists centres.

Environment liked by Tourist at the Tourists Centres

Man is not only social animal; but he is also nature lover. When one feel tired of his day to day work; he plans for tours especially environmental tours. Now a day the city people like to spend their holidays away from the cities. A few years ago, the Khandala and Lonawala near Mumbai experienced the environmental pollution. These places, which are known for cool climate, now suffer from all types of pollution. The use of plastic has eroded the equality of natural environment. The ban on use of plastic is strictly observed at hill stations such as Kodai Canal (T. N.) and Ootakmund. But still the tourists centres in Sindhudurg district have not been much polluted.

The sample respondents had stated their clear responses about the things they liked on the tourist centres. The environment things which they liked most were as under;

1. Forest and plants
2. Clean air
3. Sun set scene
4. Noiseless calm atmosphere, breeze etc.

The majority (25%) of the tourists liked the sunset in the seashore, followed by natural forest (15%) and clean air was liked by 12 % of the society. Many respondents liked all the above points. Replying to the questions whether they felt happy about the environmental status of tourist centres, they said 'Yes'. It was found that out of the total respondents 57.58% of respondents had visited the centre second time; only because they liked these centres. One lady said that her children had no chance to see sunrise and sunset in Mumbai, and hence she visits such places. This shows the utility of the environment.

Travel Cost

Considering the responses given by the tourists; the travel cost was divided into three categories, as follows:

(a) Upto Rs. 200/-

(b) Rs. 200/- to 500/-

(c) Rs. 500/- and above.

It was seen that 51.52% of the passengers had made the total to and fro cost on single passenger journey upto Rs. 200/- to visit the centre; and 24.24% of the passengers had made the cost of Rs. 201 to 500/- and the remaining number of passengers were in the last group of travel cost. The minimum, and maximum cost incurred by each passenger was Rs. 50 and Rs. 500/-. This shows that the persons from the nearest distance also visit this places. This is clear that the coastal tourist centres has attracted especially lower and middle income group of tourists. The lower income people cannot go for a long distance due to their income constraint. However, they can avail the pure environment at the cost affordable to them.

Total Cost

The total cost includes travel cost (both ways) lodging and boarding cost, cost of photography and entry fee, etc. It is very important thing to note that none of the coastal tourist centres had charged entry fee so far; hence the coastal environment is totally free of cost.

Annual Family Income

The income of the family or an individual is very important factor behind the tourism. Man first tries to satisfy his fundamental needs such as food, shelter, clothing, education and health care, and then only he thinks of the recreation and tours. It was found (Table 4) that most of the tourists (63.64%) were in the income group of more than 36000 and more while very few (21.21%) were below the income group of Rs. 15,000/- per annum. It was seen that high income group people were visiting the tourists centres. The lowest and the highest income of the sample tourist was between Rs.6000/- to 2.5 lakhs. Some industrialists from Mumbai visited the coastal centres while going to Goa. As there are no good hotels, the high income families rarely visit these tourist centres. The good and moderate hotel facilities can be made available either by the tourist authority of Maharashtra or from private sector.

Table 4: Annual Income of Sample Respondents

Amount in Rs. (000)

Sr. No.	Particulars	Income range					Total
		10 to 15	16 to 20	21 to 25	26 to 35	36 and above	
1.	No. of respondents	14	4	6	0	42	66
2.	% in total	21.21	6.06	9.09	-	63.64	100
3.	Minimum and Maximum income	-	-	-	-	-	6000 to 2.5 lakhs
4.	Per family average income						Rs. 64,848/-

Expenditure Pattern of Sample Tourists

An examination of expenditure pattern of sample respondents was made. The expenditure incurred on (1) travel, (2) staying/ accommodation, (3) photograph, (4) entry fee, etc. was studied. It was found that no sample tourist has spent on entry fee in the tourists centres. Whatever, the amount was spent that was on the personal expenditure. The table 5 shows the itemwise expenditure.

Out of the total cost incurred by all the sample (66) families, large portion (59.52%) was spent on travel made by either state transport bus, private bus or by train. Followed by accommodation cost i. e. 23.61% in total cost, while 16.86% cost was made on photography. This shows that the people were giving more significance to photography. But photography of what items? Scene and scenery. Yes; but unless, one protects the nature, there

Table 5: Expenditure Pattern of Sample Tourists

(Amount in Rs.)

Sr. No.	*Particulars*	*Travel*	*Accommodation boarding*	*Photograph*	*Total*
1.	Total cost	26724	10600	7570	44894
2.	Average cost	404	160	114	680
3.	% to total cost	59.52	23.61	16.86	100
4.	No.of families availed the facilities	66	18	26	-

would be no photography, except the personal photograph. Now a days there is no budget provision for the entry fee or pollution fee, natural conservation fees, etc. which is must.

Cost of Photography

Photography has become prestigious common hobby of tourists coming from middle and high income group. The photographs are taken of natural scene and scenery, which is God gifted to the human being. But now a day it seems that man has not done anything to protect the environment except government and few NGOs. It is said that nature is the best friend of man; but man is the worst enemy of nature. From this point it was analysed that 57.58% of the respondents were traveling without their own camera or without taking photographs, but remaining 42.42% of them had spend Rs. 250 to 500/- on photography in the travel.

One can conclude that people like natural beauty and they want to preserve only the memory of it in their camera; but they do not feel that it is their duty to pay something to nature, either in the form of money cost or labour cost.

Opinions about Entry Fee

Environment has its assimilative power. But this assimilation function has its limit. As the production process cross this limit, the process of degradation and pollution starts. Once the environment is polluted it is very difficult to improve the environment. Therefore, the main polluters of the tourists centres must be charged the fees, and the such collected amount should be spent on the management of environmental pollution.

Willingness to Pay Principle

Willingness to pay of consumers is very important. Willingness to pay of consumers depends upon the ability to pay and ability to pay is determined according to economic soundness of consumers. Each persons WT differs from person to person and place to place, as it shows the welfare of persons. If the visitors are left to them to pay the amount as per their desire or ability, then we will find that nobody will pay any amount. But the government or the authority which takes care of the centres is authorized to charge certain amount of fee; then it will be a good amount of income.

In the survey work of all the coastal tourist centres it was found that no centre was having any fee, and all centres were free of cost. But considering the future condition of such places it is necessary to charge some entry fee. For example, the Sindhudurg Fort which is more than 30 feet high is in dilapidated condition. The West side pillar has collapsed. The other sides are in critical condition. If proper care is to be taken by the Archeological Department, they should collect some amount in the form of entry fee from the visitors i.e. tourists. Hence, the respondents were directly asked (Table 6) whether they can pay at the time of visit at tourist centres. Their replies were summarised as under.

These replies shows that many tourists are neither willing to pay nor they have ability to pay. This shows that the visitors have not understood the role of environment in their life and still they consider the nature

Table 6: Willingness to Pay (WTP)/Entry Fee for Tourist Centres

Sr.No.	Particulars	Amount of fees (in Rs.)				Total
		0	5	10	15	
1.	Sample respondents	9	28	22	7	66
2.	% in total	13.63	42.42	33.33	10.60	100
3.	Minimum and maximum	-	-	-	-	Rs. 5 and Rs. 15

1. Why one should pay as these places are natural and holy places belonging to all?
2. What benefits will they get from their payment?
3. We are unable to pay the fees.
4. The centres have no sitting arrangements, drinking water facilities, hence, they won't pay.

as a free gift of nature. It is wonderful thing that on an average each group has spent Rs. 291 on photograph, but they are reluctant to pay even Rs. 5 for the maintenance of natural places.

Though the tourist has opposed to pay directly, yet it was seen that they have shown their willingness to pay some amount if charged. About 72% of them were willing to pay, while other had made the above cynical remarks.

Nature of Mental and Academic Preparation for Tour

It is always true that planning is the base of any activity whether it may be financial, educational, environmental or tour. Before, one visits the tourist centres, he has to read some related literature on the places and the literature on how to behave in nature. The National and the States Tourism Development Authorities have produced a lot of literature on this. Reading of this literature helps to see the places in detail and also it helps to protect the environment. Out of the total respondents 54.55% of them said that they have read the literature or they were heard about the places. Most of them said that use of plastic is banned in tourists centres and that was followed by them. A few respondents said that they were knowing the slogan i.e. "each one; plant one tree", or "Plant and preserve trees" etc. We feel that more awareness will be created by supplying such material by the Government at entry point of the tourist centre. This will avoid the loud shouting, throwing of stones, cutting of tree branches, making scratches to buildings, etc.

Cleanliness of Environment Centres

Out of the total respondents (Table 7) 60.61% of them said that cleanliness of the tourist centres was better, while 39.39% of them said that the places were not well maintained taken into consideration the day to day sweeping sitting arrangements, drinking water facility etc. It was observed that the visitors who were already well knowing the significance of environment, were unhappy about the cleanliness of centres. But others who were not having environment awareness were expressed their satisfaction. This shows that still large number of visitors have no knowledge of environment and its pollution. Hence, one can conclude that there is a need for environmental awareness. None of the centres have any sign boards or instructions to visitors about the use of environmental places except Sindhudurg Fort. The Tourism Authority of Maharashtra seems unaware of the damage made by visitors.

Table 7: Cleanliness of Tourist Centres

Sr. No.	*Particulars*	*Good*	*Not Good*	*Total*
1.	No. of respondents	40	26	66
2.	% in total	60.61	39.39	100

Nature of Environmental Damage made by Tourists

It is generally seen that the tourists who visit the centres usually damage the centres by many ways. Our cultural monuments such as Ajanta and Yellora have experienced the damage made by visitors, not deliberately but out of curiosity and self satisfaction. The forest places have been damaged by cutting the branches of tree and by disturbing the ecosystem of indigenous habitats. The sound pollution is another pollution taken place quickly in our country and tourist centres are no exception. With a view to know the damage made by tourists at the centres; the question was asked to the tourists, who visited the sample places and it was found (Table 8) that 70% of the respondents said that there was no any kind of pollution made by them or by another visitors. But 30% of them said that the visitors were also responsible for the environment damage such as;

1. Use and throw of plastic bags and pieces of newspapers i.e. generation of solid waste.
2. Cutting of small branches of trees.
3. Killing of sea animals and insects.
4. Use of tender coconut, water and throwing the coconut shell in open space.
5. Sound pollution by tourists vehicles.
6. Air pollution by Diesel Engine due to boating.
7. Scratches made for writing the names on historical and temple walls.
8. Pollution of Sweet water source.

Table 8: Nature of Environmental Damage

Sr. No.	Particulars	Opinions in favour of			Total
		Damage	No damage	No reply	
1.	No. of respondents	20	36	10	66
2.	% in total	30.30	54.54	15.15	100

Though the intensity of environment damage at the tourist centres was low, yet due do increasing visitors, the beauty of nature is threatened. An effort was made to enquire whether the local people had made some environmental pollution as mentioned above; but the majority of the (79%) said that the local people had not made any deliberate pollution.

Suggestions for the Improvement of Environment at the Tourist Centres

The opinions of the sample tourists regarding the sitting arrangement, lighting, drinking water facilities, public services, availability of dust bin, the plantation etc. were judged in the survey work. Majority 45.46% of the respondents (Table 9) expressed their desire regarding the cleanliness and plastic pollution took place at the centres while 12.12% said that security guards should be kept at the seashore places such as Kunkeshwar, Malwan, Vengurla, etc. As tourist has no judgment of sea water and tides. On many occasions mishap has happened. This can be avoided if such arrangement is made by the concerned centers. This can be done by charging some fees from each passenger.

Table 9: Suggestions for Improvement of Tourist Centres

Sr. No.	*Particulars*	*Suggestions*						*Total*
		No suggestions	*Benches for sitting*	*Plastic may be banned*	*Lighting facility*	*Tree plantations*	*Watchman*	
1.	No. of respondents	8	4	22	2	8	22	66
2.	% in total	12.12	6.06	33.33	3.03	12.12	33.33	100

Conclusion

It was seen that the touring hobby is more among the educated people rather than the illiterate, because there is more awareness. The recreation value is known among the educated and high income groups. The roadway is the main mode of transport, though train facility is available. To attract more passengers, the state transport should reduce its charges. About 58% of the respondents had visited this place second time as they liked the natural environment at the coastal places. The bifurcation of total expenditure shows that major item of tour cost is on travel (59.52%) and accommodation, while photography has become the regular item of cost of tour. Out of total, 72% of the respondents said that they will pay some fees if charged. The tourists have made the environmental damage to some extent such as plastic use and throw, cutting of branches, generation of solid waste, scratches to historical places, etc.

9

Environmental Laws and Policy in India

Today's generation is going through a valuable phase. Nature and environment; which gave birth to man and nursed him is in peril. Environmental preservations, on which the vary existence of mankind is dependent, is posing an overriding challenge to him. Environmental degradation is not a new problem. It has been arising ever since the human civilization began on earth and man began to exploit the natural resources for his survival. At that time the population was not so imposing a problem as it is now. Therefore, environment was not much affected. With the arrival of western culture in India, consumerist culture began to flourish, and worked havoc on environment.

Nature and environment was given great importance from the Rigvedic period. Sukta (Verse) of Rigveda states that, "The sky is like a father, the earth is like a mother and the space like their son. This, universe consisting of these three is like a family. Any kind of damage to any one of the three throws the universe off balance." (1) The aim in giving such massages was to warn people of the hazards of environmental population. In Chanakya Niti, it is said that planting even single tree with fruits and flowers makes the environment full of fragrance just as a family becomes delighted with a worthy son. Hence, we will be safe, so far the earth is full of nature. (2)

Environmental Protection: Whose Concern?

The Central Government has been given power to "take all such measures as it deems necessary or expedient for the people of protecting and improving the quality of environment" and preventing environmental pollution. It can lay down standards for quality of environment/ emissions or discharge of pollutants, specify areas where certain industries shall not be located and in other cases may lay down procedures and safeguards for prevention of accidents that may cause environmental pollution. The government may also examine manufacturing or other processes that can cause pollution, inspect, investigate and carry out related research besides establishing/recognizing environmental laboratories and institutions to carry out functions entrusted under the act. There is heavy punishment for contravention of Act, rules, direction in the form of fines of imprisonment, or both, irrespective of the fact that the defaulter is a firm, company or government department. The Government, if it deems fit, may direct closure, prohibition, or regulation of an industry, operation and process or that can stop any service such as electricity, water, etc.

Government Legal Efforts and Programmes to Contol the Environmental Pollution

There are more than 200 Central and State laws today that can be interpreted one way or other to protect the environment. The earliest of them, the shore Nuisance (Bombay and Kolaba) Act dates back to 1853. But laws enacted with the specific intention of controlling environmental degradation have been slow coming' partly because of inadequate appreciation's of environmental problems and partly because of wrong notions about legislative competence.

Until, 1976, environment protection as such did not figure anywhere in the constitution. In the 7th Schedule, which classifies various legislative entries into three groups, the Union List, the State List and the Concurrent list, there are various entries like forests and wildlife related to environment. On the face of it, it seemed that State legislatures alone are empowered to legislate on some of the most vital matters affecting environment.

Constitution and the Environmental Provisions

When the Constitution was amended for the 42nd time in 1976, certain environmental provisions were incorporated. For the first time expression "environmental protection" found a place and this led many scholars to argue that by 42nd amendment, the Central Government wanted certain powers which it did not have so far to protect the environment.

Directive Principles of State Policy

Article 48 A was added to the Directive Principles of State Policy and stated:

"The State shall endeavor to protect and improve the natural environment and safeguard the forest and wildlife in the country." In the chapter on fundamental duties, which was inserted into the constitution for the first time, Article 51 A(g) provided "it shall be the duty of every citizen of Indian to protect and improve the natural environment including forests, lakes, rivers and wildlife and to have compassion for living creatures". Besides this, the entire dealing with 'forests' and 'wildlife' were dropped from the State list and inserted in the Concurrent list. (4)

Selective List of Environmental Legislation

Powers to legislate on industry, mines and minerals, oil fields, fishing, inter-state rivers and river valleys have been assigned to the Central Government under List – I, and further, it has been authorized to social planning under concurrent list – III of schedule VII of the Constitution. The State Government can also legislate on industry, mines and mineral, fisheries, but subject to the provisions of the central legislation. Exercising the powers conferred by the constitutions, the Central Government has passed many laws. Some of the main laws passed are as foılows:

Selective List of Legislatio in Related Environment: Central Enactments

1. **Water Pollution:**

   1.1 The River Boards Act, 1956.

   1.2 The Merchant Shipping (Amendment) Act, 1970.

   1.3 The Water (prevention and Control of Pollution) Act, 1974.

   1.4 The Water (Prevention and Control of Pollution) Cess Act. 1977.

2. **Air Pollution:**

   2.1 The India Boiler's Act.1923.

   2.2 The Factories Act. 1948.

   2.3 The Mines and Minerals (regulation and Development) Act, 1947.

   2.4 The Industries (Development and Regulation) Act, 1951.

   2.5 The Air (Prevention and Control of Pollution) Act, 1981.

3. **Radiation:**

   3.1 The Atomic Energy Act, 1962.

   3.2 Radiation Projection Rules, 1971.

4. Pesticides:

4.1 The Poison Act, 1919.

4.2 The Factories Act, 1948.

4.3 The Insecticides Act, 1968.

5. Forest and Wildlife:

5.1 The Indian Fisheries Act, 1897.

5.2 The Indian Forest Act, 1927.

5.3 The Prevention of Food Adulteration Act, 1954.

5.4 The Ancient Monuments and Archaeological Sites and Remains Act, 1958.

5.5 The Wild Life (Protection) Act, 1972.

5.6 The Urban Land (Ceiling and Regulation) Act, 1976.

5.7 The Forest Conservation Act, 1980.

5.8 The Prevention of Cruelly to Animal Act.

6. General:

1.1 The Indian Penal Code, 1860.

1.2 The Environment (Protection) Act, 1986.

6.2 State Enactments:

1. Water Pollution:

1.1 Orissa River Pollution Act, 1953.

1.2 Maharashtra Prevention of Water Pollution Act, 1969.

2. Smoke Control:

2.1 The Bengal Nuisance Act, 1905.

2.2 The Bombay Smoke Nuisance Act, 1912.

2.3 The Gujrat Smoke Nuisance Act, 1963.

2.4 The Motor Vehicles Act, 1939.

3. **Pest Control:**

3.1 The Mysore Destructive Insects and Pest Act, 1917.

3.2 The Andhra Pradesh Agricultural Pest and Disease Act, 1919.

3.3 The Assam Agricultural Pests and Diseases Act, 1954.

3.4 The UP Agrocitira; Disease and Pests Act, 1954.

3.5 The Kerala Agricultural Pests and Disease Act, 1958.

4. **Land Utilisatioin And Land Development:**

4.1 The Bihar Waste Lands (Reclamation, Cultivation and Improvement) Act, 1946.

4.2 The Andhra Pradesh Land Improvement Scheme Act, 1949.

4.3 The Acquisition of Land for Flood Control and Prevention of Erosion Act, 1955.

4.4 The Delhi Restriction of Uses of Land Act, 1964.

Law of Tort and Industrial Pollution

It is said that the roots of environmental laws lies in the tort of nuisance. "Nuisance is the unlawful interference with the use or enjoyment of land or some right over or in connection with it." Excessive smoke, bad smell, sonit sludge, noise vibration, noxious vapour which causes discomfort to man or cause damage to vegetation or property is nuisance. In such a cases the owner or occupier of the land on which it originated is held liable to pay compensation to the aggravated person. Therefore, if any industry emits smoke or noxious fumes and vapour it can be held liable for tort of nuisance. The owner of the Union Carbide (Bhopal) Industry was held liable under the Law of Tort.

The Indian Penal Code and Pollutioin

Though the IPC, 1960, does not deal with any specific crimes like industrial pollution, such cases have been dealt with the public nuisance, under section 269 of the code. Section 278 of the Code also provides punishment for making atmosphere noxious to health. But the punishment provided for these offenses is too meager. Therefore, the code could not pay an effective role to prevent and control pollution. Corollary to it, Section 133 of the Criminal Procedure Code 1973 also deals with public nuisance. The magistrate is empowered under this section to order the removal of the nuisance who has caused it or can take necessary steps to prevent or abate the nuisance. Under the Section 133 of this procedure Code, Metropolitan Magistrate of Delhi ordered the closure of Shri Ram Food and Fertilizer Industry when there was a leakage of oleum gas in the year 1985.

The Public Liability Insurance Act, 1991

This benevolent piece of legislation was passed for providing immediate relief to the persons affected by chemical accident occurring while handing any hazardous substance as matter connected with these. Now the collector has been authorized to dispose of the claim for relief within a period of three months from the date of the receipt of application. At the same time, it is not necessary for the claimant to prove that the death, injury or damage was due to any wrongful act, or neglect or default of any person. This act provides security for the weaker sections of the society especially workers and wage earners. Under this act the industry or owner, who controls the handing of hazardous substance are required to take out insurance policy for the workers.

A careful study of Tiwari Committee suggests that the legislations passed so far are either inadequate or defective on the following respects:

1. They are not comprehensive in their approach.
2. They are fragmented, separated and segregated.
3. They control specific types of pollution rather than preserving and protecting the environment.
4. Laws are cumbersome rather than streamlined, simple and understandable to common man.
5. Few of the laws are outdated.

Besides bringing these defects to the surface, the committee also recommended:

1. The creation of a separate Department of Environment at the Centre.
2. The creation of posts of Environmental Advisors in all the ministries
3. Constitution of a "Cabinet Sub Committee" on the environment under the Chairmanship of Prime Minister, and
4. Review of Central and State laws on environmental management.
5. Public Awareness and Public Participation should be made key elements while making any environmental policy, planning or management.
6. To enact, and have an umbrella legislation which should take care of entire problems of pollution under one roof.

In order to fulfill the recommendations of the Tiwari Committee, the separate Department of Environment. Forest and Wild Life was created in 1985. When Late Mr. Rajiv Gandhi came to power he created two high power agencies namely The National Waste Land Development Board (NWLDB) and The Central Ganga Authority (CGA) to tackle specific environmental problems. Mr. Rajiv Gandhi was involved nature, fully devoted to the cause of environment. His strong view was that come what may, we should never compromise any thing at the cost of environment. Mr. Rajiv Gandhi noticed that in spite of number of legislation's, suitable provisions for conservation and enhancement of environment in 5th, 6th, 7th, Five year plans, there seems a continuing decline in the quality of the environment, the Bhopal tragedy which killed more than 2,700 people and injured over 20,000 people, aggravated the problem. To combat all these new Act in 1986 which is known as The Environment (Protection) Act came into force. This was the first direct legislation passed by the Government of India as the basis of the Resolutions Passed in 1972 at Stockholm at a World Conference on Human Environment.

Supreme Court and Environment Protection

Mr. M.C. Mehta, the famous public interest lawyer, who has successfully fought and won more than 50 landmark environmental cases in the supreme court says the judiciary has been very active and therefore the nation should be grateful for them. The firm stand of the court orders have helped to save Ridge in Delhi, protect historical monuments like the Taj Mahal and protects rivers like the Ganges. The judiciary is merely doing its duty caring out its constitutional mandate in protection of the environment. Environmental protection is guaranteed under Article 48-A and 51 A (9) of the constitution. The apex court has also widened the scope of Art. 21 (right to life) by stipulation that a clean environment is essential to human survival. (5)

Without a protected area network, India would today be with little or no forests. Whatever has survived has been either due to the sacred groves or to the legislation enacted in the seventies. Oil refineries, dams, mines, power plants etc. cannot be constructed within or immediately adjacent to sanctuaries or national parks. Without such land-use restrictions little would have been left in India. (6)

Role of Central and State Pollution Control Boards

The primary responsibility to control and protect the pollution lies with the State Pollution and Prevention and Control Boards. The Central Government has given the directives to the State Governments to form the Pollution Control Boards, and accordingly, most of the states have formed the Boards to protect and enrich environment. The Boards enforce the following legislations:

1. The Water Act, 1974.
2. The Water Cess Act, 1977.
3. The Air Act, 1981.
4. Environment Protection Act, 1986.

The Boards grant permission (No objective Certificates) to industries on receipt of their applications. It also keeps watch on conditions imposed in certificate. Erring industries are prosecuted by the Pollution Board. These Boards are taking the help of State Industrial and Investment Corporations, States Financial Corporations, Municipal Councils, etc. In addition, they are undertaking massive tree plantation and workshops. The Boards have full fledged laboratory and possess mobile laboratories also.

The Central Pollution Control Board has done survey work on Resource Recycling, Coastal Pollution Control, Ecological Impact Assessment, etc. In short such Boards are committed to a clean environment.

In order to enforce the law strictly, the Government needs a large enforcement machinery which is not just costly but also largely effective. The pollution control authorities are ill equipped (under staff) to monitor and regulate the small and medium industries. In many cases the authorities depend on information provided by industry rather than having an independent means of verifying such information. As a result, it is only after an incident such an industrial accident, takes place, the pollution control boards initiate action.

Defects of State Pollution Control Boards

The State Pollution Boards are not satisfied with their work as well as on the working of Central Pollution Board. One of the head of State Boards has expressed the view that the Boards did all the "dirty work" and central Board did nothing but lord over them. He was convinced that the Central Board performed no useful function and should be wound up. Inadequacy of staff as well as finances poses a big problem for the Boards. For example, The Maharashtra Board has a budget provision of Rs. 10.5 million per year and a staff of 400, which monitors 1,75,000 industries. The Board has again with additional task of air pollution control, without additional funds. (8)

Some of the Pollution Control Boards (PCBs) are not working properly. For example, the U.P.P.C.B. used wrong standards in measuring pollution levels. Similarly, the West Bengal PCB officers were found guilty and they were suspended by the State Government. In Goa, the Minister for Industries remains the chairman of PCB and hence the environmental havoc. It means, the Government is also not committed about implementation of laws.

The World Development Report 1997, has also reported that the progress in alleviating the environmental problems has been slow in developing countries because of lack of capacity and political will, at both the national and the local level. (7)

Features of the Environment (Protection) Act, 1986

This act is more comprehensive in its approach to control pollution than the earlier ones, the main provisions are as under.

1. It defines the environment, pollution and pollutant and also of hazardous substances.
2. It decides the standards for discharge of environmental pollutants and gives powers of inspection of any premises, plant, equipment, machinery etc.
3. To issue directions for closer, prohibition on regulation of industry.
4. The section 10, provides ; any person who contravenes the provisions of this act, is made punishable with imprisonment of a term which may extend to 5 years and with fine which may extend to 1 lack or both. This section further provides, that if the failure continues then the additional fine up to Rs. 5000/- per day may be inflicted.

Environmental Laws and Performance: The State Efforts

Following the courts directives, in T.N. 164 tanneries (1996) were closed down. In Rajasthan (Bichhari) about 14 villages were wiped out by the discharge of hydrochloric acid effluents from chemical industries producing dyes. The use of this chemical has been banned in developed countries. A report on water sampling in the area of this industry showed massive contamination of well; which in turn became threat to fertile land.

The PCB of Maharashtra has issued notice to about 2000 factories (1995-97) to stop their production and 14 factories were closed. The PCB has classified the factories in three categories i.e.

1. Red category : Highly polluted.
2. Orange category : Slightly polluted.
3. Green category : Pollution less.

Similarly, Government has listed the 29 highly polluted industries and such factories cab be taken away from the public at the same time for the new factories the provision of public hearing been made. Despite all these provisions, the Bombay and Thane area has been considered highly polluted in Maharashtra.

Need for Further Amendment in Environmental Laws

One time a slogan Industrialize or Perish existed Industrialize and Perish. Science which has contributed so much to human progress has also posed a serious threat to human survival. The Government of India has done a laudable work by passing the Environment (Protection) Act, 1986. This act consists of 26 sections divided into 4 chapters for prevention of hazards to human being and protection and improvement of environment. The Act is a welcome development in the legislative history of India. The act gives enormous power to the Central Government for planning and execution of a nationwide programme for the prevention, control and abatement of the environmental pollution. (9)

It is also pertinent to note that the problem of pollution cannot be tackled only by Government or Laws. An extra provision should be made in black and white in the Act itself providing:

"Every industry shall have a water treatment or effluent treatment, and air treatment plant installed in it before it starts production". This will solve half the problem.

Need for Environmental Court

In order to eliminate waste and social cost, there is a need for specialized administrative court to deal with environmental cases. The Supreme Court of India has also emphasized the need for environmental courts. Environmental court may be established in each state and union territory with an appellate court at the centre and regional branches. This court shall have jurisdiction over civil and criminal matters relating to environment. Central environment court shall have the status of the High Court and its judges may be appointed in the manner of the judges of Administrative Service Tribunal are appointed. The detailed blueprint may be worked out by the Law Commission.

It is discouraging to note that the Environment Protection Act. 1986 has not made any provision in this respect. (10)

Can Environmental Laws Bring Sustainable Development?

Article 14 in constitution of India clearly provides for equality before laws and equal protection of laws, which is one of the concepts of Rule of Law as propounded by Sir A.V. Dicey. Hence it may be safely be said that, if we adhere to the law, we can protect the environment and bring the sustainable development, because it is said in Upnishada that, "Law is the King of Kings. He (King) is not above the law. If he violates the law then he (even the King) could be punished like an other citizen. (11)

Role of Activists in Sustainable Development

The laws, have not stopped pollution of the country's air, water and land. The country's forests present a bleak picture. Poverty and crass commercialism have been responsible for the rapid depletion of the rich ecological resources of India. Specialists and environmental activists have played a useful role in generating public awareness and, attracting Government's attention to the ignorant poor and their wanton destruction by rapacious commercial interests. Their success has been dramatic, but limited. (12)

Community pressure to protect the environment is also an powerful factor than the formal rules. In many localities such efforts had set in motion sustained environmental reforms. For example, 1960 in Japan the local medical association made petition against oil refinery emissions and the health damages they caused. May factories made an agreement and they were able to crub the pollution. (13)

Laws are Many and Also the Loopholes

Taking into consideration, the above legal provisions, it seems that Indian Government is well aware of the environmental degradation. However, there are many loopholes in its implementation and also there is lack of awareness of law even in educated as well as uneducated people of our country. Some of the following examples show that still the laws remain on paper and not in practice.

1. The Bombay Municipal Corporation in its over 108 years existence, has never drawn up a comprehensive waste management plan.

2. About 50% of the sewage generated in Ahmedabad city drains into ;the Sabarmati River without treatment.

3. The case study of Gujrat's "Golden Corridor" the 450 km. Stretch Wapi to Mehsan houses 190 big industrial units including 100 of chemical units is an illustration of the manner in which environmental laws remains on paper.

4. All is not well even with garden city of India-Banglore. About 400 slum colonies in this city do not have a sewerage system. Due to the shortage of staff and vehicles it hampers the efforts of the Corporation in cleaning waste.

5. The numerous cow sheds in the city of Patna provide an ideal breeding ground for the sand fly, which transmits the deadly "Kala-azar". The same problem is in Bombay city.

6. The sanitary condition of Bhopal city is still worse except newly developed areas like Bhopal Development Authority. Only one non-government organization has made some efforts to improve the sanitary condition in Bhopal. (14)

Conclusion

Finally, it can be said that the pollution is an evil but no one can get out of it and hence it is not the responsibly of any single party. Here we can quote the observation of Justice Krishna Iyer.

"Ultimate Solution is not theoretical constitution and black letter laws but a profound movement for justice to Nature and Homosapians."

Thus, it is true that neither law nor judiciary [Rule of Law] can only bring sustainable development; unless a well mobilized public opinion [Rule of People] is created against environmental pollution by making people aware of its benefits.

REFERENCES

1. Trivedi, I.V. and Rena, Jatana (Ed.), Impact of Environment, Rupa Books Pvt., Jaipur, 1995. p .1.
2. Trivedi, I.V. and Rena – Ibid p. 2.
3. Trivedi, I.V. and Rena – Ibid pp. 2, 4.
4. Trivedi, I.V. and Rena – Ibid pp. 27, 28.
5. The Hindu Survey of the Environment, 1996 (Madras) p. 205.
6. Poachers still on the prowl: - Valmik Thapar, The Hindu Survey of Environment 96, Chennai, page 155.
7. The World Development Report 1997 published for the World Bank, Oxford University Press, June 1997, p. 138, Washington.

8. Khan, Rahmatullah, Enforcing Environmental Laws, Environmental Challenges, (ed) Wiley Eastern Ltd. New Delhi 1993 pp. 51, 53.

9. Mehta, C. S. Environmental and Law, RBSA Publishers, SMS Highway, Jaipur, 1994. P. 29.

10. Massey, I. P. Dynamics of Environmental Management and the Dialects of legal strategies. A Himachal Pradesh experience (ed) Legal Aspects of Environmental Pollution and Its Management – edited by S. Mushrraaf Ali CBC publishes and distributions Delhi 1992, p. 84.

11. Mehta, C.S. – Ibid p. 6.

12. Varshney, C.K. and Sardesai, D.R., Environmental Challenges, Wiley Eastern Limited, New Delhi, 1993 p. 55.

13. World Development Report 1997.p. 71.

14. The Hindu, Survey of Environment (Madras), 1993, 1994 and 1995.

10

Coastal Environment Acts

In the developing world "the development" has become synonymous with "deforestation and desertification" and "progress has become synonymous with pollution." But we have to encourage the process of development without destruction and protect the foundation of the life support system, including the habitats of plants, animals and microbe. Gene erosion is very dangerous because genetic diversity is the backbone of evolution."[1]

Coastal and Marine Pollution

Oceans, the treasure house of enormous riches, cover two-thirds of the world's surface. In ancient time, oceans were used only for transportation and for fishing. The various uses of the sea were known only of late. Fishing is one of the most flourishing industries in the world. With the recent scientific discoveries, the mineral wealth in the ocean has been exploited. The oil hungry world has turned oceans for oil.

Without the sea, this planet would be uninhabitable. Yet, man persists in using the water sphere of the earth as a global garbage dump for an incredible quantity and variety of human and industrial wastes with little regard for the effect on the ocean environment.

The potentially polluting materials dumped or injected into the ocean are divisible into five major types.

1. Bulk material, such as sewage, sludge or aredge spoils.
2. Phosphates and other materials that affect the biological cycles of the sea.
3. Heavy metals, such as mercury.
4. Petroleum and oil products.
5. Chlorinated hydrocarbons, such as pesticides, DDT and the industrial chemicals termed PCB.
6. Dead Animals.

Industrial and Domestic Wastes

The rising industrial and domestic wastes have resulted in heavy stress of pollution of water bodies such as lakes, rivers and coastal area. The unregulated growth of urban areas without necessary infra-structural services and proper collection, transportation, treatment and disposal of solid wastes have resulted in increased pollution and health hazard of these wastes. Based on surveys carried out, the urban municipal solid waste generated in India in 1997 was estimated at 48 million tones. The discharge of sewage into the sea can also benefit marine food chains through nutrient enrichment. There is a dilemma concerning conflicting uses of coastal zones because the choice is not simply between 'clean' and 'dirty' water but may also involve the choice between waters of low and high productivity, including food organisms for humans.

Similarly, some fishes are caught but are not good to eat; hence, such fishes are thrown away, which pollute the environment. Heavy metals such as lead and cardamom were found in Thane creek of Mumbai coast.

The Cochin region of Kerala coast has been found affected by petroleum hydrocarbons. An area of 6700 Sq. Km. under mangroves is under biotic pressure due to fishing, land use changes in land-sea interface and pollution of water. Out of 85 wetlands of international importance in the country, 45% are subject to moderate or high threat.

Sea Erosion Threat to Coastal Fishing Villages

An important impact of climate change and global warming may be the rise in sea level. The primary effect of sea level rise will be increased coastal flooding, erosion, storm surges and wave activity. Primary studies on the impact of one meter sea level rise on the Indian coastline indicate that 0.41% of India's coastal area (see Table) is inundated.

Table 1: Land Area and Population affected in India by one Meter Sea Level Rise

Sr. No.	*State*	*% of State area inundated*	*% of the State population affected*
1.	Goa	4.84	7.25
2.	Tamil Nadu	0.52	2.91
3.	Orissa	0.81	1.76
4.	West Bengal	1.88	2.35
5.	Andra Pradesh	0.19	0.93
6.	Gujrat	0.92	1.07
7.	Maharashtra	0.18	1.75
8.	Andman & Nicobar	0.72	NA
9.	Karnataka	0.15	0.56
	Total	**0.41**	**1.68**

Source: State of Environment, 1995, MOEF, GOI: Economic Survey, 1998-99 p. 162.

Severe sea erosion had occurred in some of the coastal fishing villages like Moti Danti, Nani Danti and Udwada, situated in Valsad District of Gujrat during monsoon period of 1986. Many of huts of fishermen were destroyed. Nearly 2.5 Sq. Km. area of Moti Danti village was lost due to sea erosion.

International Environmental Laws on Sea Conservation

There are a plethora of international conventions and national laws, which are concentrated and being implemented to protect our environment. The large number of international conventions at global and regional levels have adopted for the protection of biological diversity prevalent at their general nature on marine eco-system. These conventions are as follows:

Convention for protection of Mediterranean Sea against pollution adopted at Barcelona on 16th February 1976

This convention was adopted on 16th February 1976 in response to the rapid increase of human activities in the Mediterranean Sea Area, particularly in the field at industrialization and urbanization as well as the seasonal increase in the coastal population due to tourism, and the danger posed to the marine environment and to human health by pollution from land based sources, man-made off shore structures and river estuaries of the Mediterranean Sea.

The contracting parties to this protocol commit themselves to appropriate measures to control pollution of the Sea Area. The common guidelines shall take into account the ecological criteria of the parties and their need for development and the absorptive capacity of the marine environment.[2] The parties shall cooperate in scientific and technological fields related to pollution from land based sources.

The Law of the Sea Convention, 1982

This Law deals with the conservation and management at the living resources of the High Seas. Under Article 117 of the Convention it is specified that, "all States have the duty to take or to cooperate with other states in taking measures for their respective nationals, as may be necessary for the conservation of the living resources of the high seas. Further, marine mammals can also be conserved and managed according to Article 65 of the convention.[3] Under this law the exploitation of marine resources are regulated. The conservation of marine resources appears not the national but an international concern.

A General Survey of Legislations in Foreign Countries

We can summarize some of the global level laws and statutes relating to coastal environment. England was the first country, which took lead in this respect, followed by USA. Some important laws in England and USA are cited below:

England

1. The Merchant Shipping (Oil Pollution) Act, 1971.
2. The Merchant Shipping Act, 1974 (Part III).
3. The Prevention Oil Pollution Act, 1971.
4. The Petroleum (Production) Act, 1934.
5. The Mineral Working (Offshore Installations) Act, 1971.
6. The Coastal Protection Act, 1949.
7. The Continental Shelf Act, 1964.
8. The Petroleum and Submarine Pipelines Act, 1975.
9. The Dumping at Sea Act, 1974.

10. The Sea Fishing Regulations Act, 1966.
11. The Rivers (Prevention of Pollution) Acts 1951 and 1956.
12. The Control of Pollution Act, 1974.
13. The Littler Act, 1958 and the Dangerous Littler Act, 1971.

The first act was passed in 1934 to avoid the pollution by petroleum production. The separate act viz. Coastal Protection Act was passed in 1949, yet the coastal environment in England is not satisfactory.

American Law

In America, the conservation of biological diversity is important for several reasons, such as scientific, moral, aesthetic, recreational economical and environmental. The United States has tried to protect the species of these regions by imposing environmental controls on foreign assistance programs. Domestically, two types of laws were adopted, namely, species protection laws and special areas designated and protection laws. The species protection statues includes the Marine Mummal Protection Act of 1972, the Magnuson Fishery Conservation and Management Act of 1976 and the Endargened Species Act of 1973. In addition, The National Environmental Policy Act of 1969 has a direct bearing on the conservation of biological diversity in the United States. The Congress was urged to recognize that "each person should enjoy a healthful environment and that each person has a responsibility to contribute to the preservation and enhancement of the environment.[4]

Coastal Zone Management Act, 1972

The Coastal Zone Management Act of 1972 was adopted "to establish a national policy and develop a national programme for the management, beneficial use, protection and development of the land and water resources at the Nation's Coastal Zones and for other purposes" because the coastal zone was beneficial for harvesting of fish, shellfish and other living marine resources, which are ecologically fragile and extremely vulnerable to destruction by man's interference.

The Marine Protection Research and Sanctuaries Act of 1972

The discharge of dangerous chemicals, industrial waste and radioactive and various other toxic substances into marine Eco-systems may destroy the marine environment. The living resources as well as Mangroves are the critical components of tropical marine ecosystems. Mangroves protect coastal areas from erosion and reclaim from sea. Under this act, the dumping of all types of material into ocean waters is prohibited. In addition, materials containing living organisations such as biological pests, viruses, pathogenic microorganism or other agents capable of infecting or altering the normal population of the organism is prohibited under this Act.[5]

On the basis of the above discussions one can make the following recommendation that it is a known fact that the concern for international environment has been the main aim at both the developed and developing countries and for its preservation both developed and developing countries must come closer.

Marine Pollution and Legal Provisions in India

For preserving marine environment, the following Acts have been passed;

1. The Shore Nuisance (Bombay & Colaba) Act, 1853.
2. The Obstruction of Fairways Act, 1981.
3. The Indian Fisheries Act, 1897.

4. The Indian Ports Act, 1908.
5. The Major Port Trust Act 1963.
6. The Merchant Shipping (Amended) Act, 1970.
7. The Territorial Waters, Continental Shelf Exclusive Economic Zone and Other Maritime Act, 1976.
8. The Coastguards Act, 1978.
9. The Environment (Protection) Act, 1986.

Since 150 years, India has experienced the environmental laws. The laws passed in England were also applicable to India. But they are not able to help to protect the coastal environment.

Indian Penal Code of 1860, Sections Relevant to Natural Resource Managers

Section 268 on Public Nuisance

A person is guilty of a public nuisance, who does any act or is guilty of an illegal omission which causes any common injury, danger or annoyance to the public or to the people in general who dwell or occupy property in the vicinity or which must necessarily cause injury, obstruction, danger or annoyance to persons who may have occasion to use any public right.

Section 269

Negligent act likely to spread infection of disease dangerous to life.

Section 270

Malignant act likely to spread infection of disease dangerous to life.

Section 271

Disobedience to quarantine rule.

Under the above sections, imprisonment upto six months and fine is prescribed.

Section 428

Mischief by killing or maiming animal of the value of ten rupees or more. Imprisonment of two years or fine or both is suggested.

The above sections can be applied as public nuisance that can be created in respect of coastal environmental pollution. But the success of such provisions depends upon, how effectively these are implemented.

The Environmental Impact Assessment Notification, 1994 (As Amended Upto 10-4-1997) Issued By Ministry Of Environment And Forests, Government Of India, New Delhi is also useful to protect coastal environment.

The provisions in the Environment Impact Assessment Notification, 1994 reads as under:

"Whereas a notification under clause (a) of sub-rule (3) of rule 5 of the Environment (Protection) Rules, 1998 inviting objections from the public within sixty days from the date of publication of the said notification, against the intention of the Central Government to impose restrictions and prohibitions on the expansion and modernization of any activity or new projects being undertaken in any part of India unless environmental clearance has been accorded by the Central Government or the State Government in accordance with the procedure specified."

The list of projects requiring Environmental clearance from the Central Government covers 29 projects and industries, among them projects affecting seashore or marine environment are as follows:

1. Ports, Harbors, Airports.
2. Petroleum Refineries including crude and product pipelines.

3. Chemical Fertilizers.
4. Exploration for oil and gas and their production, transportation and storage.
5. All tourism projects between 200 to 500 meters of High Tide Line or at locations with an elevation of more than 1000 meters with investment of more than Rs. 5 crores.
6. Raw Skins and Hides.
7. Pulp, Paper and Newsprint.
8. Dyes, Cement, Foundries, Electroplating.

Care should be taken to prohibit such industries in the nearby sea-shore or such projects should be having clearance.

Coastal Stretches as Coastal Regulation Zone

The Coastal Regulation Zone were declared as per the powers conferred by (d) of sub-rule (3) of Rule 5 of the Environment (Protection) Rules, 1986 and all other powers vesting in its behalf. The Central Government declares the coastal stretches of seas, bays, estuaries, creeks, rivers and backwaters which are influenced by tidal action upto 500 meters from the High Tide Line and the land between the Low Tide Line in Coastal Regulation Zone. The following (13) activities are declared as prohibited with the CRZ namely;

1. Setting up to new industries and expansion of industries, which need foreshore facilities.
2. Manufacturing, handling or storage or disposal of hazardous substances as specified.
3. Setting up and expansion of fish processing units including warehouses.
4. Discharge of untreated wastes and effluents from industries, cities or towns.

5. Dumping of city or town waste, waste management shall be phased out within a period of three years.

6. Dumping of ash or any waste from thermal power stations.

7. Land reclamation, bundling or disturbing the natural course of sea water.

Guidelines for Development of Beach Resorts/Hotels in the Designated Coastal Area

Any construction work regarding the hotels/resorts in the coastal area must be approved by the Ministry of Environment and Forest. In ecologically sensitive areas such as marine parks, mangroves, coral reels, breeding and spawning grounds of fish, wildlife habitats and such other areas may be notified by the Central/State/Union Territories as prohibited areas.

Economic Instruments: The Income Tax Act

The economic instruments such as environmental tax, pollution tax, marketable permits, deposit refund system, input taxes differential tax rates and subsidies for pollution abatement can be used. The aim is to give industries and consumers clear signals about the cost of using environmental and natural resources. Alongwith the laws, use of such incentives would facilitate operationalising the standard approach of Polluter Pays Principle.

The Income Tax Act, 1961 has been promulgated to consolidate and amend the law relating to Income Tax. This Act provides 30% depreciation allowance on certain Air and Water Pollution Control equipments.[7] These provisions have been incorporated in the Income Tax Rules, 1962, with effect from 23rd February 1983. The deductions are allowed to all projects in respect of depreciation of machinery and plant owned by the assessee. Such provisions motivate to invest in pollution control devices, which helps to the public as a whole and the project owner.

Provision of Environmental Audit

Submission of an environmental statement by the polluting units to the concerned State Pollution Control Boards has been made mandatory through a gazette notification issued under the Environment (Protection) Act, 1986. The environmental statement enables the units to take a comprehensive look at their industrial operations and facilities an undertaking of material flows and focusing on those areas where waste reduction and consequently saving in input costs, is possible.[8] However the impact of such audit depends upon the efficiency of the concerned authority i.e. Pollution Control Board.

Conclusion

India has been on the lower end of the top decline of marine fishing nations in the world since 1970. In 1993, the marine fish of the country stood at 2.3 million tonnes. We have not been able to improve upon this position even with the significant improvements in technology.

Earlier, certain communities use to undertake fishing as their main job; but since recent past, especially after new economic policy and globalization, new technology and foreign capital investment is made in fishing industry. The annual income of traditional fishermen has declined as a result of which the socioeconomic problems of coastal villages have increased. This situation has forced the government to undertake some welfare measures for protecting the right and improving the livelihood conditions of fishermen. In this situation; can coastal laws and regulations solve the environmental and employment problems? The sea has become the sink of all our sins;

can the laws restrict the multi-nationals from uncontrolled fishing? Whether, we will prefer environment before the foreign currency? All these questions need further judicial thinking and action.

The experience of various countries such as USA, England and others shows that the laws regarding the protection of coastal environment were passed long back. In India, also many legal provisions have been made, even 140 years back. But, many people are ignorant about them. The laws appear like a King Cobra with large fangs but without any venom. The laws have become only paper tiger. Although the acts contain severe penalties, yet they remain on paper. There are lacunas in the enforcement and management. On the other hand, the industries also feel that the laws are unnecessary burden on them. Therefore, the programme to provide Legal Aid to needy and poor persons should be undertaken. An eminent legal scholar Shri C. S. Mehta has suggested the Government of India to create a Legal Cell in the Ministry of Environment and Forest.

REFERENCES

1. Khoshoo, T.N. Environmental Concerns and Strategies, Indian Environmental Society, New Delhi, 1984.
2. Lipton, Raje and Chellapp: Sea Erosion Threat to Coastal Fishing Villages of Valsad Dist. Gujrat, Journal published by Central Marine Fisheries Research Institute, Cochin.
3. Protocol for the Protection of the Mediterranean Sea against Pollution from Land Based Source 16th May 1980, International Legal Material Vol. 19, No. 4, 1980.
4. United Nation Convention or the Law of the Sea 1982 done at Montego Barry, December 10, 1982.
5. U. S. Environmental Laws No. 4, p. 7.
6. International Legal Material N. 42, p. 693, taken from the book A. P. Nagore, Biological Diversity and International Environmental Law, APH Publishing Corporation, New Delhi, 1996.

7. Natraj Publishers and Wild Life Protection Society of India, New Delhi, 1999.

8. Bhattacharya, S. Indian Income Tax Law and Practice, p. 225, Reproduced by Mahesh Mathur, Legal Control of Environmental Pollution, Deep and Deep, New Delhi, p. 35, 1996.

9. GOI, Ninth Five Year Plan, Draft, 1998, p. 892.

11

Education in Coastal Environment

Like global warming and ozone layer depletion, coastal pollution is also a serious global environmental problem of every country. As oceans draw the boundaries of the countries, hence a single country's pollution problem becomes a global issue. The UN had declared the 1998 as the year of the Ocean with an objective to focus and reinforce the attention of the public, government and decision makers on the importance of oceans and coastal environment as a source for sustainable development.

Man looks upon the ocean not only for food but also for energy, drugs, navigation, climate, weather forecast, waste disposal etc. It is a fact that oceans are getting polluted by the extensive human activities. In fact, man knows very little about the ocean and the coastal environment and the eco-system. Coastal pollution is caused by sewage and industrial waste disposal, hazardous waste dumping, domestic wastes, accidents involving oil spill, salt farms, fishing and the increased navigation/transport across the oceans. All these factors affect the fish life and tourism.

Some Government and Government Bodies including fisheries co-operatives have shown concern about the ecological impact of coastal pollution. The State of Tamil Nadu, Andhra Pradesh, Orissa, Maharashtra and some part of Gujrat are facing this problem. The fishing, transport and tourism should be continued but with a check on environmental degradation. This paper discusses that the sustainable coastal environment can be maintained by protecting coastal land, seawater, plant and animal genetic resources through education.

Sustainable Coastal Resource Development

The issue of Sustainable Coastal Resource Development arises in the form that the world can no longer grow more food and population [demand] should be reduced, particularly in less developed country like India. There should be 'sustainable development', 'sustainable agriculture', sustainable mining', sustainable animal husbandry', etc. Sustainable Coastal Resource Development means to have such development that does not compromise the future of the people. It is the call of the coastal resources, living in cooperation with nature and not to harm or destroy the bio-diversity in the sea. One has to consider every micro-organism as a resource. For a child must survive on breast-feed but the mother cannot be sucked to death. The same concept, we have to apply while availing the sea resources.

Indian Constitution and Environment

No country on the globe except India has given a constitutional status to law relating to environmental control, protection and preservation. In 1976 specific provisions have been made in the body of the constitution thereby making it obligatory on the State and every citizen to protect and improve the natural environment. Our Supreme Court has observed that "the constitution is in an organic document which must grow and it must take stock of the vast socioeconomic problems particularly by improving the lot of common man consistent with dignity. Right to breath in free and fresh air, consume, free water, reside, walk and travel in noise-free environment is guaranteed by Article 21 to all the residents of India. In short, Article 21 confers the right to live with dignity.

Constitutional Sympathy for Environment Preservation

In the Constitution of India, specific provisions have been made to solve the problem of environment i.e.forly second amendment of 1976. Now, it is an obligatory duty of the state and every citizen to protect and improve the environment.

Part IV of the Constitution of India deals with the 'Directive Principles of State Policy'. An Article 47 lays down that the improvement of public health is one of the primary duties of the state. Article-48-A reads; as follows;

"The State shall endeavor to protect and improve the environment and to safeguard forests and wide life of the country."

The Constitution [Forty-second amendment] Act, 1976 incorporated Part IV-A after Part IV of the Constitution of India. This part enumerates certain fundamental duties of the citizens of India. Article-51-A (g) specifically deals with the fundamental duty regarding environment. This Article provides:

"It shall be the duty of every citizen of India to protect and improve the natural environment including forests, lakes, rivers and wide life and to have compassion for living creatures." As per this statement the river and sea is also covered under natural environment.

Objectives of Coastal Environmental Educational Programme

The coastal environmental education should be directed to achieve the following objectives, which were formulated at the Tbilisi [Thailand] Conference, 1977.

1. **Awareness:** To help social groups [fisherman] and individuals to acquire an awareness of and

sensitivity to the coastal degradation and its problems.

2. **Knowledge:** To help the concerned users to take the gains but not to harm the sea, beach and rare species.
3. **Attitude and skills:** To help social groups and individuals to acquire skills for identifying and solving environmental problems.
4. **Participation:** To provide social groups [NGOS] and individuals with an opportunity to be involved activity at all levels in working towards coastal environmental problems.

To achieve these goals, the content of the curricula of coastal schools and colleges should include the economic aspects of sea wealth. The High school and college youth camps should be organized at the coastal degraded areas. The curriculum projects should be planned horizontally as well as vertically.[1] Disciplines, such as Social Sciences and Science should not be studied in isolation. The curriculum should be flexible and such material can be presented accounting to the background and needs of the students.

United Nations Conference on the Human Environment, 1972

The United Nations Conference on the Human Environment met at Stockholm from 5th to 16th June 1972. Some Principles were considered for common outlook to inspire and guide the peoples of the World in the preservation and enhancement of the human environment. Principle 7 and 19 discuss about the Marine Pollution.

Principle - 7

States shall take all possible steps to prevent pollution of the seas by substances that are liable to create hazards to the human health, to harm living resources and marine life, to damage amenities or to interfere with other legitimate uses of the sea.

Principle - 19

Education in environmental matters, for the younger generation as well as adults, giving due consideration to the underprivileged, is essential in order to broaden the basis of an enlightened opinion and responsible conduct by individuals, enterprises and communities in protecting and improving the environment in its full human dimension. It is also essential that mass media of communications avoid contributing to the deterioration of the environment, but on the contrary, disseminate information of an educational nature on the need to protect and improve the environment in order to enable man to develop in every respect.

International Conference on Environmental Education, 1981

International Conference on Environmental Education was held on December 16-20, 1981 at Vigyan Bhawan, New Delhi, it was organized by the Indian Environmental Society and the Department of Environment and Forest, Government of India. This Conference was supported by various countries and on the basis of the deliberation of the conference some points were emerged these are given as follows:

1. Environmental Education must be developed at all levels.
2. Environmental awareness is to be promoted by the voluntary agencies, professional societies, etc.
3. It is the duty of government to formulate and adopt appropriate environment policies.
4. Environmental teaching, training, research, etc. shall be strengthened at various levels.
5. World Environmental Survey Report, published by the UN is to be utilized for appropriate action plans.

This declaration call upon the coastal development authority to promote the education and training to the public, government and NGOs.

Disciplines to be Included in Environmental Education

Some of the disciplines to be covered in the environmental formal education are given below.

1. Eco-system

This may include the structure and functioning of the eco-system. The impact of man on eco-system and how he is capable of altering the systems of the earth may also be included.

2. Pollution

The impact of population on environment, migration, coastal activities, the use of resources by increasing population, the life style of population, the birth-death, etc. may be included.

3. Economics and Technology

Economic systems constitute the social arrangements for producing and distributing the goods and services that individuals and societies desire. The economic system of one country may effect the economic system of other county.

4. Environmental Decisions

The environmental decisions should seek to improve the lives of the society. How to influence the decisions which are environmentally unsound and how to take environmental decisions may be the part of curriculum.

5. Environmental Ethics and Law

Man is a part of this earth rather than careless exploiter of it. It will be difficult to support even a small population if we exploit the nature in unwise manner.

Non-formal Environmental Education

Bangladesh has initiated a non-formal environmental education and training programme both for young people and adults through mass media. Due to successful national media, more seminars and workshops for coastal people and for journalists were held.[2] In India also number of NGOs are active in environmental training. These organization should be financed by the government. The primary and secondary school should have one or two teachers trained in the coastal degradation. The colleges and universities should conduct the case studies from their region. The reading materials should be produced according to the local needs and in local language.

Each Coastal District should have the Coastal and Martine Development Boards under the direct control of State Pollution Boards., the Board can appoint the instructors who can undertake coastal environmental training to the fishermen, industry and the people in their area. The 2-3 days seminars, one–day rally, discussions should be organized. This scheme will create awareness among the public, who are responsible for the coastal and marine pollution. Care should be taken to appoint lady educators also. The tourist should also be properly instructed by the tour organizers.

Mass Media: Successful Method

In many countries mass media efforts have been tried with a variety of success. Daily newspapers have generally proven the materials and generally are read more closely by rural people. The use of radio has proven successful in several countries in South America and India, but the material must be well chosen and often the presenter must have first hand knowledge of the specific area in which the programme is to be used. Television has generally not been effective in reaching most rural audiences. It appears that in coastal area a well planned mass media approach can be used if it is coordinated with the ground extension workers.

Extension Programmes in Coastal Environment

The term 'extension' is sometimes reduced to mean only technology transfer but usually, in international settings, includes educational efforts as well. In few countries, extension covers many functions of governmental agencies including enforcement's efforts. It is rather a problem solving, action oriented education that instructs, demonstrates and motivates. The extension programme motivates the people to bring changes.

Before we start any extension programme, we have to think on what is the need of the coastal people? Is it a regional need or a local need? Do the people in the affected region have the need and recognize it? Unfortunately, many administrators have made the error of deciding the results from one area to another in spite of variations in soils, water quality or fishermen's preferences.[3]

People's Participation in Environmental Management

Public participation is an essential ingredient of environment management along with other components like regulation and use of economic instruments. Public participation is facilitated by various environmental education and awareness programmes. The MOEF implements formal as well as informal education programmes and conducts various environmental awareness programmes. The usefulness of public participation is highlighted by the success of programmes like Join Forest Management. In Japan, the consumers' cooperatives popularize green products which are recyclable, biodegradable, rechargeable, ozone friendly and unleaded.[4]

The above discussion shows that the MOEF also believes in education, training and extension of environment. People's participation for coastal environment protection should be taken. The fisheries cooperatives, especially the National Federation of Fisheries Cooperatives (New Delhi) can implement the programme.

Conclusion

Developing countries such as India have great advantage in having vast coastline. Although India is a nation of farmers, with availability of land for agriculture yet, agricultural practices for sustainable food requirements of the increasing population have been a limitation. The various aspects such as nutrition, reproduction, genetics, bio-technology, diseases, production system, economics, extension and marketing are related with the marine products i.e. fish. However, care must be taken by the scientists to find out the best methods of aquaculture and sea fish, which would we economically viable, socially acceptable, environmentally safe to provide reasonable priced, safe and highly nutritious food to expanding population.[5] For the sustainable coastal development there is need for formal as well as non-formal education. The measures suggested by national and international conferences and by experts must be brought into practice. The mass media and NGOs can contribute more in the protection of coastal environment.

REFERENCES

1. Mathur, Mahesh: Legal Control of Environmental Pollution, Deep and Deep Publication, New Delhi, 1996, p. 100.
2. Mathur, Mahesh: Ibid.
3. Davis, J.T.: Cooperative Extension Programmes in Aquaculture, Aquaculture Research Needs for 2000 A.D. (etl) Oxford & IBH Publishing Co. Pvt. Ltd., New Delhi (1992), p. 382.
4. GOI, Economic Survey, 1998-99,pp. 168-69.

5. Jackson, R.D.: Aquaculture Research for the year 2000, Inaugural Session, A Joint US-India International Symposium, New Delhi, 15-18 November, 1988.

12

Sources and Consumption of Energy in Rural Area

India is a land of villages in which more than 70 per cent of the total population still resides in these villages. Most of the total energy consumption by these people consists of non-commercial fuels such as fire wood, cow dung and agricultural wastes and these non-commercial fuels comprise more than 40 per cent of the total energy consumed in the country. The continuous and widespread use of these non-commercial sources of energy in the rural areas is resulting in the large scale destruction of the environment. The rural people get non-commercial fuels at almost zero private cost, the social cost for meeting their energy needs has been increasing over the years.

Consumption Pattern of Energy in Rural Area

The intensity of consumption of energy in rural area is much lower as compared to the Urban areas. A large share of population in rural area is too poor to buy commercial energy such as electricity. The unlimited growth in population has resulted in serious environmental problems which include widespread deforestation, soil erosion, loss of fertility and loss of biodiversity, etc. The scarcity of kerosene has also hit the rural people.

Is World Facing Energy Crisis?

It is incorrect to say that the world is facing energy crisis. Energy crisis can never arise because energy is neither created nor destroyed. The real problem is not the availability of energy but the availability of energy in the readily usable form. Hence it is more appropriate to call this a technology crisis rather than an energy crisis. It is true that the fossil fuels are depleting fast and soon be extinct. Hence, the research on renewable energy is mooted and the various possibilities can be tried.

New Thrust on Renewable Energy in India

The Ministry of Non-convential energy sources was created in 1992 by upgrading the erstwhile Department of non-convential energy sources. The main responsibility of this ministry includes the development and utilization of the entire spectrum of renewable energy sources from the traditional to the modern technologies, from draught animal power, improved woodstoves, biogas to hydrogen energy, including solar, wind, biomass, small hydro power, congeneration ocean energy and alternate fuels. The main activities include research and development, development of standards, operation of test facilities, promotion of manufacturing and development of markets commercialization of technologies, operational programmes, awareness creation, information dissemination and international co-operation.

The most appropriate method of non-conventional energy to be used in rural area is biogas plant. The central government gives subsidy to these plants. The subsidy varies according to the size of the plant, category of beneficiary and area. The rates of subsidy are shown in Table 1.

Emissions from Traditional Energy Use

One popular latin proverb says, "The Kitchen Kills

Table 1: Amount of Central Subsidy in Rs.

Capacity of Plant Cum of gas	*For Assam*	*NE Region except Assam, J & K, UP etc.*	*plain, UP Western Ghats, A & N Islands*	*For Other Area*		
				SC/ST & desert districts	*Small marginal landless labourers*	*For all others*
2 C.Mtrs.	4000		2400	2000	2000	1700
3	5100		3600	3100	3100	2200
4	6200		4300	3600	-	2600
6	7300		4900	3600	-	2800

more than the Sword." This is clear from the above proverb that the problem of indoor air pollution was recognized even 2000 years ago. It is reported that five million children below the age of five years die of pneumonia every year in developing countries. An indoor air pollution is an important cause of death. But this problem has not received the attention of national and international governments. This might be due to low status given to woman in such countries. Indian rural women has little political and economic status even though laws are passed for equal status. The hazardous fuelwood collected by women and children causes indoor air pollution. Proper training and awareness about the benefits of improved stores will be the solution to this environmental problem.

Table 2: Adverse Health Effects and Emissions of Traditional Stoves as compared with Improved wood stoves

Fuel	*Nst*	*Co*	*Ch*	*TNMOC*	*RSP*	*Health*
LPG Store	0.70	0.02	Neg	0.02	0.01	0.01
Charcoal stove	0.30	0.73	0.30	.10	0.23	0.22
Kerosene stove	0.50	0.05	0.01	0.13	0.17	0.16
Traditional stove	0.15	1.00	1.00	1.00	1.00	1.00
Improved stove	0.25	0.20	0.20	0.20	0.20	0.20

Table shows that improved wood stove have a distinct advantage over traditional stove both with regard to health and to the global environment. In India about 15% of rural households had adopted improved stoves, though the stoves and improved chullas were offered at highly subsidised rate.

An Experience

With a view to getting the idea about the sources of energy in rural area in Kolhapur region, a mini survey was carried out, in two villages. These villages were from Kolhapur and Satara Districts. The various sources of renewable energy as well as present use of traditional energy were studied.

Methodology

The two villages viz. Majale (Kolhapur) and Jamb (Satara) were covered under study. The population of these villages as per 1991 census was 3010 and 3781 respectively. The total number (55) of purposive sample household selected were 25 and 30 respectively. The field work was made with the help of schedule. The data collected have been analysed with simple mathematical tools.

Village Set-up

Both the villages are having Gram Panchayat, Primary Schools, drinking water facilities, cooperative societies, etc. The main occupation of these villages is agriculture, while about 13 to 15 of the household were having the jobs in nearby small scale industries such as spinning mills, sugar cooperatives and private industries.

Occupational Pattern of the Villages

An important indicator of economic development is the occupational structure and livelihood pattern of a community. An economy with a diversified occupational structure affords scope for more employment and hence higher income. In case of the two villages selected for the following occupational pattern was found.

Table 3 shows that the percentage of agriculture income in both the villages is more than other occupations viz. Services and other sources. The other occupation ranks the second; while employment ranks the third. About 22 to 25 per cent of the village income is now contributed by the employment. As compared with the occupational structure, the present position of agriculture seems declining. The table also indicates that the average income of the sample family is more than Rs. 63,231/-, which is three times more than the income fixed for the poverty line i.e. Rs. 20,000/-. The per capita income of each person was Rs. 11,358/- and Rs. 10,670/- in respective sample families.

Table 3: Occupational Pattern and Sectorwise Income of Sample Families

Sr. No.	*Occupation*	*Income Rs. Jamb*	*Income Rs. Majale*
1.	Agriculture	9,16,350	71,4,000
	Average per family	43,635	28,560
		(48.30)	(43.74)
2.	Employment	4,80,600	3,62,400
	Average per family	60,075	14,496
		(25.33)	(22.19)
3.	Other Sources	5,00,000	5,56,080
	Average per family	29411	22243
		(26.35)	(34.6)
	Total	18,96,950	16,32,480
	Average per family	63,231	65,299
	Per Capital Income	(100.00)	(100.00)
		11,358	10,670
		(167 members)	(153 members)

Note: Figures in the brackets show the per cent in total.

The above figures show that in Majale village about 88% of the sample families were using Kerosene, followed by wood, electricity and LPG Gas. This was seen that the total annual cost incurred on LPG Gas was Rs.16,224/- which was more than any other source of energy. The villages which are nearby towns, are generally in habit of using the non-renewable energy such as gas. Due to

Table 4: Sources of Energy in Sample Villages

	Non-Renewable				Renewable					
Village	*Kerosene*	*LPG Gas*	*Coal Agri.*	*Electricity*	*Wood Forest Chulla*	*Dung Cake Less*	*Smoke Gas*	*Goober*	*Solar Cooker*	*Others*
Majale	No. of Family (22)	06 (24)	0 (0)	23 (92)	24 (96)	13 (52)	08 (32)	2 (8)	0 (0)	0 (0)
	Annual Expenditure Rs. 10,728	16,224	-	15,680	15,060	21,600	-	-	-	-
Jamb	No. of Family (29) (96)	14 (46.6)	01 (3.3)	19 (63.3)	27 (90)	26 (86.3)	01 (3.3)	01 (3.3)	0 (0)	0 (0)

Note: Figures in the brackets show the percentages.

private transport facilities, it becomes easy for them to get this energy. If we look at the renewable resources, it shows that wood is being used by 96% of the families. This was found that wood was made available either from nearby forest or from their own farms. About 80% of the families were using the firewood of nearby forest. More than one sources of energy were being used.

It was seen that hardly 32% of the families were using smokeless Chulla and 8% Gobar Gas, while the use of Solar Cooker was nil. This clearly shows that still people are not using renewable energy. The same results were seen in Jamb village. It was possible to use Gobar Gas as 50% of the families were having animals at their homes.

The Expenditure on Renewable and Non-Renewable Sources

Efforts were made in the field work to collect the sourcewise amount of money spend annually on renewable as well as non-renewable energy sources. The sourcewise figures are given in Table 5.

Table 5: Sourcewise Expenditure on Energy

Amount in Rs.

Village	*Wood (Purchased)*	*Dung Cakes*	*Kerosene*	*LPG Gas*	*Electricity*	*Total*
Majale	15,060 (18.99)	21,600 (27.24)	10,728 (13.53)	16,224 (20.46)	15,680 (19.77)	79,292 (100.00)
Jamb	32,160 (34.42)	30,024 (32.13)	6,882 (7.36)	12,519 (13.40)	11,840 (12.67)	93,425 (100.00)

Note: Figures in the brackets shows percentage.

The table shows that in Majale village the maximum amount was spent on dung cakes, LPG Gas (20.46%), electricity and wood, while in Jamb the maximum amount was spent on wood and dung cakes. This shows that the main source of energy in villages is wood and dung cakes followed by LPG Gas.

Share of Energy expenditure in Total Annual Income

Table 6: Share of Expenditure in Annual Income on Energy

(Amount in Rs.)

Village	*Total Annual Income of Sample Families*	*Total Expenditure on different sources of energy*
Majale	16,32,480	78,328 (4.80)
Jamb	18,96,950	93,425 (4.92)

An effort was made to know the amount spent on all the sources of energy in rural areas. It was found that out of the total annual income about 4.80 to 4.92 per cent of the income was spent on all sources of energy. This shows the expenditure of villages. Of course, this amount seems less due to the free firewood collected by the villagers.

Highlights in Brief about Sources and Consumption of Energy (Conclusions/Suggestioins)

A examination of the sources and consumption of energy in sample rural households can be highlighted as follows:

1. In both the villages more than 90% of the household were using wood either from their farm or from the nearby forest.
2. The dung cakes were used in majority (80%) of the families.
3. Hardly 3.3% families were using wood coal, which is rare in this area.
4. Improved Chulla was used in 32% of families in

Majale village (Kolhapur) and 6.6% in Jamb (Satara) village. This shows that there is lack of extension work in this respect.

5. Still 88 to 96% of the rural household use kerosene which is easily available on their ration cards. A few people also run their diesel engine on kerosene.

6. The most economical and subsidised source of energy is gobar gas. However, 3 and 8% of the sample families were using this source. There was misunderstanding about this source, on the ground that it gives bad smell and it goes often out of order. This mis-concept needs to be removed by the Khadi and Village Industries Commission and Gram Panchayat. This seems there is lack of extension work.

7. The educated and employed families use LPG Gas, as they get it even from private gas companies.

8. The use of electricity was common, except few families; but this source was mainly for house lighting and rarely for fan, freeze and mixer and ironing purpose. Still few poor households are without electricity.

9. The average size of the family was 5.56 persons and land size of 3.54%.

10. Renewable sources of energy such as improved Chulla, Gobar Gas, Solar Cooker is not popular among the villages though it is environment friendly. Instead they depend upon the non-renewable sources such as kerosene, dung cakes, LPG gas, electricity etc.

In short, still there is need for popularizing the renewable source of energy among the rural areas. Rural area is such area, where there is scope for use of renewable energy rather than urban area. More sincere efforts need to be taken by Government, Co-operatives and by NGO's in this respect. The respondents expressed that the solar cooker, water heater and even gobar gas needs more investment, which is beyond their reach. Hence, subsidy schemes should be still continued.

REFERENCES

1. Kamble, V.B. Energy Today and Tomorrow, Gujrat Energy Development Agency (GEDA), Baroda.
2. Vidyu, Lata, IREP, Overview, Delhi, 1998.
3. Balkrishnan Latika, Social Welfare, GOI, Oct, 1997.
4. Surya Cooker Manual, GEDA, Baroda.
5. Opportunities and Guidelines for Foreign Investors in Non-Conventional Energy Sector (Booklet) Ministry of Non-Conventional Energy Sources, GOI, New Delhi, Feb, 1996.
6. Shastri, R.A. Southern Economists, November, 1998.
7. Sengupta, Ramprasad, Commercial Energy in India, International Conference Paper, November, 1989, New Delhi.
8. Yojana, Special Issue on Energy, GOI Marathi Mumbai, January 1993.
9. Urjapatra, GEDA, Baroda, Jan-Dec., 1997.
10. Kurukshtra, GOI, New Delhi, July, 1992.
11. Wind Pumping, GEDA, January, 1998.
12. Social Weifare Biomedical Ethics, AIBA, February 2000, Chennai.

13

Co-operative Institutions and Environment Protection

Introduction

It is a beautiful world that we live in. Mother nature has provided us with everything in abundance that we need to live. It gives us food, clothing and shelter. Unfortunately, we have disturbed the ecological balance to satisfy some of our modern technological and personal needs. As Mahatma Gandhi has rightly said that Nature is able to satisfy our needs; but not our greeds. It is our own hands to make our life pleasant and comfortable and leave something more pleasant and comfortable for our future generation.

Although we, as individuals, can play our roles independently, yet we being the members of co-operative world, can also play role in correcting the environmental degradation in a co-operative way. There is a need for co-operatives to develop ways and means which could protect the environment. It is for all the co-operative organizations and co-operators to follow the ways and listen to the new demands and needs of the society. (1)

Meaning of Environment Protection

In a simple term, environment protection means healthy life for everyone, a better way to life and prosper, not only to human being but to animal, birds and every biosphere on the earth. But how this can be achieved is the problem before the society. This can be achieved by providing the following things:

1. Better standards and quality of life.
2. Natural life support system.
3. Conservation and regeneration.
4. Pollution free environment.

This chapter discusses the efforts made by some foreign and Indian co-operatives in environment protection. In developing countries especially, consumers co-operative stores are putting 'Consumer Care' labels on their products. They are keeping 'pollution free' materials for sale. The chapter gives the work done by some noteworthy co-operatives in respect of forest and soil protection. Before we go for detailed discussion, we can understand what are the ways and means of environment protection in the hands of co-operatives?

Participation of Co-operatives in Environment Protection: Way and Meals

Co-operative institutions as people's organizations can play a significant role in creating awareness among the people. These roles could be:

1. Creating awareness among co-operatives and co-operative members through extension programs;
2. Developing educational and training programs for board members and staff members;
3. Co-operating with government agencies in suggesting new measures and implementing environment-related programmes;
4. Giving publicity to environment-related successful measures taken by co-operatives; and

5. Collaborating with co-operatives abroad in exchanging information and techniques.

Activities Co-operatives can Undertake

The following activities can be undertaken:

1. Creating awareness among the people on the consequences of increase in population;
2. Creating awareness among the people on the consequences of cutting down trees indiscriminately;
3. Creating awareness among the people on the consequences of flow of waste water in village streets;
4. Creating awareness among the people on indiscriminate mining and digging up soil and brick-kline etc;
5. Educating farmers on the use and handling of chemical fertilizers, insecticides and pesticides, e.g., DDT';
6. Educating people on the importance of washing vegetables and fruits before using them;
7. Informing people on the use of alternative sources of energy for cooking;
8. Encouraging people to develop social forestry programme; and
9. Encouraging people to participate in community development programmes e.g., rural sanitation, cleaning of school premises, cleaning of village streets, repairing the leaking water taps, discussions with the nearby factories or mills.
10. Developing modest rural health programmes, better management and regreening of wasteland etc.

Scenerio of Co-operatives in India

The impact of Government support on co-operatives has been both positive as well as negative. The multi-directional growth and expansion of co-operatives through establishment of 5.45 lakhs (2001) societies of all kinds covering almost every aspect of socio-economic life of the people, with a membership of 23.6 million and working capital of more than Rs.3400555 million indicates a solid and positive impact of Government support. The important segments of co-operative sector that have emerged in the country are: (a) agricultural co-operatives – credit co-operatives both for short-term, medium-term and long-term agricultural credit; marketing co-operatives; agro-processing co-operatives e.g. co-operative sugar factories; co-operative spinning mills; dairy co-operatives; co-operative godowns and storage; (b) urban credit co-operatives - urban co-operative banks; salary earners and credit societies; (c) Consumer co-operatives; (d) Artisan/ Workers' Co-operatives – Weavers Co-operatives and non-weavers co-operatives; (e) Non- artisan workers' Co-operatives (unorganised labour co-operatives)- Construction labour co-operatives; forest labour co-operatives; (d) Co-operatives for Weaker Sections – Fishery co-operatives: women co-operatives: co-operatives for tribals: co-operatives for scheduled castes/scheduled tribes; (g) Housing Co-operatives; and (h) Integrated Co-operative Industries – IFFCO; KRIBHCO; PETROFILES; NHEC. Such a vast network and the federal organizational structure of co-operatives has facilitated integration of rural economy.

Co-operative Institutions Engaged in Environment Protection: Some Examples

Co-operative Forestry Societies

In India small steps have been recently taken. Several co-operative organisations, notably among them the fertilizer, dairy and sugar industrial units have responded to the call. One such project is in the Sultanpur district of Uttar Pradesh where forestry co-operatives organized by poor farmers within the short span of three years. Afforested large tracts of salts-affected westland and where not a blade of grass grew until recently, and have brought even ravines under tree cover. The project began as an effort for some greenery on 15 hectare of saline soil, but has already afforested over 12,000 hectares of degraded and salt-affected land.

The Tree Growers' Co-operatives in Gujrat, M.P., A,.P., Orissa and Karnataka are also making efforts for improving the environment. As on March 2001, there were 633 tree growers cooperatives with its 49618 members providing employment to the villagers.

IFFCO And Environment Protection

Krishak Bharathai Co-operative Limited (KRIBHCO), is a national level multi-state co-operative society jointly promoted by Government of India, IFFCO and co-operative societies from all over the country. Apart from the production and marketing of fertilizer by KRIBHCO, its contribution towards agricultural production, rural development and environment protection is significant.

Although conceived initially by the Indian Farmers Fertilizer Co-operative (IFFCO), it is today an entirely people's programme with local people banded together into co-operatives taking all decisions as well as the responsibility for implementing them. The benefits seem to have been manifold: the developing forests yield timber, fuel and fodder, the soil quality has changed to the point of supporting the cultivation of cash crops like turmeric; the once-unskilled villagers have acquired enviable expertise in afforestation and perhaps most important of all, the greening of the soils has lifted the people out of despondency and stimulated term into attempting other ventures like acquaculture to increase their income.

Use of Fertilizer and Soil Testing

In order to propagate efficient and balanced use of fertilizers, the society collects and tests soil and water samples with the help of 07 mobile testing vans and the recommendations are given to farmers free of cost. This saves the soil degradation.

Development Projects

The society has carried out a number of activities in 199 adopted villages and 13 Commercial Area Development Projects, 14 Rural Development, Programmes with provision for drinking water, tree plantation, social forestry, etc.

Indo-British Rainfed Farming Project

Under this project, a landmark has been achieved through people's participation in various development activities, such as crop management, soil and water conservation, water resource development, tree plantation and programmes including Joint Forest Management, livestock development and skill building.

In bringing about socio-economic changes and environmental protection, co-operatives play a pivotal role through spirited co-operatives efforts. KRIBHCO proves as it is a model. (2) With the lead provided by organisations like IFFCO several social forestry programmes have been undertaken in desert-dominated areas like Rajasthan where several forestry co-operatives have been organized.

Fisheries Co-operatives

Fishery Co-operatives in India have introduced a number of innovative programmes. Some of the measures taken are, among others, proper maintenance of fishing crafts, keeping the engines in good order, strict hygienic conditions at landing platforms, systematic salting and drying of fish procedures, packaging and marketing. Training programmes in fishing craft management, handling and marketing of fish and health programmes at fishermen's settlements are given to fishery co-operative members, board members and staff.

Role of Housing Co-operatives

Arrangements for proper maintenance of improved slums can be made effectively and though co-operatives of residents. Co-operatives of slum dwellers on other hand can be made responsible for proper maintenance with some financial and technical assistance from local bodies. Co-operatives can be expected to make slum dwellers understand their responsibilities, and adequately train them for understanding necessary action in this regard. They can make the arrangement of disposal of garbage. They can plant trees and maintain gardens. In addition to natural environments the housing co-operatives bring healthy social environment as they live as one family even they belong to different religious, caste or language groups. (3) There were 92000 all types of housing cooperatives in the country providing 66,00,000 houses to members.

The Role of Co-operatives in Environment Protection in Maharashtra: A Regional Review

The Co-operative sugar factories in this region have made positive impact on the socio-economic conditions of the rural people. It is always charged that the co-operative sugar factories have polluted the rivers in their areas, and it is true. Because Maharashtra is having about more than 140 factories in operation and they are subject to water pollution. For example, The Rajaram Co-operative Sugar Factory, Kolhapur, Shree Datta Co-operative Sugar Factory, Shirol. The Bhogavati Co-operative sugar Factory,

Parite, etc. have been charged by the State Pollution Control Board, and they were held responsible. The paper plant unit of Shree Datta Co-operative Sugar Factory which was running in profit has been closed due to pollution. The molasses in these sugar factories is drained out into the rivers in rainy season. Therefore, it is the responsibility of these factories to undertake the treatment on their effluents. It is worthy to be noted that the Warna Sugar Co-operative Factory has done the remarkable work in this direction. With the help of private company, the factory is able to generate about 6000 to 10000 units of electricity through the waste molasses and bagass. Similarly, the factory is using the waste material for bio-fertilizers, which is supposed high quality fertilizer. Apart from this about 5 to 6 acres of land has been brought under horticulture by using the waste water. The sugar co-operative at Akluj in Solapur district has converted the barren land of 25 acres into forest. The factory has so far constructed about 30000 gobar gas plants, which generates non convential energy. This work has been done by all the sugar factories in western Maharashtra. The "Area Development Fund" created by the factories plays important role in this respect.

Dairy Co-operatives

Similar type of responsibility has been undertaken by the Dairy Co-operatives, as they are also responsible for water and air pollution. The waste water in such plants directly goes to the streams and finally to the rivers, which are already polluted. The co-operative dairies such as Warna Dairy, Gokul Dairy, Shivamrut Dairy in Kolhapur and Solapur districts have already spent some amount out of their budget on environment protection. All these dairy plants are famous for their gardens. The Warna Dairy has won several prizes for its garden. The garden at Shivamrut Dairy (Akluj) can be acknowledged as the best example of rural gardens in Maharashtra. It is observed that except the co-operative agro-processing units in Maharashtra, no work has been done by other types of co-operatives such as urban banks, district banks, service co-operatives, consumers, etc. A survey of 10 village service co-operatives was recently conducted, wherein it was found that, the authorities of these societies were not even knowing the word environment, and it was said that to plant a tree is a job of Village Panchayat or Youth Clubs. This shows that there is a need for creating awareness among the village co-operatives. Also, there is a need to create separate fund for environment protection.

Co-operatives and Environment Protection: Some Objections

Many a times, objections are raised by critics stating that co-operatives in India cannot protect the environment; because many co-operatives are in loss. The answer to this criticism is that all the co-operatives are not in loss. About 40% the societies are in loss and hence atleast 60% of the societies which are in A and B audit class can devote some of their profit to this cause.

The second objection raised is that the co-operative spend extra vagant money on politics, elections and court cases rather spending money on real needs of the society. This can be checked by strong legal provisions, The third objection is that co-operatives are not giving remunerative prices to the producers and how they can spend on environment protection? Sugar factories are polluting the water and not paying pollution tax. But we have some examples of sugar co-operative like Warna and dairy co-operatives like Amual, Dudhsagar who had laid good impact on the minds of members and public. We can conclude by saying that 'Yes' what work has been done by co-operatives in India in respect of environment protection is insufficient, but not negligible. It is also true that co-operatives have failed in environment protection; but they must succeed and they will succeed.

Conclusion

The foregoing discussion shows that if co-operatives spare atleast 1% of their net profit every year, they can undertake several environment protection activities within their area of operation. Thus, co-operatives are the best and most appropriate institutions to generate a favourable climate in favour of the movement- a movement to save the earth and to make it a place to live. Of course, there is a need for research, debate and training of members and employees of co-operatives in India.

REFERENCES

1. Daman, Prakash: A place to live. Roles co-operatives can play in protecting the Environment, ICA, New Delhi (1993).
2. Dharmarajan, S. Rural Development Through Co-operatives; Role of KRIBHCO in Agricultural Promotion and Rural Development, The Maharashtra Co-operative Quarterly, Pune, Vol. LXXXIIII, April-June-2000, pp. 28, 29.
3. Khurana, M.L.: Housing Co-operatives and Environment Awareness. The Co-operator, NCUI, New Delhi, November, p. 205.

CHANGING DYNAMICS OF INDIAN FEDERALISM

CHANGING DYNAMICS OF INDIAN FEDERALISM

ZEENAT ARA

ABHIJEET PUBLICATIONS
DELHI 10094

ABHIJEET PUBLICATIONS
2/46 Tukhmeerpur Extension
Delhi 110094
Phones: 011-22960492, 65698474
e-mail: abhijeetpublication@gmail.com
abhijeet_singh1@indiatimes.com

CHANGING DYNAMICS OF INDIAN FEDERALISM

First Published 2008

ISBN 978-81-89886-58-5

PRINTED IN INDIA

Published by J.K. Singh for Abhijeet Publications, Delhi 110094, Lasertypeset by Gaurav Graphics, Delhi and Printed as Himanshu Printers, Delhi.

Dedicated

To My Parents

for their love and support

Preface

Adoption of federal structure in India was conceived as a necessity to meet out exigencies arising out of plurality of Indian situation. Elements of heterogeneity and plurality could be managed through bringing about reconciliation between national identity and those of constituent units. Federation was an answer to that. Politics of accommodation was the catchword in the process of political institution building.

In political context, balancing the relationship of centre and states became evidently important, particularly after 1956, when cultural identities were provided a political personality in terms of reorganisation of states on cultural lines.

In the scenario of working of Union-State relations in India, it was envisaged that conflicts would arise and to mitigate such challenges, some structural devices were carved out for conflict resolution between the Centre and States like provision of the supremacy of the Constitution, independence of Judiciary, Judicial Review, amendment process etc. However the in-built mechanism of resolution of conflict between Centre and States did not prove to be adequate. This point can be elaborated by evaluating some of the important steps taken by various governments during post-independence phase. For example the appointment of a study team on centre-state relations by the Administrative Reforms Commission in 1969 and the Rajamannar Committee appointed by the Tamil Nadu Government in the same year. But these efforts did little to reconcile the severely strained relations between the Centre and the States, A proper solution to the problem of the centre-state relations demands an approach which will devise a federal framework substantially different from that provided by the makers of the Indian Constitution. The Sarkaria Commission (1983), no doubt in dealing with the problem had a sufficiently wide perspective, but its approach was limited to the founding fathers. It aimed at correcting some of the distortions emerging out of the functional aspects of the Constitution, but ignored the basic factors causing strains in the relations between the Union and the States, specially in the post-Nehru period. After initial two decades when no challenge—cultural, religious or regional—was posed to the integrity of the country, the whole political environment underwent a change giving place to tensions and strains almost threatening the federal system. The Commission failed to show a comprehensive understanding of the factors responsible for the change in atmosphere and an appreciation of the causes responsible for their growth, primarily because of its faith that constitutional management itself will provide a satisfactory solution of the problem. It ignored the dynamics of prevalent context. The emergence of new factors in the form of regional elites have also affected the working of the Federal System.

Inspite of all this, certain other functional factors emanating from the political culture have influenced the conflict resolution syndrome. This study is primarily looking into these processes emerging out of various situations. For this purpose models of U.P. and Kerala are put under enquiry in this case.

Though there have been a number of studies about the centre-state relations in India, most of the studies are confined to the study and dynamics of constitutional structure with an emphasis on either the role assigned to the Centre in the Constitution, or that of the Congress Party. For instance, analysts like K. Santhanam, Justice K. Subha Rao, S.P. Aiyar and Asok Chanda have based their interpretations on an analysis of the provisions of the Constitution. They observed that the Union is excessively powerful vis-a-vis the States and exercises considerable control over them. These constitutional studies have ignored the processes affecting the working of this system. Apart from some legal constitutional studies e.g. of Paul Appleby, there are studies on the working of the Federal System as of C.P. Bhambhri, A. Krishnaswamy and others while K. Subha Rao have pointed out the constitutional portion and the authority of the Planning Commission.

However the studies of Iqbal Narain and Marcus F. Franda are in sharp contrast, as they pointed out that Union-State relations in India have in the last two decades been marked by tensions. Some other scholars like K.R. Bombwall, Rasheeduddin Khan etc. have also observed centrifugal trends in the Indian polity. Thus, it is clear that largely the context of the working of Union-State Relations is ignored. It seems desirable to assess this issue in an over all environment, necessary for the operational viability of political institutions and more specifically the case of Union-State relations in India. Such an attempt demands an evaluation within a micro-level universe of the study. It is attempted to reduce the universe by taking up only two contrast models of Centre-State relations in terms of Uttar Pradesh and Kerala. In U.P. same party was in power for a long time since independence, none of which could complete its term of five years, although, there is a decline in its voting strength. Political unrest and governmental instability have been the characteristic features of Kerala's history since independence. Kerala is the first state to vote communists to power through parliamentary process. It has witnessed the largest number of changes of governments. In Kerala no single party could come to power after 1959 and barring Achyutha Menon ministry, none could complete its term. Secondly religion and caste are the two major social divisions in U.P. Hindu-Muslim conflict has become a common occurrence in the State. For example, the controversy over Ram-Janambhumi- Babri Masjid issue has been there since long. Religion is the technique here for political mobilisation, while ideology is the dominating factor in Kerala, as Communist Party of India-Marxist (C.P.I.-M) has ideologically emerged as a more homogenous party. Thirdly geographical proximity has also affected the relationship between the Centre and the States. Fourthly, economics have affected the context to the extent of threatening the stability of the system. Kerala has been described as a 'problem state' of India, as its economy is plagued with various problems like over population, increasing unemployment, poverty and chronic food shortage, which has increased due to the Gulf crisis. It was pointed out repeatedly that Kerala's economic problems are due to the malfunctioning of the processes. U.P.'s economy is characterised by agricultural stagnation and industrial decline. Within the state, different regions have different levels of economic development. Inspite of long same party rule it is lagging behind with regard to many social and developmental services.

Here, an effort is made to look into these models and draw conclusions, valid in proving that Indian Federation has gradually changed its character from Cooperation Federation model to Conflict Frame. With 1989 elections, began an era of coalition governments coincided with the politics of accommodation and adjustments, thereby changed the whole context sharply.

This work is divided into five chapters. Chapter I deals with factors for adopting a federal set-up for India. Views of the provinces and the nature of the proposed federal structure are dealt in this. Chapter 2 is about the analysis of the functioning of the Constitution regarding administrative and legislative relations of U.P. and Kerala with the Centre. The reasons of the emerging trends and their comparative analysis in two different contexts is done in Chapter 3. How the political parties change the relations between Centre and States is analysed in Chapter 4. One of the major issues of Federation i.e. economic dynamics is analysed in Chapter 5. To what extent are these States financially subservient to the Centre and to what extent, central assistance to the State is based on the 'need' or the bargaining strength of the State and to what extent, do the financial relations reflect a conflicting model, are analysed in this chapter.

I am finding it difficult to put in words my deep sense of gratitude to all those who in one way or the other, enabled me to complete this work. First of all, I would like to record my sense of gratitude towards Prof. Zahoor Mohammad Khan for his encouragement and expert advice in writing this book. His guidance was a process of constant learning and improvement for me. I am again especially thankful to him that even in the midst of pressing engagements, he provided me proper guidance and rendered some very important suggestions.

My special thanks is, undoubtedly due to my friends, Amalji Sahay, Dhananjay Verma, Dr. Parveen Sabharwal, Dr. N. Balakrishnan, too many to name individually, who have constantly helped me. Their continuous inspiration for hard work, helped a lot.

I also owe thanks to all the library staff members of the Nehru Memorial Library—Teen Murti House, Jawaharlal Nehru University Library, Central Reference Library—University of Delhi, Zakir Husain Library, Jamia Millia Islamia, Indian Council of Social Sciences Research (Documentation) Library, Central Secretariat Library—Shastri Bhawan, Parliament House Library, National Institute of Public Finance and Policy, and Yojana Bhawan Library, Library of Indian Institute of Public Administration, Library of the Institute of Constitutional and Parliamentary Studies, Indian Council of World Affairs (Sapru House) Library, for their help in collecting the valuable research material. I am also thankful to Uttar Pradesh Information Centre (New Delhi) and Kerala Information Centre (New Delhi) for providing me necessary material and information for this work.

In the end, I express my profound gratitude to my parents and other members of my family who gave me tremendous love, support, encouragement and understanding all the time.

Zeenat Ara

Contents

1

Historical Perspective

In the process of political institution building, context is vital in terms of structure and functioning of an institution. For this perspective studies are needed. Most striking is the historical perspective of evolution of Indian political system since 1945. This period was marked by the collapse of colonial order and the successful culmination of the national liberation struggle. It covers an important phase of British imperialism in India. It exploited for its own ulterior motive, the economic backwardness of dependent countries. India was not an exception to it.

Post Second World War era witnessed the beginning of decolonisation of the Third World. During this phase, though political liberation in many countries was achieved and new nations appeared on the map of the world, these could hardly enjoy economic self-reliance. It was a difficult situation of imbalance between political independence and economic dependence. However, a serious effort was launched for carving out new political structures and to use them for achieving stability in political terms. These countries were formally independent but lacked the instrumentalities of translating their independence into political reality. The attainment of economic independence was the basic requisite for consolidating political sovereignty. Alien rule continued to influence the way of thinking and the formation of political institutions even after decolonisation.

In the 1917 Montague-Chelmsford Declaration, the British Government accepted the progressive realisation of responsible government which,however, neither envisaged any federation nor meant 'self-government'. But in 1919 people started demanding for 'self-government' against the provision of the Government of India Act, 1919. Indian leaders wanted to secure full self-governing dominion status for India under the British empire and autonomy for the units. Subsequently there was a shift in British policy when they asked the Indians to produce a constitution with a general consensus among the leaders of India. Afterwards the Nehru Committee in 1928 produced a constitutional framework, where the word 'federation' was not used at all. However, the idea of a federal set up for the whole of India, consisting both of princely states and the British India was suggested for the first time by the Simon Commission (1927-29) and later by the Indian States (Butler) Committee (1927-30) in 1930. The idea of federation was discussed in detail by the successive Round Table Conferences convened in London by the British Government, from 1930-33, and was approved later by the Joint Parliamentary Committee (1934).

The Britishers were aware of the developments in India and realised that some well timed action was required to pacify the Indians. So a Commission with Sir John Simon as the Chairman was constituted. The Commission asserted: "The ultimate Constitution of India must be Federal, for it is only in Federal Constitution that units differing so widely in constitution as the Provinces and the States can be brought together while retaining internal autonomy."[1] It made two basic recommendations:

(i) provincial autonomy should be strengthened by further devolution from the Centre,

(ii) No change should be made on the Central Executive; but the Central Legislature should be reconstituted on a federal instead of a unitary basis.

But "the Commission did not suggest the establishment of an All-India Federation including the Indian states, nor even refer to dominion status, though in 1929 its attainment had been officially declared to be the 'natural issue' of the declaration of 1917."[2]

The most striking fact about the proposed federation was the disparity of the federating units in geographical terms. It was clear that "what the Princes really wanted, was not federation but a loose form of alliance or 'confederation'. They were reluctant to place at the disposal of the federal government, a long list of powers, and even in respect of those powers they were inclined to keep up to some extent at least their individual authority and jurisdiction".[3]

The Indian provinces were never enthusiastic about the federal idea. They were willing to work out the scheme for the sake of unifying India under one common government at the Centre, Sardar Ujjal Singh, a representative of the Sikh community from Punjab said, "In coming to a decision on the type of federation, we must not forget that India is now rapidly advancing towards nationhood. Nothing should be done which might stifle the process of unification and nationhood. We must guard against any disintegrating tendencies on the part of various units".[4]

In view of the implications, arising from the introduction of responsible government at the Centre, regarding the relationship of the responsible central government to the provinces and to the states, Sir Tej Bahadur Sapru made a respectful appeal to their Highness, who, he declared, were patriots first and princes afterwards and said: "Let them move forward with the vision of an India, which will be one single whole, each part of which may be autonomous and may enjoy absolute independence within its own borders, regulated by proper relations with the rest. I, therefore, ask them to come forth on this occasion and say whether they are prepared to join and All-India Federation".[5] The ruler of Bikaner gave a positive response to Sapru's appeal. He said: "We of the Indian states are willing to take our part in, and make our contribution to, the greater prosperity and contentment of India as a whole. I am convinced that we can best make our contribution through a federal system of government composed of the states and British India."[6] He also declared that the princes "will come into the Federation of their own free will and on terms which will secure the just rights of their states and subjects".[7] The Maharaja of Kashmir said: "To my mind, there is today no alternative to Federation".[8]

The First Round Table Conference was, thus, able to find a solution to the problem of adjusting the relations of Indian states with British India, but failed in handling the communal issue. The deliberations of the Round Table Conference revealed that the communal problem had become more complicated since the Nehru Report was rejected by Indian Muslims. "Taking their cue from Muslim communal ists, other minority interests had also raised their voices",[9] Under B.R. Ambedkar's leadership, the so-called depressed classes began to press for separate electorates and reservation of seats.[10] However, the Hindu-Muslim question remained the major issue of the communal problem. Sir Mohammad Shafi, one of the leading spokesmen of Muslim communal ism, at the conference on the one hand emphasised the necessity of a federal polity in India, and on the other hand declared that "it was natural for the seventy millions of His Majesty's Mussalman subjects to insist upon this, that in the constitutional and administrative evolution of India, they must have their legitimate share both in the provincial and the central governments."[11]

Muslims were dissatisfied with the report of the committee appointed by the All-Parties Conference as they were in favour of federation. After the failure of this Conference, Mohammad Ali Jinnah formulated his "Fourteen Points". One of the points related to the claim that "the form of the future constitution of India should be federal with the residuary powers rested in the provinces".[12]

Then, the Raja of Parlakumadi pressed for the establishment of a separate province for the Oriyas in the First Round Table Conference. His main argument was that since Orissa was an area with Oriya a single language, and a well-defined historical and cultural association, it should be under one administration instead of being parcelled out among four different provinces — Bihar and Orissa, Bengal, the Central Provinces and Madras. The demand was accepted without much difficulty but this was done more as a counter-measure to the creation of Sind as a separate Muslim province, than as a concession to the linguistic principle.

Maulana Mohammad Ali, a British Indian delegate stated: "The Mussalmans desire — and this is the crux of their fourteen points and not separate electorates that there should be federal governments, so that the central unitary government with a permanent Hindu majority should not override them everywhere",[13] with complete Provincial Autonomy, they would be able to pursue the development of their own community.

During the Second Round Table Conference, Mahatma Gandhi tried to resolve the communal tangle through talks with the representatives of various groups. But on 8th October, 1931 he announced to the Minorities Committee "with deep sorrow and deeper humiliation, the utter failure of his efforts to secure an agreed solution."[14]

He further suggested that "the Minorities Committee be adjourned sine die and that fundamentals of the constitution be hammered into shape as quickly as may be".[15] This was rejected by Sir Mohammad Shafi, one of the leading spokesmen of Muslim communalism. He declared that it was impossible to frame a constitution for India "without first settling the various communal problems involved".[16] Dr. S.K. Dutta, a liberal and nationalist Indian Christian, warned that "this fragmentation of India with religious communities is going to have the most disastrous results on our future."[17]

In the Second Round Table Conference session, in a

separate memoranda, the Raja of Bobbili and V.V. Giri presented a powerful case for the constitution of a separate province for the Andhras. V.V. Giri declared: "Andhras belong to a very ancient race and have as brilliant a past as any other nation in the world",[18] and recalled that they had once ruled over a great kingdom. The Raja of Bobbili based the demand for Andhra province on a sense of grievance, "unless a separate province is created, their interests could never be really looked after".[19] He maintained that the Andhras had all along felt that "they could not develop and emphasise the special features of their culture except by being a separate political and administrative unit and that such development of the Andhra culture could only be possible by education being imparted through the medium of Telugu and also by public business being transacted in that language".[20] On the same lines, B. Shiva Rao also pressed for the establishment of a separate Karnataka Province.[21]

In each case it was claimed that the proposed new province would be administratively and financially viable. It was V.V. Giri, however, who clearly linked the issue of linguistic provinces with success of a federal polity in India, This formation of a separate Andhra province, he declared was in consonance with the ideal of provincial autonomy.[22] The Maharaja of Patiala said: "Outside the matters of common concern, we shall preserve our internal autonomy intact".[23] Their determination to treat their territories as personal fiefs and to withhold the benefits of democracy from their subjects was reflected in the attitude of the Maharaja of Bikaner who said: "That is our affair, we know our states and our people... we shall know how and when to adjust our system to any changing conditions; but we will do it in our own time and in our own way free from all external interference.[24] The question which agitated the princes "was not whether federation would enable them to contribute to the benefit of India as a whole, but whether their own position would be better and safer inside the federation or outside it".[25] One important issue on which the Princes were not at all prepared to compromise was federal finance. Two committees were appointed for examining various aspects of the federal finance[26] and came to the conclusion that only a policy of "give and take" could solve the difficult problem of federal finance. Besides, the imposition of some sort of a tax, preferably a corporation tax or surcharge on income tax was suggested by Peel Committee[27] as a federal source of revenue.[28]

There were two difficulties in evolving a constitutional settlement in regard to regional units in India. One was to meet the aspirations of the Muslims for regional autonomy in Muslim majority provinces. The other was to integrate the Indian native states with the then British Indian provinces under one common central administration. But these native states wanted to maintain their identity and autonomy which was possible only in a new set up similar to federal system. Eventually, probably federalism was the only way out of this imbroglio. It was designed to meet both these necessities.

The Government of India Act, 1935 provided the basic framework for Indian Federation. But it could not be put into operation owing to non-participation by the requisite number of states and also due to the sudden outbreak of the second world war. Only autonomous provinces were created as the first step towards the establishment of the Federation.

After the passing of the Act, it was proposed that "Instruments of Accession" should be called "Treaties of Accession" and regarded as bilateral agreements requiring the British Government to "preserve and safeguard the whole of their sovereignty and internal autonomy from any encroachments in future".[27] Under the Act of 1935, the first ever attempt was made to give the provinces an autonomous status by freeing them from external interference. Theoretically the entire executive and legislative authority was transferred to the people. But this autonomy was not absolute or unqualified. Externally, the Governor-General could interfere in the administration of a province to the extent of seeing that it did not threaten the peace and tranquility of India. Internally, the Governor's powers of discretion and unilateral judgement meant a drastic cut in the powers of the ministers. The provinces were separate and only partly autonomous. It made the Governors more powerful than the ministers. The Indian National Congress dubbed it "a prodigy of imperialist statesmanship devised to secure the continuance of British Rule in India". Jawaharlal Nehru condemned the Act as "a new charter of bondage"[*30]

The changes made by the 1935 Act in the financial relations between the centre and the provinces did not make the provinces financially independent. However, there was a significant improvement in the financial status of the provinces by making them independent in the raising of revenues and the ordering of their expenditures, thereby injected some firmness into the financial backbone of provincial autonomy.

In 1937 elections, the Congress got absolute majority in six provinces - Madras, Bihar, Bombay, United Provinces, Orissa and Central Provinces, but they refused to form ministries as they argued that with special powers reserved to the Governors, Provincial Autonomy had become a mockery. The Congress Working Committee advised the Congress legislature parties not to accept office unless the Governors promised that they would not use their powers of interference or set aside the advice of the Ministers in regard to their constitutional activities. However the deadlock was solved by two statements, one by the then Secretary of State, Marquess of Zetland, and the other by the Governor-General, Lord Linlithgow. According to these, it was affirmed that the scope of intervention by the Governors was restricted to the narrowest limits possible. The Congress Party accepted this assurance and joined office. But there was a change in Congress policy of nonintervention in the affairs of Indian states to a "forward" or "activist" policy or "a policy of undisguised hostility" to the state governments and of open encouragement of agitation within and without the states, against them."[31]

The autonomy of Indian provinces had limitations even in the sphere reserved to them by the Constitution, the Central Government could exercise an appreciable measure of control. But this autonomy could be entirely suspended if the Governor-General issued a proclamation of emergency declaring that "a grave emergency exists whereby the security of India is threatened whether by war or internal disturbance".[32] Few problems arose out of the operation of· Provincial Autonomy. What happened in practice was that constitutional federalism was superseded by political unitarianism, "freed from the control of the legitimate centre, the provinces were subjected to a far closer and stricter control by the Congress centre".[33] This Act not only established a strong Centre with wide discretionary powers to the Governor-General but also granted discretionary powers to Governors which greatly curtailed the autonomy of the Provinces. The establishment and the functioning of the federation were made conditional to the willingness of the autocratic Indian rulers of Princely states. As Dr. Ambedkar said "without real responsibility at the centre, Provincial Autonomy is "an empty shell".[34] For example, in Orissa, the Governor proposed to proceed on leave ordering the chief secretary to work as acting Governor during the period of his absence. The Congress Ministry objected to the subordinate officer being promoted to work as head of the Executive and declared that such a step was inconsistent with constitutional practices. When the Congress Ministry threatened to resign on this issue, the Governor acted discretely by getting his leave cancelled. In 1938, there occurred a clash between the Governor and the ministries in U.P. and Bihar over the question of release of political prisoners. The Congress Ministries of United Provinces and Bihar determined to release them but the Governor-General issued a directive to the Governors under section 126 of the Act, not to accept the advice of the ministers. Hence the Governors did not agree to the release of political prisoners. The ministries resigned in protest on February 16, 1938, as centre's undue intervention was quite evident. The Congress held that the interference of the Governor-General was a clear violation of Section 126(5) of the Act. The Governors made more active interference in non-Congress provinces, and during the course of the military operations after 1939, the office of the ministers became precarious. In the province of Sind, Allah Baksh, the Chief Minister, surrendered his title "Khan Bahadur" as a protest against the British war policy. The Governor was infuriated and dismissed him even though he commanded a stable majority in the Legislative Assembly. There were as many as five changes in Sind during 1937-43 and in 1946 the Governor called the leader of the largest single majority party to form the ministry even though the existing coalition ministry had a stable majority in the legislature. Another conflict arose when Sir Sikandar Hayat Khan, the Chief Minister of Punjab, broached the subject of the release of political prisoners in United Provinces and Bihar with the Governor, the latter informed the Governor-General that the Chief Minister of Punjab had advised him against such release lest peace and tranquility of the province be disturbed. When questioned in the Legislative Assembly, Sir Sikandar Hayat Khan denied having ever tendered such an advice. This shows the extent to which the Governor of Punjab took liberties in his relations with the Chief Minister. Jawaharlal Nehru has very aptly compared the working of Provincial Autonomy in the Congress and in the non-Congress provinces. He says: "This difference between the Congress provinces and Bengal and Punjab was immediately apparent in regard to civil liberties and political prisoners. In both Bengal and Punjab there was no relaxation of the police and secret service *raj* and political prisoners were not released. In Bengal, where the Ministry often depended on European votes, there were in addition thousands of *detenus* that is, men and women, kept indefinitely for years and years in prison without charge or trial. In the Congress provinces, however, the very first step taken was the release of political prisoners."[35] The Governor-General exercised decisive legislative powers.

Section 45 of the Act of 1935 authorised the Governor-General to issue a proclamation by which the entire constitution of the federation could be suspended. After the issue of this proclamation, the Governor-General could assume all the powers.

Indeed the most striking feature of the working of Provincial Autonomy during this period was the behaviour of the Governors who functioned as constitutional heads of states. There was "substance of independence in the provincial field and the two cardinal principles of a parliamentary government. Representative character and the executive responsibility to the legislature were for the first time found in practice. Provincial Autonomy worked satisfactorily in the Congress provinces while in the non-Congress provinces it was just a mockery, and it was expected that the Governor-General would not interfere in the provincial affairs. But he was equipped with special responsibilities which could enable him to dominate the provinces. The directives of the Governor-General to the Governors of United Provinces and Orissa over the release of political prisoners bear ample testimony to this fact. Jawaharlal Nehru rightly observed, "... the position of a popular government was extra-ordinary. There were all the checks of viceregal powers and our irresponsible central authority."[36] Moreover the Governor-General could afford to be assertive as certain kinds of Bills could not be initiated in the provincial legislatures without his previous sanction and certain Bills duly passed by the provincial legislatures could be reserved for his consideration. Reservation of "Orissa Amending Bill" by the Governor for the consideration of the Governor-General which entailed controversy between the Governor and the Chief Minister of Orissa is an example.

The character of the federal system under the India Act of 1935 can be understood only by referring to the conflicting interests of both parts of India. Whereas the British Indian provinces with the mature political system of centralised administration were desirous of creating a strong central government but the princely provinces viewed such a move with alarm as an attack upon their authority and were willing to accede only limited powers over few subjects to the centre. In 1939, the princes declared that they left no one in any doubt about their determination to insist "that in any future constitution for India, the essential guarantees and safeguards for the preservation of the sovereignty and autonomy of the states... should be effectively provided".[37]

Shortly after the Second World War, a Cabinet Mission was deputed to negotiate a Constitutional Settlement in India, The provinces were to be grouped as A,B, C and each group having the right to secede from the Union. The states were to retain all subjects and powers other than those ceded to the Union, namely foreign affairs, defence, and communication. This Act gave the rulers of Indian states, the choice to join or not the proposed All-India Federation. The Congress was not opposed to an All-India Federation but to the federal scheme embodied in the Act of 1935. Jawaharlal Nehru explained the Congress standpoint as:

> "Utterly bad as the Act is, there is nothing so bad in it as this federation and so we must exert ourselves to the utmost to break this and thus end the Act as a whole.... The development of this federal scheme is worthy of consideration. We are not against the conception of federalism. It is likely that a free India may be a federal India though in any event there must be a great deal of unitary control. But the present federation that is being thrust upon us is a federation in bondage and under the control, politically and socially of the most backward elements of the country".[38]

The federation which is about to be established by the Act of 1935 marks a complete departure from the laws and regulations under which India has been governed since the advent of the British in India".[39] According to H.V. Pataskar — "at the time of the second reading of the report of the Union Powers Committee, we developed a fear complex... . The autonomy of the states or their semi autonomy came to be looked upon as a matter of national danger. We kept the form of federation but we changed the substance or the context of the federation."[40]

When the Constituent Assembly first sat, there were two major problems in constructing a federal polity. The first is the communal sentiments of the Muslims and the erstwhile semi-independent Indian states. Hence in order to bring them under the Federal Scheme, it was inevitable that the Union should have only a minimum of enumerated powers and the residual should be left to the units. Consequently, in the Objectives Resolution which was adopted in the Constituent Assembly on January 22, 1947, it was announced that the Union should have only those three powers viz., Defence, Foreign Affairs and Communications, which had been conceded to it by the Cabinet Mission.[41] That the States of the Federation shall be "autonomous units" having all residuary powers left,[42] after assigning to the Union the three aforesaid subjects, together with those powers which followed by implication from the powers assigned to the Union.

It was unfortunate that the contemplated Federation was never established; had it been operative for a few years, habits of cooperation might have developed between the Indian States and the provinces and among the different communities in limited governments. It might have minimised the separatist tendencies and prevented subsequent partition of India. In fact since 1937 all provinces whether they were ruled by the Congress or the Muslim League had moved into the Union. Their cooperation in the interests of the nation was equally sincere as was evident from the various conferences convened by the Government of India for mutual consultation and exchange of views.

This was not to be when the Cabinet Mission of 1946 laid down the blueprint for a constitution to be drawn up by the Constituent Assembly; they provided for a very feeble centre whose jurisdiction was to be confined to defence, external affairs and communications with powers for raising necessary finances for them. The residual authority was to be vested in the provinces who were required to share powers with them.

Thus it is clear that the Objective Resolution adopted by the Constituent Assembly contained a provision to have a federal set-up with autonomous constituent units. This resolution had supported the idea of strong autonomous provinces and a weak central government. This concept was altered upon the recommendation of the "Union Powers Committee" of the Constituent Assembly which proposed that the residuary powers of government be vested in the Centre rather than in the States. The committee's explanation for the change in the location of the residuary powers in the Centre was suggested to accommodate the Muslim League in its demand for minority protection. It was pointed out that after the resolution of the partition issue, "this reason was no longer compelling and, therefore, it was preferable to have a strong centre with residuary powers lodged there."[43]

In presenting the Report of the Union Powers Committee to the Constituent Assembly on the 20th August, 1947, Jawaharlal Nehru, the Chairman, said "we are unanimously of the view that it would be injurious to the interests of the country to provide for a weak central authority, which would be incapable of ensuring peace of coordinating vital matters of common concern and of speaking effectively for the whole country in the international sphere. At the same time, we are quite clear in our minds that there are many matters in which authority must be solely with the units and that to frame a constitution on the basis of a unitary state would be a retrograde step both politically and administratively".[44] The committee had, thus, prescribed a federal structure with a strong centre. When the Constituent Assembly was convened on December 13, 1946, it officially endorsed the principle of federalism as the structure of the new India. It supported the resolution offered by Jawaharlal Nehru wherein "the said territories shall possess and retain the status of autonomous units together with residuary powers, and exercise all powers and functions of government and administration, save and expect such powers and functions as are vested in or assigned to the Union, or as are inherent or implied in the Union....[45] In India, liberation from British rule brought in its wake peculiar consequences. The legacy of foreign rule continued to influence the way of thinking and formation of political institutions even after India became free. Moreover, the administration could not change itself immediately to suit the indigenous conditions without impairing the morale of the personnel. The implications of the process of change is succinctly put in the following lines:

> "The British set in motion forces which were more powerful than they themselves realised and it is these forces rather than the British policies and influences, which really created modern India".[46]

Being a big country accompanied by the element of unity in diversity, historically and geographically India was bound to be a federation. While borrowing the principles of other constitutions, it also showed a great fidelity to the 1935 Act, which had been designed to suit a highly centralised authority. Later on, the necessity to integrate the Indian states and the need to grant responsible government in various categories piece by piece and the test of bringing together all the units under a fairly uniform pattern within an All-India framework, brought about an entirely different political climate little dreamt of by the constitution-makers.

REFERENCES

1. *Report of the Indian Statutory Commission.* Vol. II, Para 21.
2. Asok Chanda, *Federalism in India* (London: George Allen and Unwin Ltd.), 1965, pp. 18-19.
3. N.C. Roy, "The Indian Princes and All-India Federation" in *The Modern Review,* September 1932, p. 258.
4. *Proceedings of the Indian Round Table Conferences,* 12 November 1930-19 January 1931, p. 91.
5. *Ibid.,* p. 28.
6. *Ibid.,* pp. 36-37.
7. *Ibid.,* p. 37.
8. *Ibid.,* p. 245.
9. Ram Gopal, *Indian Muslims: A Political History,* (Bombay: Asia Publishing House), 1959, p. 229.
10. Regarding the attitude of Ambedkar, Mahatma Gandhi said: "I can understand the claims advanced by other minorities, but the claims advanced on behalf of the untouchables is to me the unkindest out of all". *Proceedings of the Federal Structure Committee and Minor ities Committee,* 1932, Vol. Ill, p. 1384.
11. *Proceedings of the Indian Round Table Conferences,* op.cit., p. 49.
12. Mohammad Ali Jinnah's "Fourteen Points", 28 March 1929, Gwyer and Appadorai, *Speeches and Documents on the Indian Constitution* Vol. I, p. 246.
13. *Proceedings of the Round Table Conferences,* (First Session), Appendix I to the Minority Committee Report, pp. 163-64 (letter written to the British Prime Minister).
14. Indian Round Table Conferences (Second Session), *Proceedings of the Federal Structure Committee and Minorities Committee,* 1931, Vol. Ill, p. 1345.
15. *Ibid.,* p. 1346.
16. *Ibid.,* p. 1351.
17. *Ibid.,* p. 1370.
18. *Ibid.,* p. 1449.
19. *Ibid.,* Annexure 2, p. 1446.
20. *Ibid.,*.pp. 1445-46,

21. *Ibid.*, Annexure 4, pp. 1450-53.
22. *Ibid.*, p. 1448.
23. *Proceedings of the Round Table Conferences, op.cit.* n.4, p. 73.
24. *Ibid.*, p. 31.
25. V.P. Menon, *The Story of the Integration of the Indian States,* (Calcutta: Orient Longman), 1956, p. 33.
26. Sir Eustace Percy's Committee comprised, apart from the Chairman, L.J. Kershan, A. Hyderi, K.N. Haksar, F.P. Robinson and V.S. Sunderam. And the Indian States Enquiry Committee (Financial) consisted of the Rt. Hon. J.C.C. Davidsen, Sir Maurice Gwyer, Sir Charles Stuart Williams, etc.
27. *Report of the Federal Finance Committee,* 1932, Government of India Press, Simla, p. 27.
28. Percy Committee was appointed in continuation of the Sub-Committee of federal structure Committee under the Chairmanship of Lord Peel to examine the question of federal finance, *Ibid.*, p. 1.
29. *Views of Indian States on the Government of India Bill* (1935), p. 17.
30. In his address at the 50th session (Faizpur) of the Indian National Congress, December, 1936. Quoted from Sir Maurice Gwyer and A. Appadorai, *Speeches and the Documents on the Indian Constitution,* Vol. I, London, 1957, p. 386.
31. R. Coupland, *Indian Politics 1935-42* (Madras: Oxford University Press) 1944, p. 5.
32. *Government of India Act,* 1935, Section 102 (I).
33. R. Coupland, *op. cit.* p. 96.
34. B.R. Ambedkar, *Federation versus Freedom,* Poona, 1939 p. 156.
35. Jawaharlal Nehru, *Discovery of India* (Oxford: Oxford University Press), 1946 pp. 374-75.
36. *Ibid.*, p. 370.
37. *Resolution of the Chamber of Princes,* 12 March, 1940, Parliamentary Papers, (1939-40) (cmd 6196), p. 42.
38. Address at Faizpur Congress, *op. cit.* n. 30.
39. Sir Shafa'at Ahmad Khan, *The Indian Federation,* London, 1937, pp. 24-25.

40. *Constituent Assembly Debates* (hereafter *C.A.D.)*. IV,6, Appendix 'A' pp. 671-72.

41. D.D., Basu, *Commentary on the Constitution of India,* 6th edition, Vol. A, p. 6.

42. I. *C.A.D.,* pp.57-58; II. *C.A.D.* p. 300.

43. Official Reports, *Constituent Assembly Proceedings,* Vol. V, Appendix A, pp. 60-61.

44. *C.A.D.* (1947), 20 August, 1947.

45. Official Reports, *Constituent Assembly Proceedings,* Vol. 1, p. 57.

46. Norman D. Palmer, *The Indian Political System* (London: George Allen and Unwin), 1961.

2

Constitutional Structure

Independent India's primary task was to find a suitable constitution that can meet the requirements of a country which stands united amidst diversities. After prolonged discussions it opted for a federal arrangement as a feasible mechanism. The federating states entered into a contract and formed a 'nation state'. The entire structure was meaningfully regulated through Indian Constitution which formed the fundamental law of the country.

India, inspite of its unitary character upto 1919, experienced perceptible changes in the relations between the central and provincial governments in the form of transfer of certain responsibilities to the provinces. Though the provinces continued as administrative units of India, these were autonomous in provincial subjects.

Some efforts were made in late 1940's to find out an adjustable constitution for Independent India. For this the first step was the appointment of Cabinet Mission Plan in 1946 to devise a constitutional framework under which independence could be granted. It rejected the demand for Pakistan and proposed a federal constitution for the whole of India. The Plan limited the jurisdiction of the Central Government to defence, external affairs and communications with powers to raise necessary funds while the rest of the powers to be vested with the units. The Constituent Assembly of India was elected under this plan and started working. The Constituent Assembly constituted a Union Powers Committee to define the subjects of jurisdiction of the Centre and the units in the proposed federation. The Constituent Assembly officially endorsed the principle of federation as the structure of the new India. It supported the resolution by Jawaharlal Nehru, that the provinces shall possess and retain the status of autonomous units along with residuary powers, and exercise all powers and functions of government and administration except such powers and functions as are assigned to the union. This resolution had supported the idea of strong autonomous provinces and relatively weak central government.

Close on the heels of Partition, various problems emerged which threatened the very existence of the new State. The Union Powers Committee in its report, altered the idea of strong autonomous provinces and declared that "the soundest framework for the constitution is a federation with a strong Centre".[1] In its second report, the Union Powers Committee declared: "Now that Partition is a settled fact, we are unanimously of the view that it would be injurious to the interests of the authority which would be incapable of ensuring peace, of coordinating vital matters of common concern and of speaking effectively of the whole country in the international sphere".[2] Jawaharlal Nehru accepted this explanation and pointed out that "after the resolving of the partition issue, this reason was no longer compelling and therefore it was preferable to have a strong Centre with residuary powers".[3] Although the Constituent Assembly accepted this decision but there were differences of opinion regarding the nature of the proposed Indian federation. Dr. Ambedkar, the Chairman of the Drafting Committee, while introducing the Draft Constitution, said, "The form of the constitution is federal in as much as it establishes a 'Dual polity' consisting of the Union at the Centre and the States at the periphery, each endowed with sovereign powers to be exercised in the field assigned to them respectively by the constitution. The Union is not a league of States, nor are the States administrative units or agencies of the Union Government. The Constitution has sought to forge means and methods whereby India will have federation and at the same time will have uniformity in all basic matters which are essential to maintain the unity of the country".[4]

But his views were not accepted by many members. For instance, one of the members said "The constitution was laying the foundation more for a formidable unitary constitution than a federal one. It gives nothing to the individual, nothing to the family, nothing to the villages, nothing to the districts, and nothing to the provinces. Dr. Ambedkar has taken everything to the Centre".[5] Ambedkar's view that a list of concurrent powers was a device to reduce the rigour of rigidity and legalism was not accepted by K. Santhanam who said that in was an inevitable political tendency of all Federal Constitutions that "the Federal list grows and the concurrent list fades out, because when once the central legislature takes jurisdiction over a particular field of legislation, the jurisdiction of the provincial legislatures goes out".[6] He asked surprisingly "... whether this is what we want? and whether this is desirable".[7] Some of the members were not agreeing even to call it a Federation.[8]

The Federal Obsession

The founding fathers were not sure on the point of labelling the constitution as unitary or federal. They realised that with the Partition, a federal form was unwarranted and at the same time to fall back to a unitary form would be a retrograde step, both politically and administratively.[9] Then the Constituent Assembly adopted an objective resolution and pledged itself to framing a federal constitution with autonomous constituent units. In the words of K.C. Wheare, "If there is to be a federation, one condition must be fulfilled. There must be some matter, even if only one matter, which comes under the exclusive control, actual or potential, of the general government and something likewise under the regional governments. If there were not, that would be the end of federalism."[10]

The pattern introduced by the 1935 Government of India Act continued to remain as the basic framework of the new constitution. Besides it incorporated many features of other federations of the world. But this new constitution was neither federal or unitary nor presidential or parliamentary. However the uniqueness of our Constitution lies in the fact that for the first time in the world, a Constitution with borrowed features of many other constitutions was evolved; characteristics, each of which was designed to function in a given set up, were picked up and absorbed to suit the Indian conditions. A very strong centralised government was given to the Indian subcontinent, which is multi-ethnic, multi-religious and multi-linguistic. The concept of a nation that was yet to strike, was introduced to a common chord geographically as well as emotionally. The constitution has borrowed heavily from other sources and this was intended, as declared by Nehru, that "We should learn from their successes and avoid their failures".[11]

Union-State relations are significant to the pattern of political processes in a federal system. There are evidently two models in Indian federal system. First, there are different parties in power in Centre and State as in Kerala. Secondly, the same party holds power at both levels like in Uttar Pradesh (hereinafter U.P.),

In a federal system, the States are influenced by the national set-up and in turn affect it. U.P. and Kerala present a clear understanding of political experimentations and of the factors which affect political institutions and determine the behaviour of politicians in India. An analysis of the functioning, presents some common features which are present in other States also despite difference in context.

It is true that the constitutional provisions empowering the Centre to encroach upon the powers of the States have led some observers to conclude that "the States in India are not more than the units of a unitary governmental structure".[12] But the federal theory presupposes a political capacity congruent with the constitutional competence of each federated unit; and it is not rare to find an Indian State exercising considerable influence and bargaining with the Centre on a number of issues. The State leaderships have often assumed strategic importance and have influenced the national decision-making process including the choice of Prime Ministers.[13] No where the national government is so much dependent on its sub-ordinate units as in India. In fact, "it is the leadership in the State which plays a decisive role in the shaping of major policies and in determining national programmes, although ostensibly the political set-up at the Centre appears to be an ail-powerful force".[14]

As the Centre-State relations were unfolded after the operation of the constitution, its functional analysis brings forth various stages.

The beginning is characterised by the dominance of a single political party namely the Indian National Congress. Because of the political dominance of the Congress Party, there was a tendency to tilt towards centralisation of power and thereby hampering the state autonomy. There is a change in the relationship among the Centre and States and the Constitution was operated in a manner contrary to the intentions of the framers. "... the actual relations between the Union and the States have been very different from those postulated in the constitution. India has practically functioned as a Unitary State though the Union and the States have tried to function formally and legally as a federation. This State of affairs can continue so long as the Union and most of the State Governments are dominated by a single political party and the Union continues to finance economic and social developments in the States in the same massive scale as they have done during the first and second five year pians".[15]

Various issues generated controversy and strained the relations between the Centre and the States. These were more prominent in the states where a non-Congress party is in power like Kerala.

In 1952, after the First General Elections, Congress formed a government in Travancore-Cochin with the support of the Travancore Tamilnad Congress. However, after some time, Tamilnad Congress withdrew its support which led to the defeat of the ministry. The Rajpramukh[16] dissolved the Assembly. Criticising this action the leftists argued that the Government could have been formed by the opposition instead of dissolving the legislature.

The Central Government tried to extend its power and deepen its direct involvement in the political future of the state of Kerala through various means in this phase. The most common is the imposition of President's rule. In 1957, Communist Party came to power through the ballot box in Kerala. With a sense of warning, it was pointed out that if the Central Government and their henchmen in the State create obstructions to the first Communist Government or oppose their policies, the Communist Party will be compelled to give up their belief in the ballot box and face the challenge once again shedding blood".[17] But just after two years, in 1959, President's rule was imposed after the dismissal of the Namboodiripad Ministry. It may be relevant here to quote what Morarji Desai commented on this dissolution way back in 1974. He said that "the Kerala Assembly was dissolved at the insistence of the then Congress President Mrs. Indira Gandhi, though the then Prime Minister Jawaharlal Nehru was against the dissolution."[18] This Ministry was dislodged from power even though it enjoyed the confidence of the members of the Legislative Assembly. In a parliamentary form of government, once a party is elected to power, it should be allowed to remain in office so long as it enjoys the confidence of the Legislative Assembly.[19]

In fact in Kerala there was no constitutional breakdown.

But a political crisis was created by the opposition parties. Hence 'political breakdown' became a pretext for the Centre to intervene.[20] The Centre's stand against the non-Congress Government is on the basis of political and ideological differences between the State Communist Ministry and the ruling Congress Party at the Centre. This way it prevented the opposition party from holding the rein of power in the state ministry.

During the Lok Sabha Debate on March 30, 1959 the criticism of the opposition was vociferously voiced by Ashok Mehta (Praja Socialist Party hereinafter referred to as P.S.P.), A.K. Gopalan (Communist Party) and others that emergency provisions of the constitution were being misused to protect partisan interests of the Congress and to permanently damage parliamentary democracy. They said that principles were changed and standards varied from state to state and from time to time in the same state to suit the convenience of the Congress Party. It was said that the Government's principle was: "Either Congress Ministry or no ministry at all".[21]

The role of the Governor was also came under criticism. In 1959, President's rule was imposed on the explicit advice of the Governor, though he could not justify the reason. As in a democracy there is only one way to measure the confidence of the people in the popularly elected government through testing its strength on the floor of the State Assembly, the Communist Government was not given a chance to prove its majority.

Again in 1965, no single political party secured absolute majority in Kerala. The left communists[22] were 11 seats short of an absolute majority, but the problem was the formation of a stable government in the state. The Governor recommended President's rule and the newly elected coalition ministry was dissolved. The denial of an opportunity to the leader of the single largest party to try to form a government became an issue of intense political discussion in the country.[23]

The Kerala happenings reinforce the view that during the Nehru-era, the norms, the goals, and the policies and programmes of the government were laid down by the Centre. The other example is the fate of 'Kerala Education Bill' (1957). This Bill was reserved by the Governor for consideration of the President. But the question is, whether a Governor can reserve a Bill for the assent of the President even when such reservation is not assented to by the State Government?. This Education Bill was reserved for Presidential assent inspite of the fact that the State Government was against it. "This was totally unconstitutional".[24] The Centre wanted this Bill to be reserved and the Governor is told to reserve the Bill either formally or informally.

In the case of U.P. , during this period, the Governors acted in a formal way as the constitutional head of the state, but in reality they functioned as an instrument of the centre. None of the four Governors[25] of U.P. K.M. Munshi, V. Venkatagiri, R.K. Rao Burgula and Biswanath Das had any occasion to use their discretionary power in appointing the chief ministers and the council of ministers, as the Congress enjoyed a majority in the State Vidhan Mandal (Legislature).[26] In fact the Governors refrained from using their powers even when the situation called for the use of such powers. For instance, in 1963, the Governor, on the advice of the Chief Minister C.B. Gupta, demanded the resignation of A.R. Shastri, the Minister of State for forests, but he refused to resign. Instead of exercising his power to dismiss the minister, the Governor visited the capital to seek the advice of the Congress leaders, and after two weeks of hectic activity, the Prime Minister used his influence to make Shastri submit his resignation. This shows how the Governor remained contended with functioning as an instrument of the centre like "a bird in the golden cage".[27]

In another case, as the Governor has the discretion to reserve a Bill for the assent of the President under Art. 200 and it is compulsory for him to do so under Articles 31(A),

33(3) and 288 (2) of the constitution. But on the contrary this provision was used to strengthen the hold of the Centre over the state.[28] During this period, the Governors adopted the strategy of reserving Bills for the assent of the President, for besides being convenient, it helped to show their allegiance to the Prime Minister and served to control powerful chief ministers like G.B. Pant and C.B. Gupta.

In the mode of selecting a Chief Minister of the state, the Party High Command preferred to nominate a person as Chief Minister instead of asking the State Congress Party to elect its leader. The appointment of Sampurnanand as the chief minister in 1954, inspite of the popularity of C.B. Gupta in the state can be cited as an instance. He was a choice imposed on the state by the Congress leaders in the Centre.[29]

In 1964, the U.P. High Court came in conflict with the Vidhan Sabha (Legislative Assembly) over the complicated question of the powers and jurisdiction of the High Court and its judges in relation to the powers, privileges and immunities of the State Vidhan Mandal and its members.[30]

The functioning of the Constitution in U.P. from 1950-67 was merely a formal affair. Whatever may be the issues, were solved amicably within the party. This is precisely due to the same party rule in the State as well as in the Centre. The people had no voice in choosing or removing the Governor from office. He was more loyal to the centre than to the people. Several chief Ministers were not the choice of the people, as they were the nominees of the central government, directly or indirectly. Sampurnanand in 1954, C.B. Gupta in 1960, and S. Kriplani in 1963 etc. were appointed chief ministers not because they enjoyed the patronage of the Congressmen in the state or were elected by the people but because they enjoyed the patronage of the Congress leaders at the centre.

So long as the Congress Party was in power at the Centre as well as in most of the States there was little need to use the constitutional provisions which are available for managing Centre-State or inter-state conflicts. This trend was broken in the year 1967.

The 1967 General Elections were a landmark in the evolution of Indian federalism since for the first time, the overwhelming dominance of the Congress Party met with a challenge. The States had began to be vociferous in their demand for more powers and autonomy. The organisational machinery of the Congress could no longer be used for resolving Centre-State differences now. For the first time, the provisions of the Constitution were put to severe test and Centre-State relations assumed the proportion of a burning issue.

This period witnessed tensions, stresses and strains in Centre-State relations as the Congress began to lose its political grip over a number of States and also because planning was almost put under suspension, the Central Government lost any definite ideological direction and leadership and in a state of desperation sought to assert its authority over the State through various other means.

When we look at the post-1967 period, it is essential to discuss the term of the second Namboodiripad Ministry (1967-69) and the Achyutha Menon (C.P.I.) Ministry.

In the first one, State Government showed affirmation against the policies of the Central Government, For example there was a movement protesting against the Centre for insufficient quota of food grains per capita and delay in releasing food grains for distribution. Another conflict arose over the State's demand for equitable share in the foreign exchange earned by the Centre through Kerala's contribution. It was pointed out that 'the Centre earned more than Rs. Fifty crores from cashewnut exports alone and Kerala's demand was justiciable, and if Kerala were denied justice it should secede from the Indian Union."[31]

Two other issues were also brought up at that time. First concerning the State Government's policies in handling popular agitations and second with regard to the demand for financial devolution.

The Articles in Part XVIII "Emergency Provisions" of the Constitution arm the Union with powers to ensure the unity and integrity of the country. These are meant to be used in a spirit of mutual trust. Article 355, which comes under this part should not be interpreted as enabling the Union Government to assume direct control over law and order in a state but as imposing a duty on it to make available the assistance of its armed forces in aid of the civil power in the state. As a matter of general policy, armed forces of the Union should be deployed in a state with the consent of the State Government concerned. When the central government employees went on a strike in September 1968, the Union Government, without informing or seeking consent of the Kerala Chief Minister, moved the Central Reserve Police (CRP) in the State. The Namboodiripad Ministry was against using police as a means to suppress popular agitations. The Union Government, on the other hand, wanted law and order to be maintained and its assets and property protected. Both sides accused each other of transgressing constitutional provisions. As maintenance of law and order is the obligation of the states, this step of the Centre was considered as a serious violation of the constitutional provision.[32] Similarly it was alleged that in the absence of equitable financial devolution, the states were no better than municipalities. C.P.I.(Marxist) (formed in 1964 after a split in C.P.I.) especially contended that the Centre would not allow the States more so the C.P. I. (M)-led State of Kerala to be independent and viable financially for fear of losing its grip on the politics of the State. The Kerala Chief Minister, along with him Tamil Nadu counterpart, held unanimous views in the National Development Council (N.D.C.).

The Achyutha Menon Ministry had to tolerate situations and in which it had to pressurise and persuade the Centre to concede Kerala's rightful demands whereas the Centre chose to go slow. Some of the major issues related to: Centre's consent to bills for nationalisation of private forest and of plantations owned by the foreigners, granting constitutional protection to Land Reform Act; raising price of locally grew rubber etc.

The question of the formation of new All-India Services has been an important area of friction between the Central Government and the States. Three reasons were put up for this resistance by the State Governments: (a) the creation of new All-India Services cuts at the effective spread of state services, thus reducing the employment opportunities for the sons of the soil: (b) the All-India Services encroach upon state autonomy and (c) they also involve larger expenditure because of high salary scales. Indeed, the All-India services are already becoming suspect in the eyes of leftist parties. E.M.S. Namboodiripad, openly questioned the validity of the All-India Services the members of which "are recruited and trained by the Congress Government at the Centre and posted to states in many of which are non-Congress Governments".[33]

When K.M. Mani was the Finance Minister in Kerala, he argued about Finance Commission's alleged 'discrimination' against Kerala[34] and the failure of the Planning Commission to do 'justice' to them. He said that there has been 'discrimination' against Kerala and the Planning Commission has done little to correct it. Besides, Kerala's per capita income being below the national average and its 'peculiar' circumstances, it is forgotten that, what is being estimated is income 'originating' in a state and not income 'accruing'.[35]

In the case of U.P. this period was a significant phase in its political history. It is important also as after twenty years of unbroken Congress rule it failed to win a majority of seats in the Legislative Assembly. The opposition parties had for the first time been able to combine their efforts and take advantage of the growing popular discontent and anti-Congressism in the State. It was during this period critical issues and constitutional controversies were raised in the State. The political situation in the State was precarious and political parties were formed on the basis of regional, local and personal considerations. For example, the Bharatiya Kranti Dal (hereinafter referred to as B.K.D.) was formed by Charan Singh in 1967 after he had defected from the Congress. Over and above in 1967, monopoly of power ended and power was transferred to different parties and coalitions in U.P.

The Constitution vests complete power with the President for the selection and appointment of the Governor, making him a nominee of the Central Government. The essence of the Governor's role lies not much in what has been formally laid down in the Constitution but rather in the political dimension that this office has acquired, in the context of States which allow coalition parties to power and follow policies opposite to that of Central Government. The Governor has often tended to use his discretionary power to seek information from the Chief Minister relating to administrative and legislative matters which go beyond the intentions of these provisions in the Constitution. Similarly the Governor has often taken recourse to referring back to the Council of Ministers, decisions made by individual ministers mainly because he as a representative of the Central Government feel compelled to intervene in the ongoing process of administration at the State level. In 1967-68 the Governor played precisely this role as the agent of the Central authority and received orders from the Central Government which could in no sense be regarded as neutral and which carried the indubitable stamp of the party in control of its power. The interventionist character of the Governor's power to return bills passed by the State Government on matters other than money votes, for reconsideration and/or reenactment in amended form has become more and more pronounced over the years. This is specially true in its application to state governments which are controlled by non-Congress parties.

After 1967, the Governor became an active participant in the politics of the State and played a crucial role. The Chief Ministers could not complete their full tenure and the Governor had to choose the Chief Minister each time. This brought the office of Governor into limelight[36] on the one hand and made him act as an agent of the Central Government to safeguard the interests of the party in power at the Centre, on the other hand. But the decisions of the Governor were not uniform and in accordance with any fixed norm. For example, B. Gopala Reddy took different decisions in identical situations in 1969 and 1970.[37]

In 1967, the office of the Governor had become more controversial, when Governor Biswanath Das had invited C.B. Gupta, Leader of the Congress to form the government[38] and his decision was criticised by all the opposition parties as unjust and undemocratic.[39]

In 1970, both Charan Singh and Girdhari Lal put forth their claim to form the government.[40] But the Governor called Charan Singh to form the ministry inspite of the fact that Girdhari Lal had the majority. His action was condemned as unparliamentary.[41] S. Nijalingappa, President of the Congress(O)[42] alleged that "the Governor had acted under pressure from New Delhi",[43] S.S. Kothari of Jan Sangh said that "the institution of Governor was getting into discredit and the people were gradually losing their faith in it, for the Governors were being reduced to the instruments of the ruling party at the Centre and were not acting according to the Constitution." One of the remarks was that the Central Government exercised pressure on the Governors to instal the governments of its choice or alternatively asked them to recommend the imposition of President's rule.

Again in October 1970, the Governor invited T.N. Singh to form the government.[44] The Governor did not accept the advice of Kamlapati Tripathi, leader of the Congress(N) who said that the Congress(N) being the largest party in the House, should be given the chance to form government.[45] The Governor was accused of political discrimination and Nath Pai of the P.S.P. said that "The fate of a government shall not be decided in the gubernatorial palaces which is the resting house of the retired politicians but on the floor of the Assembly of the State".[46]

Another crisis cropped up when Chief Minister Charan Singh (of coalition cabinet), demanded the resignations of twenty seven ministers belonging to the Congress(N) and on their refusal to quit, asked the Governor to dismiss them. While he assured the Governor that he enjoyed a majority in the Vidhan Sabha. But the Governor Gopala Reddy, wrote to Charan Singh that the coalition, in which Congress(N) was the major partner, no longer existed as he (Governor) took away their portfolios, so he should resign. The parliamentary process was completely paralysed when the Chief Minister refused to resign and was ready to show strength. But the Governor refused to judge the majority on the floor of the House and recommended President's rule instead.[47] This action of the Governor was criticised as the President was out of the country and unaware of the conditions prevailing in the State.[48] It was described as an abuse of power "committed on the mere asking of the Central Government" giving benefit to one party and disadvantaging other parties.[49] M.P. Tripathi, leader of the Jan Sangh doubted the impartiality of the Governor and alleged that he had violated the Constitution. A.K. Sen of the Congress said that the Governor of U.P. had acted in a partisan way.[50]

Governor may dismiss a ministry if he has the reasons to believe that it is engaged in activities which are likely to endanger national security and solidarity.[51] But in this case the Governor had no reason to dismiss the ministry or to ask for the resignation of the Chief Minister. It is improper for a Governor to recommend President's rule on the advice of the Attorney General, because he can dismiss ministry only if the Chief Minister refuses to resign after a vote of no-confidence has been passed against the ministry, and if he has a reasonable ground to believe that the Chief Minister no longer enjoys the confidence of the Vidhan Sabha and avoids facing it on the pretext or the other.

Governor B. Gopala Reddy should not have exercised his discretion because Chief Minister Charan Singh was willing to face the Vidhan Sabha on the fixed date or earlier, and this leads to the conclusion that the Governor had acted on extra-constitutional basis.[52]

During this period the Governor, took almost all decisions in accordance with the directives of the Central Government and did not pay much attention to the interests and aspirations of the people of the state. The role of the Governors not only adversely affected the working of Parliamentary democracy but also strained Centre-State relations. They just remained confidential agents.[53]

The appointment of B. Gopala Reddy as Governor was announced before the formation of the new Cabinet headed by Charan Singh. In Lok Sabha, S.M. Banerjee wanted to know, whether Charan Singh would be consulted and this appointment would be reconsidered.[54] Y.B. Chavan, the then Home Minister, however, said that there would be no consultation.[55] Here Chief Minister was not consulted at all inspite of the fact that the Governor should be appointed in consultation with the State government concerned.

There was a perceptible change from 1971 i.e. when Mrs. Gandhi's position became politically strong. Gradually she started centralising all powers in her hands. The legislatures were completely ignored in the matter of electing their leader and were compelled to accept the imposed leader. Even those who enjoyed the support of the majority of the party legislatures, had to depend on her for their survival. In a way she acquired the position of the de-facto leader of the state cabinet. Chief Ministers worked only as her representatives in the State. All the Chief Ministers in U.P. from 1950 onwards have been nominees of the Centre. The following statement of some of the M.L.A.'s made in October 1973, when the Prime Minister had not yet announced her choice of the new Congress Chief Minister for the State vividly depicts the then prevailing state of affairs: "Who are we to voice our views in public over such delicate matters as the choice of our leader? We can only whisper our wishes in Tripathi's ears, who can in turn pass them on secretly to the Prime Minister. It is her prerogative to name the leader and it is our duty to elect him.[56] However the state leaders have never rebelled openly against the Centre's decision.

Centre has also intervened in another way, through U.P.C.C. election. Open contests between candidates are rare, in most cases, a person is nominated by the Centre and then unanimously 'elected' by the State Congress. We can cite here the election of U.P.C.C. President Baijnath Kureel in December 1972 as an example.

In 1973, after Tripathi, H.N. Bahuguna was appointed as Chief Minister of U.P. Mrs. Gandhi was the sole decision maker of the affairs of U.P. Mrs. Gandhi was convinced about Bahuguna's loyalty to her.[57] The Prime Minister's influence could be clearly seen in the proceedings of Congress(R) Legislative Party in 1974 which was called to elect Bahuguna as the leader. Bahuguna declared that "the Prime Minister would be sitting in judgement on the day-to-day functioning of each Minister in the State. She would decide how long a Minister would last.[58] This shows the loyalty and the dependence of the Chief Minister on the Prime Minister. In the same way as a Chief Minister is elected, his fall is also brought about by the Prime Minister. H.N. Bahuguna resigned after being asked to do so by Indira Gandhi.

The 1977 General Elections marked a watershed in the political history of the independent India, It brought about a historical change by catapulting the Janata Party to power by replacing for the first time the Congress at the Centre. In U.P. the Congress suffered a major setback, while it drew blank in Kerala.

The first act of the Janata Government was the dissolution of nine State Assemblies which were under Congress rule, and the imposition of President's rule in those States inspite of no reason for its imposition. This was the most flagrant case of misuse of Article 356, when there was neither a breakdown of constitutional machinery, nor a loss of majority, nor a mass upsurge against the governments in those States, The phrase 'or otherwise' in Article 356[59] helped the Central Government to resort to the extreme measure of dismissing a popularly elected ministry.

In U.P. Legislative Assembly, the Janata Party won over 60% of seats, all of which were earlier controlled by the Congress Party. No other incidence of constitutional distortion had occurred in U.P. barring the misuse of Article 356.

This phase had no impact on Kerala politics as the same coalition of Ruling Front maintained its majority. But this phase witnessed frequent changes of ministries and Chief Ministers were installed by the central leadership.[60] The split of the Congress Party after 1978 and formation of Congress (Urs, hereinafter 'U') by Dev Raj Urs was very much anti-Indira and had its impact on the Kerala politics also. The State Congress leader, A.K. Antony, resigned from the chief ministership in protest against the ambiguous and unprincipled stand of the central Congress leadership in the Chikkamagalur by-election in which Mrs. Gandhi contested in 1978.

The March 1977 General Elections that swept Indira Gandhi away from the Centre did not have any impact on the state with regard to the functioning of Constitution. To sum up during the phase of Janata Party rule, no major controversy regarding constitutional provisions occurred in U.P. and Kerala barring the controversy of misusing Aticle 356 in U.P. and other eight states.

With the breakup of the Janata Party and its electoral defeat in 1980, the Congress was voted back to power once again at the Centre but had lost more states including Kerala, while in U.P. it regained power.

In 1960, Congress Party behaved in the same way as Janata Party did in 1977. It also dissolved nine state assemblies under Janata Party rule and imposed President's rule without any specific reason.

In 1981, a controversy arose in Kerala regarding the formation of ministry by a minority party. It is against the basic concept of the Constitution that a minority party can form a government. Instead, the leader of the largest political party should be invited to form the government. In 1981, K. Karunakaran, a Congress (I) leader was appointed as Chief Minister of the minority government of the United Democratic Front (U.D.F.). There were widespread demonstrations in the state against Governor's action. But after his exit the Governor did not give the opposition a chance to form the government.[61]

Even after the submission of the report of the Sarkaria Commission in which it was recommended that the Governor should be appointed with the consultation of the concerned state chief minister,[62] Rajiv Gandhi appointed six Governors to the states in 1988 without prior consultation with the Chief Ministers.[63] E.M.S. Namboodiribad, C.P.M. General Secretary, pointed out that the appointment of Mrs. R.D, Sinha as Kerala Governor was not done in consultation with the State Chief Minister.[64] The Sarkaria Commission has also suggested that a politician from the ruling party at the Union should not be appointed as the Governor of the State which is being run by some other party or a combination of other parties.[65] Inspite of this specific recommendation Mrs. Sinha was appointed. Namboodiribad criticised this action of the Rajiv Gandhi Government very much.[66] In the same year, the Kerala State Committee of the Left Democratic Front (L.D.F.) in a resolution adopted at the end of its three-day meeting held in Kerala in February 1988, declared that the appointment of Mrs. R.D. Sinha as grossly undemocratic and such actions of the Centre would not be helpful for healthy Centre-State relations or the smooth functioning of the democratic set-up, the committee warned.[67]

The practice of imposing chief ministers in the Congress (I) governments in U.P. continued during this period also.

Mrs. Gandhi nominated only someone who suited her most. In this process, loyalty to her own person was the first and foremost criterion for selecting the Chief Minister. The nominated person got elected by the Congress (I) Legislative Party only to justify the democratic claim. V.P. Singh was appointed as Chief Minister of U.P. because of the 'pairavi' (support) done in his favour by Sanjay Gandhi and his friend Sanjay Singh.[68] Similarly S. Misra was nominated as a compromise candidate between Vir Bahadur Singh and Lokpati Tripathi. Both of them were M.P.'s at the time of their nomination. The practice of nominating the chief minister touched its height in the case of N.D. Tiwari (the Minister of Finance at that time), when he was ordered over telephone to come back from his official tour to Vienna and to join chief ministership of U.P. when S. Misra resigned on health grounds in 1984. In 1985, however, Vir Bahadur Singh's nomination for chief ministership was not significant in the real sense of the term. The Centre did the right thing by not imposing once again a nominee of their choice on U.P.[69]

So it is clear that within the Indian Constitution, the states are not given a totally independent position, comparable to that of the American States. In many ways, the States are dependent on the Centre and closely related to it. Moreover the Congress Party is federally organised, and its constituent State units are independent. Yet it is a highly centralised party. The Congress High Command has always played an active role in the internal affairs of the party units at the State level. In the case of U.P. this trend has been more pronounced because of its size and as it has always been the Prime Minister's "home State". Central intervention occurs because Central and State Congress politics are interwined. Faction leaders at the State level belong to a particular faction and pay allegiance to a particular leader at the Centre. Hence all their political decisions at the State level are influenced by decisions made at the Central level. Further national party organs always consider a matter from the national angle and not from the view point of the interest of the concerned State.

While in the case of Kerala, the Centre being geographically remote also became politically distant and the situation in Kerala is viewed as if from the Himalayan heights, removed from the realities of the present.

Actually the framers had viewed the federation in legal and constitutional than in ethnic, linguistic or cultural terms. They relied heavily on the Act of 1935 and thought that problems could be satisfactorily solved within that framework. But Centre-State relations or the federal structure in actual practice gets under strains on account of not only there being different parties in power but also because of the great deal of infighting and different policy preferences within the major parties. It is also clear that the Centre-State relations have not been entirely in tune with the formal constitutional arrangements. The working of the Federation has been marked by centrifugal trends which are discussed in the next chapter.

REFERENCES

1. *Report of the Union Powers Committee,* Para 2.
2. *Constituent Assembly Debates* (hereinafter *C.A.D.)* V, 3, Appendix 'A', p. 58.
3. Official Reports, *Constituent Assembly Proceedings.* Vol. V, Appendix-A, pp. 60-61.
4. *C.A.D.* Vol. VII, pp. 33-35.
5. *Ibid.,* p. 241.
6. *Ibid.,* p. 263.
7. *Ibid.*
8. For example: B.M. Gupta, Member of the Constituent Assembly, said that the kind of Federation could not be called a Federation but a decentralised Unitary State. See *C.A.D.,* Vol. XI, p. 844.
9. Shiva Rao, *Report of the Union Powers Committee of Constituent Assembly,* Vol. II, p. 777.
10. K.C. Wheare, *Federal Government,* third edition, (London: Oxford University Press), 1953, p. 79.

11. Jawaharlal Nehru, *C.A.D.*, Vol. I, Government of India Publication, New Delhi.
12. K.V. Rao, "Centre-State Relations in Theory and Practice", *Indian Journal of Political Science*, Vol. XIV, No. 4, October-December 1953, pp. 352-55.
13. Michael Breacher, *Nehru's Mantle; The Politics of Succession in India* (New York: Praeger), 1966; Rajni Kothari, *Politics in India* (Orient Longmans Ltd.), 1970, pp. 310-15 and R.J. Venkateswaran, *Cabinet Government in India* (London: Allen and Unwin), 1967, pp. 127-39.
14. Paul H. Appleby, *Public Administration in India; Report of a Survey* (New Delhi: Government of India, Cabinet Secretariat), 1963, p. 21.
15. K. Santhanam, *Union State Relations in India* (Bombay: Asia Publishing House), 1960, p. 70.
16. In 1950, when the Constitution came into existence, the constituent units of the Indian Union were divided into four parts. The Head of the Part A States was the Governor while the Head of the Part B States was Rajpramukh. Travancore-Cochin was in Part B. Part C and D States were administered by the President through a Chief Commissioner or a Lieutenant Governor.
17. A polit bureau member, Sri Sundarayya, *Malayala Manorama*, April 7, 1957.
18. Mr Desai's statement issued on 11 March 1974, when he began his indefinite fast demanding the dissolution of the Gujarat Assembly, *Asian Recorder*, 1975, p. 11943.
19. Shri N.V. Gadgil, then Governor of Punjab, publicly expressed the view that the Communist Government of Kerala had the right to continue in office for the term of five years, unless it resigned of its own accord or was voted out of office. *The Tribune*, Ambala, July 7, 1959.
20. Amal Ray, Kerala episode is different from the state emergency of any other state. In this case central action was adopted against an opposition Government which had not suffered, technically viewed, a political breakdown. Naturally the opinion was sharply divided as to the reasonableness of such action, and it was alleged in some quarters that this action was tinged with political prejudice, *Inter Governmental Relations in India*, (Bombay: Asia Publishing House) 1966, p. 110.

21. *The Statesman,* March 30, 1956.
22. After a split in Communist Party of India (C.P.I.) in 1964 into two factions - C.P.I. and C.P.I. (M), the C.P.I., is considered as right faction while the C.P.I. (M) as left faction or left communists.
23. Robert L. Hardgrave, Jr. "The Communist Parties of Kerala: An Electoral Profile" in Myron Weiner and John Osgood Field (ed.) *Electoral Politics in the Indian States,* (New Delhi: Manohar Book Service), 1975, pp. 182-84.
24. K. Santhanam, *op.cit.* p. 23.
25. S.R. Sen, *Dictionary of National Biography,* 1973 and 1974 (Calcutta: Institute of Historical Studies), Vol. II (E-L) and Vol. III (M-R), pp. 70, 175-76 and 467-69. All the Governors were active members of the Congress Party.
26. U.P., Report, on the General Administration of U.P., 1952-1967 (Lucknow: Superintendent, Printing and Stationary).
27. "The States" *Link,* Vol. V, No, 53, 11 August 1963, p. 21, Para 9.
28. See *U.P. Gazette Extraordinary,* 1950-64 and *Lucknow Law Times,* 1964-65, 1965-66, 1966-67.
29. Marc J. Swartz, (ed.) *Local Level Politics; Social and Cultural Perspectives,* (London: University London Press Ltd.) 1969, p. 330.
30. With reference to Article 143, Constitution of India, Keshav Singh Vs. State of U.P., *All India Reporter.* Supreme Court, 1965, Vol. 52, p. 755.
31. *Economic and Political Weekly (E.P.W.),* Special No. August 1967, Bundhs were organised all over the State and demonstrations held at the residence of the Prime Minister and the Union Food Minister.
32. *Ibid.,* 28 September, 1968, pp. 1465-66.
33. *The Statesman,* 23 February, 1969, p. 7.
34. The broader issues of financial relations between the Centre and States are discussed more exclusively in the Fifth Chapter on "Economic Dynamics of Centre-State Relations".
35. K.N. Raj, "Kerala's Problems in the National Context" *Mainstream,* July 13, 1985.

36. A.K, Ghosal, "Forum : The Role of the State Governors in India", *Indian Political Science Review,* Vol. II, No. 1-2, October 1967-March 1968, p. 178, Para 4.

37. S. Chatterjee, "The Role of Governor in Indian Politics Since 1967", *Indian Journal of Political Science,* Vol. XXXII. No. 4, October-December 1971, p. 523, Para I.

38. B.K. Mukherjee "Constitutional and Parliamentary Developments", *Journal of Constitutional and Parliamentary Studies,* Vol. I, No. 2, April-June, 1967, p. 92, Para 5.

39. *The Statesman* (Delhi), 14 March, 1967.

40. *Asian Recorder,* 9-15, April 1970, pp. 9480-81.

41. Charan Singh had the support of 235 M.L.A.s whereas Girdhari Lal had the support of 236 M.L.A.s. The Governor did not disclose the reason. In view of democracy being the government by the majority, the decision should have been in favour of Girdhari Lal and not Charan Singh. See "Legislative and Constitutional Role of Governors in Ministry Making in U.P. and Bihar", *Journal of Parliamentary Information,* Vol. XVI, No. 2, July 1970, pp. 166-68.

42. In 1969, due to internal dissensions at the Centre, the Congress Party was divided into two groups, one [Congress (O)] by the Congress President (S.N. Nijalingappa) and other [Congress (N)] by the Prime Minister.

43. *The Hindustan Times,* New Delhi, 18 February, 1970.

44. *Lok Sabha Debates,* 9-23 November 1970, New Delhi: Lok Sabha Secretariat, 1970, Vol. 45, No. 1, Series 4, pp. 229-30.

45. *The Statesman,* 8 September, 1970.

46. *Lok Sabha Debates, op. cit.,* 15 November 1967, Vol. IX, Series IV, Col. 810.

47. *Lok Sabha Debates,* 9-23 November 1970, *op. cit.* The report of the Governor of U.P. dated 29 September 1970 was laid on the table of the Lok Sabha on 9 November 1970.

48. The President V.V. Giri was on an official visit to the Soviet Union; the communique was sent to him and he signed it in Kiev on 7 October 1970.

49. *The Statesman,* 7 October 1970.

50. *Op. cit.* n. 42, p. 167.

51. *India: Administrative Reforms Commission, Report on the Centre-State Relations,* June 1969, (New Delhi: Manager of Publications), 1969, p. 30.
52. "Role and Position of the Governors and Centre-State Relations", *Proceedings of the Indian Parliamentary Symposium,* Parliament House, New Delhi, 2-3 May, 1970, pp. 23-25.
53. V.K. Varadachari, *Governor in the Indian Constitution* (New Delhi: Heritage Publishers), 198O, p. 34,
54. *Lok Sabha Debates,* Vol. II, 1967, Col. 2794.
55. *Ibid.,* Col. 2795.
56. *The Statesman,* Delhi, 18 October, 1973.
57. H.N. Bahuguna himself declared that he was the Chief Minister at the pleasure of the central leadership, *National Herald,* 29 March, 1975.
58. *Ibid.,* 6 March, 1974.
59. Article 356 - The Constitution provides that if the President, on receipt of a report from the Governor of a State or otherwise is satisfied that a situation has arisen in which the government of a State cannot be carried on in accordance with the provisions of the Constitution, he can declare failure of the constitutional machinery.
60. In March 1977, K. Karunakaran was appointed as Chief Minister, followed by his resignation in April 1977, A.K. Antony was installed as Chief Minister, followed by his resignation in 1978, P.K.V. Nair became Chief Minister followed by his resignation in 1979, Mohd. Koya was appointed as Chief Minister and when he resigned after two months, Assembly was dissolved and President's rule was imposed.
61. B.J.P. to demand Governor's recall, *Indian Express,* 20 February, 1988.
62. *Sarkaria Commission Report on Centre-State Relations,* Part I, Government of India Publications, 1988, pp. 123-24.
63. Brahmananda, "State Governor", *Indian Express,* 15 February, 1988.
64. "E.M.S. flays overriding of Sarkaria Commission Report", *Indian Express,* 20 February, 1988.

65. 'Panel against Politicians as Governors", *The Times of India*, 5 February, 1988.
66. "Governor's Role under Fire", *Indian Express*, 15 July, 1988, "Jan Morcha should decide itself; Advani", *Indian Express*, 16 February, 1988.
67. Kuldip Nayar, "The Pattern for 1985 Poll", *The Tribune*, 3 June, 1982, p. 4.
68. Sanjay Singh is the son of the Raja of Amethi which was the parliamentary constituency of Sanjay Gandhi.
69. *Pioneer*, 25 September, 1985.

3

Emerging Trends in Indian Federal System

The relationship between the Centre and the States in India has always remained under review as it is a sensitive matter. The Constitution created a central authority to maintain and consolidate national political integrity, to secure rapid and planned economic growth and to give the States an effective and autonomous role in designated fields.

In the post-Constitution period, both centripetal and centrifugal tendencies operated in full vigour in India. This created stresses and strains in the federal relationship. The question of Centre-State relations received serious attention mainly due to the context of emerging development since 1950. On the one hand, there has been an inexorable trend towards more powers and functions for the Central Government, partly due to the attitude of expecting the Government to be all in all, so that the States have looked up to the Central Government for help and to take over matters in the State's area of responsibility. Another reason is the nature of modern economy which requires planning and coordination and consequently centralisation.

Various factors such as the single constitution, emerging strength of the Centre, its power to alter the name and boundaries of the State, to appoint Governors and to issue directives to the State Governments, strong Central political leadership, monolithic party system, planning process, financial strength of the Centre, have all contributed to the overall supremacy of the Centre. Due to these factors various trends emerged, some of which have taken serious shapes.

Although these trends are generally seen in most of the states, but here it would be appropriate to select two models, U.P. and Kerala for assessing these trends. It will be interesting that despite differences in these models along with their context, the trends do not show differences in kind but only in degree.

The most important trend of the Indian Federal system is towards centralism, i.e. the Union Government is gathering more powers and functions in its own hands and thus has weakened the federal structure. This development is not new. The Constitution itself has provided certain provisions which are strengthening this trend. Further uni-party rule upto 1967 had also provided pillars to it. An analysis of the functioning of the Constitution presents some common features which are present in other States also despite different context. In U.P., the Congress Party was in power since independence. In this type of model, the States had no hesitation in accepting the direction, leadership and authority of the Central Government, There was a tendency to abdicate even their constitutional authority in favour of the Union, For example the Government of U.P. has recorded that it is not only desirable but necessary to give the Union, the supervisory role over the States. To be precise, uni-party rule at both the levels upto 1967, has helped through various ways in making the Centre more powerful. Further the use of Article 356 and the partisan role played by the Governors were some of the means of controlling States by the Centre. These became controversial in States, ruled by a different party as in the Centre. For example in 1959, the dismissal of first democratically elected Communist ministry in Kerala and the imposition of President's rule in the State, was clearly the violation of the constitutional provisions. The ruling Congress Party at the Centre brought the non-Congress Governments under the President's rule on the grounds of political and ideological differences between the State Communist Ministry and the ruling Congress Party at the Centre. In a parliamentary form of government, once a party is elected to power, it should be allowed to remain in office so long as it enjoys the confidence of the legislative assembly. The action of dismissing the ministry was thus criticised by many non-Congress political parties.[1]

Thus the abuse of the provision of Article 356, has been one of the main reason for conflict between the Centre and States. This has particularly strengthened the trend of centralisation. Especially after 1967 there has been a repeated misuse of this Article. In some cases, it was justified but on many occasions it has been exercised for ulterior political purposes. It has been indiscriminately used making a mockery of the States' autonomy. The first use of Article 356 in 1951 in Punjab to oust G. Bhargava, pointed out the relevance of the comment made by Ambedkar in the Constituent Assembly in these words: "The people have got a very legitimate ground for suspicion that the government is manipulating the Article in the Constitution for the purposes of maintaining their own party in office in all parts of India".[2] This is a rape of the Constitution.[3] V.R. Krishna Iyer said that "Article 356 must go".[4]

In U.P. and Kerala, governments have been dismissed on unconvincing grounds, even when they were ready to prove their majority on the floor of the House at a short notice. For example, Naraboodiripad in Kerala (1959), Charan Singh in U.P. (1970), E.K. Nayanar in Kerala (1981), K. Karunakaran in 1982, and in U.P. N.D. Tiwari (1977) and Banarasi Das (1980), by the Janata Party and Congress (I) respectively.

The power of declaring failure of constitutional machinery has also been misused by the Governors, who have been giving priority to the interest of the ruling party at the Centre, Whenever the ruling party at the Centre felt that it would be in a position to form an alternative ministry either by maneuvering defections or otherwise, the Assemblies were suspended, or, dissolved. For example Kerala Assembly was dissolved in 1965 and 1970 and in 1982. The arbitrary dismissals of the Governments, suspension and dissolution of the Assemblies on partisan consideration reveal that it has been misused by the Central Government. This is one of the very important factor which led to the trend of centralisation.

Another very effective way of grabbing power is through the office of Governor. The Constitution vests complete power with the President for the selection and appointment of the Governors, making him as the representative of the Central Government. The role of the Governor is viewed as a device for an authoritarian Centre to curtail the autonomy of the States. Instead of balancing the pulls and tensions of a federal polity, he is identified as an agent of the Centre. "Governor must be made to act as the President acts at the Central level."[5] The prevailing mood can be understood from the following statement by the non-Congress (I) opposition parties. "The institution of Governor has been misused...". The record proves beyond a shadow of doubt that, in most cases, the Governors have used their office to serve the interests of the ruling party at the Centre."[6]

It is the discretionary power of the Governor to appoint Chief Ministers but in the case of U.P. the Governor did not use this power even when the situations are called for it. At times, he had to seek the advice of the Congress leaders at the Centre.[7] "Governors have been reduced to mere 'yes men' of the Centre being made to dance to its tune.

Their fate is made or marred at the Centre's pleasure. S.S. Dhawan's term in West Bengal was abruptly ended as he was supposed to be soft towards the Jyoti Basu Government, evidently not to the liking of the Centre."[8] They were nominees of the Central Government rather than the choice of the people. Similarly in U.P. also Chief Ministers were appointed as they enjoyed the patronage of the Congress leaders at the Centre. Even all the Chief Ministers of U.P. from 1950 onwards are a nominee of the Centre. The Members of Legislative Assemblies had no choice and they accepted the person as Chief Ministers whom the Central Leadership chose.[9] However the state leaders have never rebelled openly against the Centre's decision. In Kerala, however, the Chief Ministers were not nominated by the Central Government as in the case of U.P., but sometimes as pointed out earlier, even the leader of the single largest party was not invited to form the government. According to Sampurnanand, "the spheres of the Central and State Governments are, on the whole, clearly demarcated in the schedules attached to the Constitution but "there is a steady attempt on the part of Central Ministers to encroach on the jurisdiction of the Component States."[10]

Centre-State relations have been steadily deteriorating, with the Rajiv Gandhi's Government's policy of appropriating greater powers and control for itself, increasing its authoritarian stance. Centre has been particularly hostile to the opposition ruled States, most particularly to the left-led States. In November 1988 Kerala State Cabinet sat on dharna to protest the blatant and shameless discrimination practised by the Centre against them. K.R. Narayanan said in an interview to *People's Democracy* that the Governor R.D. Sinha from the very beginning has been taking a partisan attitude towards the L.D.F. Government in the State, according to the advice he gets from the Congress (I).[11] The Kerala Government has demanded revamping of Centre-State relations and abolition of the post of Governor.[12]

The balance of Indian Federal Finance is also tilted in favour of the Centre. This development is, however, not new. The Constitution provides that the Centre can levy taxes on state heads of revenue as well as a surcharge for its own benefit.[13] Even in the obligatory shareable income tax receipts, the actual proportion to be made is left unspecified; leaving it to the Finance Commission[14] to recommend and Parliament to accept, while the excise revenue is available to the States only at the discretion of the Centre. In the VIIIth Schedule, certain large taxing powers are vested in the Centre.[15] Further Article 275 gives it power to make grants. These are the ways and means through which Centre can enter into the financial structure of the State, e.g. in the matter of education, the Centre by its readiness to encourage it subsidises it more easily. Further Central Welfare Board, the University Grants Commission are other examples whereby the Centre is able to influence the policy of the State Government on subjects in the State List which are entirely the concern of the Units. The States have a number of limitations, e.g. in the matter of getting loans, its power is limited by the Union.[16] The States also have no power to borrow outside India, even with Union's consent. This was not so in the Act of 1935.

Revenues of the State Governments in India are derived from other distinct sources: state taxes, non-tax revenues and transfer of funds from the Centre to the States. There is a problem of inelasticity of state revenues. The U.P. Chief Minister, Kalyan Singh had called for the redefining of Centre-State relations so as to give more financial powers and resources to the States. He said that "at present the States were like municipalities earning revenue from just three sources - excise, sales tax and stamp duty".[17] He said that "this has led to the State becoming dependent on the Centre for funds for development. The Centre uses this fiscal power to dictate terms to the Chief Ministers resulting in a situation where all powers get centered with the Central Government much against the ethics of democratic functioning of the states".[18]

There has not been uniformity in the distribution of revenue between the Centre and States and among the States by the Finance Commission. For example the divisible pool had stagnated at the twenty percent level till 1977-78 when the Seventh Finance Commission recommended to raise the State's share to 40 percent.[19] In 1977, West Bengal

Government submitted a memorandum and demanded that "the Articles regarding Finance Commission and the distribution of revenues should be amended to provide 75 percent of the total revenues raised by the Centre from all sources for allocation of different States by the Finance Commission."[20] The B.J.P. pointed out that "the taxing power of the States is woefully inadequate to finance any ambitious scheme of development. If the Central Government or rather the political party to which it belongs decides upon a cause of hostility to any state government, it can, by use of those constitutional provisions, destroy the latter's economic viability and gradually make it so unpopular and intolerable as to compel it to get out of office".[21] The P.V. Rajamannar Committee had also recommended that corporation tax should be included in the divisible pool, like income tax and the surcharge on income tax be merged with the basic rate of income tax and be shared with the States and all excise duties, whether basic, special or regulatory or otherwise should be compulsorily distributed to the States.[22]

Over a period of time, State Governments starting with relatively inelastic sources of revenue, had become more and more dependent on assistance from the Centre and increasingly susceptible to the latter's tying of such assistance to particular projects. The States no longer enjoy any initiative in matters relating to economic development. Namboodiripad (and Jyoti Basu) in particular drew attention to Central bias against state governments actively committed to expanding the public sector. He said that the process of structural change could not begin unless the following basic premises were accepted:[23]

1. India consists of a number of sub-nationalities;
2. Each State has its distinctive characteristics and is a centre of loyalty in addition to the nation as a whole;
3. Since a state government is more directly acceptable to the people of the State than the Central Government, it should be given enough scope for

initiating socio-economic changes according to its own policies and programmes; and

4. To deny the state governments their autonomy in the sphere of economic development and social change would be tantamount to circumventing or suppressing democracy at the State level.

As a matter of fact, financially the States are in a very tight position. Hence regional aspirations in the form of subnational assertions will continue so long as their grievances are not duly attended to. The basic the problem is that the States lack sufficient resources to discharge their responsibilities. Naturally they have to rely on central assistance. This trend of centralisation discriminate the States especially those ruled by opposition parties. This results in conflicts and tensions and create strains in Centre-State relations. C.P.I.(M) especially contended that the centre would not allow the States especially the C.P.I.(M) led state of Kerala to be independent and financially viable for fear of losing its grip on the politics of the State. The Chief Ministers of Tamil Nadu, Kerala and West Bengal demanded a revision of the Constitution to endow the States with greater political freedom and larger financial resources. The cry was that "for a country like India with its multi-1ingual and multi-cultural character, it is essential that the various regions into which it is divided should have the largest measure of autonomy possible. To administer it as a unitary state would be to invite disaster."[24]

The Constitution has been put into practice in a manner contrary to the intentions of the framers. It is worthwhile here to recall the remark of C. Rajagopalachari that "the independence of the State is being forgotten and a unitary state is being established in India thoughtlessly."[25] A former Union Minister, M.M. Shah observed that "the Centre is becoming a streamroller and the States appear to be in a pitiable condition."[26]

The landslide victory of the Congress under the leadership of Mrs. Gandhi in 1971 and her style of politics qualitatively changed centre-state relations. In the 1970's, again a period of enormous centralisation of political power in the Prime Minister and her secretariat began. Not only did Mrs. Gandhi established her absolute control over the national government, she also created a 'Pyramid like structure'[27] of the Congress party, which was reduced to merely an instrument of her personal power. This trend prompted the noted political analyst to remark that: "This process of centralisation transformed centre-state relations from one of 'political bargaining' to the ones akin to feudal tutelage".[28]

Her mass political base enabled Mrs. Gandhi to wipe out regional political leaders. State Chief Ministers became her nominees and all major decisions in the states needed her approval. Decision making came to be centred more and more in the "kitchen cabinet" or the "coterie" of the few political leaders and bureaucrats close to Mrs. Gandhi.

Mrs. Gandhi's successor Rajiv Gandhi succeeded in eroding the federal structure even more. In the beginning of 1987, he began to address district magistrates and collectors in different regions, stressing the need to return to a system in which the collector was to once again become the kingpin of governance for the sake of "development", modernization etc. bypassing the State Governments.

The bureaucracy also played a significant role in strengthening the trend of centralisation. The first three decades of relationship between political leaders and bureaucratic elite were of a different kind than the emerging challenge of the eighties. As bureaucrats are professionally trained and experienced, the political leaders had to depend on them. As a result, the bureaucrats began to work in a manner they like. The bureaucracy got hold of the centre stage of policy formulation and its implementation. The concept of welfare state has also helped in its expansion. Even every important economic decision and distribution of funds require bureaucratic approval. This has made the system more unitary.

The above analysis of the working of the Indian Federation makes us to conclude that decentralisation should be effected only to the extent, that the autonomy of the states is respected. The demand for state autonomy is more prevalent in India as here centralisation has become a companion to authoritarianism. In a country of India's size and diversities, federation and autonomy of the federal units are not only necessary but highly desirable. To quote Carl J. Friedrich: "Vigorous development of the several languages combined with retention of the increasing pluralism of such an increasingly federal India, might become a source of strength as the component states mature into vigorous democratic societies".[29] Frustrated with slow economic progress and the dominant Congress Party rule, the leaders of the regional parties in the States have consistently clamoured for more and more autonomy for the States. For instance, the leader of the Pragati Party in Orissa said on 26 December 1973, that "the States should have 'concurrent economic powers' and that since the people of India lived in the States and not in the archives of New Delhi,there should be some decentralisation of economic authority by making the states more responsible and more responsive, to meet the problems of their own areas".[30] Bhartiya Kranti Dal (B.K.D.) leader Charan Singh also asked for greater autonomy for the states in financial matters.[31] In 1966-67, the Akalis demanded that "this newly created Punjab state be accorded the same status and powers which are given to the state of Jammu and Kashmir under the Indian Constitution of 1950".[32] In October 1973, the Akali Dal Working Committee passed an important state autonomy resolution. "In this new Punjab, along with other states, the Central sphere should be limited to the subject of Defence, Foreign Affairs, Railways, Post and Telegraphs and Currency. Rest of the subjects should be within the jurisdiction of Punjab and for whose management, the Punjab should have the right to frame its own constitution".[33]

The West Bengal Government document on Centre-State relations[34] demanded a thorough revision of the Centre-

State relations and called for amending the articles concerning the distribution of resources between the Union and the States. Under the Janata Party rule, guidelines were sent to the States as prescribed by the Planning Commission, for the formulation of their plans and the Prime Minister's letter to them regarding their performance in family planning, the West Bengal Government, in order to secure greater autonomy, has intensified its campaign for the revision of Centre-State relations. The West Bengal Finance and Planning Minister declared that "the Planning Commission had no mandate to issue such guidelines and these were not applicable to them".[35] Karnataka Finance Minister in the State Assembly, while discussing the budget for 1978-79, pleaded for a proper fiscal federalism and observed that the fiscal relations between the Centre and the States required reconsideration.[36] "The concentration of all economic power in the hands of the Centre has made the State Governments a supplicant at the door of the Union Government. Their economic programmes, their agricultural programmes all are at the mercy of the Centre. The CPI(M) warns that this monstrous concentration of power in the hands of the Centre is creating the danger".[37]

This all shows that the growing self-consciousness and self-assertiveness of the regional governments, strengthened by the reorganisation of the states on a uni-lingual basis, act in India as an important decentralising force.[38]

States are organised on linguistic groups and consequently have acquired a regional identity. But the process of centralisation and personalisation of political authority resulted in an increased inability of the system to accommodate regional demands. It placed limits on the system's capacity to deal effectively with the demands of regional and ethnic groups, as is evidenced in its dealings with the situation in Punjab, Assam and Kashmir.

Regional parties play a significant role at the state level. Their role becomes much more relevant in the Indian context as it is a "Continent of many Communities united through shared experience but powerfully motivated by parochial and regional considerations".[39] Regionalism first emerged in Tamil Nadu as the aftermath of an entirely different phenomenon the non-Brahmin movement started by the Justice Party, and later taken over by the Dravida Kazhagam, for a more equitable distribution of educational and job opportunities to the non-Brahmins of the State, who formed 95 percent of the population. The movement slowly transformed itself into one of language, Tamil vs. first Sanskrit as the original language of the Brahmins and then Hindi of the North.[40] The division of States on linguistic lines accentuated the developing problem considerably. On the crest of language fanaticism and language riots, regional parties, first the Dravida Munnetra Kazhagam (D.M.K.) and then the All India Anna Dravida Munnetra Kazhagam (A.I.A.D.M.K.), came to power in Tamil Nadu. Absence of rapport between the Centre and State Governments left many needs of the state unfulfilled and projected regionalism as the major issue of the centre-state relationship.

The problems of Assam also have compelled the emergence of acute regionalism there. Distant location from the Centre, poor transportation facilities and inadequate investments have always been their grievances. But the situation was further aggravated by the balkanisation of Assam and continuing influx of foreigners and others into the State rendering the local residents in effect into a minority in their own land. Situation became complicated in 1979-80 with the agitation spearheaded by the All Assam Students Union (A.A.S.U.) and the All Assam Gana Sangram Parishad (A.A.G.S.P.) . The most glaring results of over-centralisation and political manipulation of over forty years are now manifest in Kashmir whose denial for political rights and constitutional integration has resulted in the collapse of entire administrative and political system. "Political profligacy turned out to be the surest way to alienation of the people of the valley which became the breeding ground of militancy and happy hunting ground of infiltrators from across the border".[41]

Kashmir sustains India's now vulnerable view of itself as a secular democratic country. Nothing unites Indians more than the determination to "hold" Kashmir, comments JAMES CLAD of the *Washington Post,* and nothing unites Kashmiris more than a desire to get rid of India, a tragic impasse that results mostly but not entirely from the manipulation of Kashmiri politics during the last three decades.[42]

With the continued fall out of the linguistic division of the country, the States of Punjab, Haryana and Himachal Pradesh were formed. The new State of Punjab became the homeland of the Sikhs. They felt that their State was treated badly by not redressing their territorial, social and regional grievances, which formed the platform of the regional Akali party. Then Khalistan movement appeared. The Akali demands got mixed up with the extremism of Khalistanis.[43]

Within the region itself, the feelings of sub-nationalism have become a force in Indian politics. It is in its extreme form of regionalism that a region demands that it wants to break away from the Indian union. The D.M.K. in Tamil Nadu, the Akali Dal in Punjab, the Mizos and Nagas in North East India, the supporters of Khalistan movements and the Kashmiri Muslims have been demanding succession from India.

Sub-nationalism has gained grounds in Kerala also. The people are proud of Kerala's identity, the Malayalam language, contribution of Kerala to the growth of India, Indian nationalism, Indian culture and Indian economy. But at the same time Kerala very often and very seriously raises the complaint that she being in the deep south and far away from Delhi, is neglected by the Centre and does not get a fair treatment. Once Kerala seriously thought of asserting her independence and seriously considered the question of becoming an independent sovereign state. At the time of independence, Sir C.P. Ramaswamy Iyer, the Dewan of Travancore tried to sell the idea, but it was rejected by the people. Then Kerala Socialist Party took up the issue but failed because of the lack of popularity and response. Again in 1961 it was pointed out that the south had been ignored and neglected by the Centre in plans for India's industrial development. So the States of Kerala, Andhra Pradesh and Madras should secede from the Indian Union to form an independent Republic.

There has been a demand of separate statehood in U.P. also. The hill areas of U.P. have been demanding a separate state to be carved out of the present state of U.P. The point was that it has a very distinct economic, geographical and cultural identity, which distinguishes them from the plains districts of the state. Another demand is the partition of U.P. since long. In 1954 Sardar K.M. Panikkar in his minute of dissent to the Report of the States Reorganisation Commission[44] suggested the bifurcation of U.P. He said that if U.P. was bifurcated, there would be greater uniformity in the sizes of states, failing which "the excessive size and weightage of U.P. would prove detrimental to the unity and integrity of the country". He further added that unless this was done, the "problem of India's internal tranquility could not be solved".[45]

Unlike Kerala, U.P. was not formed on the basis of language. It is not a uni-lingual state. As it is a Muslim dominated state, controversy over making Urdu as second official language was raised many times.

The organisation of Kerala State on the basis of language made the people conscious of the importance of their own language and they began to feel that the study and promotion of their own language would get them better fruits. So instead of developing a nationalistic outlook they became chauvinistic. "The formation of linguistic states has brought about a strong emotional attachment of the people to the states and has become the real federal force."[46]

Regionalism began to acquire critical shape during Mrs. Gandhi's time especially in Punjab and Assam. The erosion of so many institutions and conventions and turnabouts in the whole conception and strategy of nation building, remarks Rajni Kothari, has led to a "gross neglect of issues of growing disparities, deprivation, discrimination and destitution".[47]

The trend of regionalism is becoming critical to the future of the country as there is a demand of greater autonomy for the states on the one hand and growing violence and lawlessness deriving support from regional interests on the other. Demands of distributive justice in the face of scarcity and regional economic imbalances, assume the form of regional and sub-regional movements.

The linguistic division of the country maximized state autonomy which means, partial isolation of the states from one another in the federation and their 'linguistic' independence of the centre. It gives the state political machines more authority and power and drives them further away from the overall of the centre. "The state reorganisation has no doubt intensified group loyalties and has set in motion the consolidation of political parties at the state level".[48] It has strengthened the states as units of power[49] and helped to bring political consciousness and to think about their region than India as a whole.

Another important trend which has been emerging is the political mobilisation on caste or religion. In fact this laid the foundation for the division of India. "Communalism is the political assertiveness of a community to maintain its identity in a plural society undergoing modernization".[50] This trend is more prevalent in both U.P. and Kerala inspite of the fact that the context in both these States is different. In U.P. unlike Kerala, ideology cannot come into prominence as its system depends for its functioning on religion and caste as the two main social divisions and on appeal to independents and political entrepreneurs. Here religion dominates politics very effectively.

The year 1986 has been a period full of challenges. It had to face a number of communal incidents during the year. The question of Muslim Personal Law, 'Rath Yatra', and the activities of terrorists in Punjab during 1984-85 led to creating tension among the religious groups. One major example is the controversy on Ram Janambhoomi-Babri Masjid. Conflict and tension increased during the last decade and later over this issue. Hindu-Muslim riots, often resulting in many deaths became a common occurrence in the life of the state. This bitterness which developed between the two communities has continued to be an important trend in U.P. politics.

The trend of communalism is not confined to U.P. alone but it has national ramifications. Kerala is a state where despite its reputation of being a left stronghold, communalism has continued to hold the whip hand in political conflicts. The communal parties have grown from strength to strength with successive elections. In the peculiar situation of the state where no single force has been able to hope for a legislative majority, it has thrived on a syndrome of chronic instability. Mobilisation along religious lines became a legitimate part of social and political movements. People organised themselves on communal lines in the belief that they were in a better position to protect their interests as a collective.

There has been a resurgence, to some extent of a common identity based on language, culture and even ecology. Within mainstream political movements, certain groups are encouraging this trend. An important feature of the Kerala social structure is that all the major communities in the state have their own powerful organisations to safeguard their interests. The fall of the first Pattom A. Thanu Pillai ministry was mainly on account of friction and rivalry among the major communal groups in the Congress Party. Instead of being loyal to their party leader, the ministers supported the leaders of their communities. Since then communalism has been growing in the Congress organisation.

Communalism in Kerala is at the political level unlike U.P. where it is in the society. In Kerala, each communal organisation used to have its own lobbies in the Congress leadership. So it is possible for them to topple a particular leader on a government, who, they thought was not in their interests. "Communalism has become the dominant influence in the state and the major communities look at each other with suspicion. The division has gone deep in the Congress organisation also".[51] Robert Hardgrave rightly observed that "Indeed it is the politics of caste which forms the fundamental reality of political life in Kerala".[52]

These emerging tendencies shows that the days of centralised rule and integration measures are coming to an end. Never before has the Indian polity been more multi-centric than now. With so many states being governed by different parties and with many of them becoming more assertive vis-a-vis the Centre than was earlier the case, the upsurge of regional identities, the clear weakening and growing vulnerability of the central authority in the face of so many challenges and above all, with the decline in the authority of the Prime Minister (who has always been the symbol of central rule and dominion) in his own party and extending all the way to the electorate at large, unitarianism is on the decline.

As the writ of the Congress Party does not any longer run in all parts of the country, and as no other political party is in a position to play the same role as the Congress Party did in the past, the relationship between the state and civil society is also informed by a decline in the dominance of the government over social formations and the increasing assertion of the latter for acquiring greater say and autonomy for themselves.

Such assertions, Rajni Kothari argues[53] have taken three different forms: First, there is a gradual return to the tradition of voluntarism that has been the characteristic of Indian society for long. Second, the demand for decentralisation of power and resources, not just to the state level but to levels below it, is on the increase both because everyone argues that centrlaised state apparatus has failed to deliver the goods. Third, there is the rise, in large parts of the country, of ethnic identities which are demanding more autonomous spaces for themselves, with some of them even asking for new regional arrangements including independent statehood within the federal set up.

Political parties played an important role in strengthening some trends e.g the trend of centralisation has been due to uni-party rule at both levels. Regionalism also got pushed up thorough regional parties. The demand for state autonomy was also first raised by a regional party (Dravida Munnetra Kazhagam of Tamil Nadu). These trends can take serious shapes if a serious effort is not taken to abort them. The role of political parties in the overall working of the Centre-State relations is analysed in detail in the next chapter. As a matter of fact, financially the states are in a very tight position. Hence regional aspirations in the form of subnational assertions will continue so long as their grievances are not duly attended to.

REFERENCES

1. *Lok Sabha Debates,* 30 March 1959, criticised by Praja Socialist Party (P.S.P.) and Communist Party.
2. He said that "such Article will never be called into operation and that they would remain a dead letter".-*C.A.D.,* Vol. IX, p. 177.
3. J.R. Siwach, *Politics of President's Rule in India,* (Simla: Indian Institute of Advanced Study), 1979, p. 29.
4. *Newstime,* 13 June, 1984.
5. *Ibid.,* views of V.R. Krishna Iyer.
6. On Centre-State relations, "The statement adopted by the Srinagar Conference of opposition parties on October 5-7, 1983", p. 2.
7. For example in 1963, at the time of dismissing Algu Rai Shastri, Minister of State for Forests, on the advice of Chief Minister C.B. Gupta, the Governor visited the capital to seek the advice of Congress leaders. Afterwards due to Prime Minister's influence, Shastri had to resign.
8. *Newstime,* op. cit.
9. *The Statesman,* Delhi, 18 October, 1973.

10. Sampurnanand, *Memories and Reflections,* (Bombay: Asia Publishing House), 1962, p. 155
11. See for details *People' s Democracy,* "The Partisan role—The Governor Plays", 18 December, 1988.
12. *Indian Express,* (New Delhi) 16 June, 1988.
13. Article 269, Constitution of India.
14. Article 280 of the Constitution provides for an independent Finance Commission appointed by the President after every five years. It makes recommendations to the distribution proceeds of compulsory as well as voluntary shareable taxes between the Union and the States.
15. For example Article 269, 270 of the Constitution of India.
16. Article 293, Constitution of India.
17. *The Hindu,* New Delhi, 1 May, 1992.
18. *Ibid.*
19. D.D. Panigrahi, *Centre State Financial Relations in India* (Delhi: Vikas Publishing House), 1985, p. 45.
20. A memorandum on Centre-State relations which was adopted by the West Bengal Government on December 1, 1977, para 8.
21. *About Us*. B.J.P's Official Publication, Vol. II, No. 28, August 1985, (New Delhi: Nav Chetan Press), pp. 31-32.
22. *Report of the Centre-State Relations Inquiry Committee,* Madras, Government of Tamil Nadu, 1971.
23. In the course of interviews with Mr. T.V. Sathyamurthy, Namboodiripad came back to this thome on a number of times.
24. R.N. Sapru "Centre-State Ties on More Regional Basis", *Amrita Bazaar Patrika* (Calcutta) 24 April, 1969.
25. Quoted in "A South Indian Review", *The Hindustan Times,* 17 April, 1962, p. 7. In a similar strain, the D.M.K. leader, C. Annadurai has alleged that the working of the Federal Constitution is endangering the powers of the states which have been reduced to the position of dolle-getting Corporations". Quoted in 'A South Indian Review', *The Hindustan Times,* 5 February, 1963, p. 7. Since the D.M.K. abandoned its demand for a sovereign state of the south, Annadurai has frequently urged that the Constitution should

be reshaped to provide for a real and purposeful Federation. *The Hindustan Times,* 14 December, 1965, p. 5.

26. In an address at the Harold Laski Institute of Political Science, Ahmedabad, *The Hindustan Times,* 12 October, 1959, p. 4.

27. Stanley A. Kochanek "Mrs. Gandhi's Pyramid: The New Congress" in Henry C. Hart (Ed.) *Indira Gandhi's India: A Political System Reappraised.* (Boulder, Colorado, West View Press), 1976.

28. W.H. Morris Jones "India—More Questions than Answers" *Asian Survey,* August, 1984, p. 811.

29. Carl J. Friedrich, *Trends of Federation in Theory and Practice,* (London: Pall Mall Press Ltd), 1968 p. 140

30. B.L. Fadia, *Indian Government and Politics,* Sahitya Bhawan, 1992, p. 191.

31. *Ibid.*

32. *Shiromani Akali Dal da Aadesh Patar* (Election Manifesto) 1967, Amritsar, Shiromani Akali Dal.

33. *Shiromani Akali Dal da Nawan Policy Programme* (New Policy Programme), passed by the Dal's Working Committee on 16-17 October 1973, at Anandpur, 5-6.

34. Information and Public Relations Department, Government of West Bengal, No. 1010 (450) IRT/P.

35. *The Times of India,* 24 June, 1978.

36. B.L. Fadia, *op. cit.*

37. C.P.M. Manifesto, *Seminar,* February 1971 (138) p. 37.

38. Amal Ray, *Inter-Governmental Relations in India,* (Bombay; Asia Publishing House), 1966, p. 148.

39. Lewis, P. Fickett Jr., "The Politics of regionalism in India" in *Pacific Affairs,* Summer 1971, p. 193.

40. Duncan B. Forrester, "The Madras Anti-Hindi Agitation, 1965" *Pacific Affairs,* Spring, 23 (1966).

41. Nikhil Chakraborty, "Solving the Kashmir Tangle", *The Hindustan Times,* 29 November, 1991.

42. James Clad, *Guardian Weekly,* April 19, 1991.

43. M.S. Dhami "Political Parties and State Autonomy Issues" in K.R, Bombwall (Ed,) *National Power and State Autonomy* (Meerut: Meenakshi Prakashan), 1977, pp. 144-60; Pradeep

Kumar "Communal Dimension of Regionalism in Indian Federation: A Study of Trends in Akali Politics" in Akhtar Majeed (Ed.) *Regionalism: Developmental Tensions in India* (New Delhi: Cosmo Publications), 1984, pp. 145-50.

44. States Reorganisation Commission was appointed in 1954. Its members were K.N. Kunzru, Fazal Ali and K.M. Panikkar.

45. *The Statesman* (New Delhi) 13 June, 1991.

46. K. Santhanam, *Union-State Relations in India,* (Delhi: Asia Publishing House), 1960 p. 69.

47. Rajni Kothari, *State Against Democracy; In Search of Humane Governance,* (New Delhi: Ajanta Publications) 1988.

48. Over Street, Gene & Tinker Irene, *Political Dynamics in India,* Chicago, 1957, p. 44.

49. The effect of reorganisation was to give state politics more intensely regional character and to make states a much more important level of power—Hugh Tinker, *India and Pakistan,* p. 134.

50. Robert Melson and Howard Wolpe, *The American Political Science Review,* Vol. 64.

51. *Link,* July 26, 1964.

52. Robert L. Hardgrave Jr., "Caste and the Kerala Election", *The Economic Weekly,* April 17, 1965, p. 672.

53. Rajni Kothari, *Seminar* (357) May 1989.

4

Role of Political Parties

The functioning of the federal system depends on various factors which in turn influence the political process in the country. In the over all context, the political parties play a vital role. In fact, the relationships between the two *working levels of the federal* system are largely dependent on the kinds of relationships that the members of the parties at both levels establish with each other. Often the party members operating the governmental structure at the federal level are co-partisans of those operating the structure at the regional level. As a sequence, inter-party relationships assumes importance for the development and functioning of the federal system. At times the ruling parties at the regional level may be different from the one at the Centre, The confrontation between the political parties influence to a great extent the legislative, administrative and even financial relations between the central and state governments. W.H. Riker rightly observed: "Whatever the general social conditions, if any, that sustain the federal bargain, there is one institutional condition that controls the nature of the bargain... this is the structure of party system, which may be regarded as the main variable intervening the background social conditions and the specific nature of the federal bargain."[1] He further said that the centralising and decentralising tendencies in a federal system depends upon the degree to which the parties (or party) operating the Central Government, control parties in the constituent governments.[2]

Most of the major political parties pre-date the establishment of India's federal republic. The Congress developed the characteristics of a political party in the late 1920s. A certain ideological polarisation then emerged in Indian politics and a more organised revolutionary force came into existence. The leaders of the Congress became apprehensive about maintaining unity and sought to promote more central control. In 1937 when the Congress assumed power in several provinces under the Government of India Act (1935), there was renewed emphasis on party discipline and central dominance. Then in 1946, when Congress members again assumed power in several provinces, the party characteristics of the Congress began to assert themselves. Besides, the Communist and the Congress Socialist parties, which have been operating under the same or some new labels in India's pre-independence period, had their origins in the pre-independence period.

The structure of Indian federalism which provides the framework for the operation of the political parties has a strong orientation towards centralisation. The evolution of India's political economy had helped to produce new political elites from rural areas. "A powerful challenge to "New Delhi's continued dominance" in the working of federal structure has recently come from them who, in collaboration with the mainly state-based political parties, have formulated demands for greater federalisation of India's political system."[3]

As long as the same political party is in power, at both levels, only intra-party factors are important in determining the centre-state relations. But in an emerging multi-party system where few of the state governments are under different parties, inter-party factors determine the centre-state relations and tend to make them more complex.

The Congress Working Committee played an important role in formulating all-India policies and coordinating Union-State relations. Its decisions served as guidelines to all the states even on subjects like Zamindari abolition, land reforms, cooperative farming and primary education which were constitutionally within their own jurisdiction. Some observers have pointed out the significance of unitary rule as the crucial factor in the growth of the predominance of the Centre in the period upto 1967 and after 1980, "By and large, the effect of the Congress organisation on the Union-State relations was to emphasise the strength of the Central Government and the relative subordination of the state Governments".[4] Asok Chanda, Chairman of the Third Finance Commission, remarks: "One has facilitated and even encouraged Parliament to consider itself as the apex of a legislative and executive pyramid. The Prime Ministers and other Ministers have not hesitated to take an indirect and sometimes even a direct hand in settling and deciding issues which are constitutionally the responsibility of the States, The limited sovereignty of the states is thus being surrendered by usage and sufferance and it would be difficult for a State later to reassert or regain its constitutional authority. It may be claimed that the 'advice' tendered by the Union Ministers is in their capacity as members of the Congress High Command and that there has thus been no infraction of the sovereignty of States. The sophistry will hardly delude many."[5] So as a result the alternative and extra-constitutional channels have led to a high degree of centralisation in the working of federal structure. What the Centre could not impose on the States through the Constitution it could enforce through the party channels. The changing dimension of the federalising process in India can be seen in the dynamic context of political parties. There have been two kinds of instabilities in the Indian States. There are situations in which no one party has been able to win enough votes in the assembly to form alone, or in stable coalitions with others, an enduring government. The most extreme situation has been in Kerala where there has been a succession of party and coalition governments.

In the second kind of instability, the Chief Ministers have been unable to sustain support within the Congress Party and conflicts within Congress have been so intense and overt that there have been frequent changes in ministries e.g. Uttar Pradesh (U.P.).

The Dominance of the Congress Party

During the period from 1950 to 1967, a single political party, the Indian National Congress was dominant. The Congress was the dominant force in the U.P. politics also. Actually it has been a multi-party system with one party dominance. Although it has experienced a steady decline in its voting strength, no opposition party by itself has acquired sufficient strength to represent a threat to the Congress barring the Jan Sangh.

Since independence, however, personal and factional politics have come to dominate the internal affairs of the State Congress. According to Paul R. Brass: fractional conflicts within the Congress Party are so great that the State Government is in a state of paralysis since almost any governmental action is likely to disturb the balance of power among the party factions. Factionalism, lack of commitment, and a low degree of loyalty pervade Congress politics in U.P.[6]

Immediately after independence, differences which had existed earlier among Congressmen in U.P. surfaced and manifested in the form of internal political crisis. The first crisis was the defection of a group of socialists from the Congress in 1948. Their departure brought to an end the ideological conflict in U.P. Congress politics. Next the election of P. Tandon as the President of Indian National Congress precipitated another political crisis. "He was the symbol in his home state (U.P.) and in the country of Hindi and Hindu culture, of Hindi revivalism as opposed to secularism. The resignation of Tandon under pressure and the assumption of the seat by Jawaharlal Nehru in 1951 made an important impact on the Congress in U.P."[7]

Gradually with no issues of importance left, politics in the U.P. Congress started revolving around personalistic group or factional politics. In the period of conflict and crisis in the years immediately after independence, a generational change in political leadership also took place. The leaders of the nationalist movement from U.P. either joined the opposition or the Central Cabinet. After the departure of G.B. Pant from Central Cabinet the whole tenor of U.P. politics changed. Authoritative political leadership was replaced by group and faction leadership.

Since 1955, the internal politics of the Congress Party in U.P. has revolved around a struggle to gain or control the office of Chief Minister by dominating the party organisation. In 1962, a political conflict over the passage of a land tax bill in U.P. dominated the political life of the state throughout the year. Division within the Congress over the bill existed at every level in the Congress Party organisation and the government in U.P, and Delhi. Another source of opposition to the state government from within the Congress came from Congressmen from U.P. in New Delhi. The leadership of the New Delhi Congressmen from U.P, was provided by Keshav Deo Malaviya, a Central Minister at the time and Mahavir Tyagi, a prominent M.P, Both of them had quarrels with Chief Minister Gupta. A significant campaign against the state government's tax proposals was carried on among Congress members of Parliament from U.P. Thirty M.P.s signed the letter which was sent to the Chief Minister urging him to withdraw the Land Tax Bill.[8] This shows that the Chief Minister of U.P, was under great pressure from members of his own party.

The ineffectiveness of the Congress government in U.P. in the face of internal factionalism and determined opposition was further demonstrated in September and October 1963 when the land tax controversy was resumed.

In the case of Kerala, this period includes its formation and Communist-led-governments in opposition to the party in power in the Centre.

These were two important aspects of the first CPI-led ministry in independent India. First of all the taking of power by the C.P.I. in any part of India through the electoral process was profoundly unacceptable to the Congress Party and the Central Government. Even Nehru, the champion of bourgeoisie parliamentary democracy, was unhappy that an Indian state should have elected a CPI-led government to power. This meant that both the organisation of the Congress Party at the national level and the Central Government controlled by that party had a vested interest in bringing down the Kerala CPI-led Government at the earliest possible opportunity. In the Communist Party National Council Meeting[9] in 1958, the Council adopted a resolution viewing the "tactics and methods of the Congress against the Communist Ministry in Kerala" as a challenge to all healthy norms of public life and to the future of democracy in India. It said that the Congress Working Committee's resolution on Kerala showed that "Constitutional propriety and democratic norms have no place in the affairs of the Congress High Command, the moment their monopoly of power and vested interests are affected. Further, it added that "the danger in Kerala is not merely the right of a non-Congress Government to exist and function, but the very fundamentals of democracy and democratic institutions are challenged. By their actions, the Congress leaders have put the Constitution to a severe strain. The greatest damage to the Constitution and to democracy is being caused by the utterances and acts of leaders of the Congress Party and Central Government which amount to instigation of officials in Kerala against the State Government or otherwise demoralize them."[10]

Second, the serious intent on the part of C.P.I. to introduce reform measures of a far reaching nature in order to achieve certain ends to which the Congress Party had got into the habits of committing itself in rhetoric achieved the result of quickly polarising politics within the Kerala state. This meant that all the reactionary and counter revolutionary forces as well as political forces which would have been prepared to accept a mild dose of radicalism from any source other than a C.P.I. in power combined together to confront the government. Their realisation that the government could not possibly be brought down in a constitutionally sanctioned manner, simply shattered by bringing it down, if necessary, by anti-constitutional means.

After 1950, in view of its futility of direct action, the CPI decided to contest the elections to central and state legislatures with the purpose of opposing the government from within. On the eve of the elections, the CPI proclaimed that it was not for the establishment of socialism in the country under prevalent conditions. The party declared:

> The party now aims at the replacement of the present anti-democratic and anti-popular government of people's democracy created on the basis of a coalition of democratic and anti-feudal and anti-imperialist forces in the country.[11]

The Congress which came to power in 1947 failed to give a stable government to the state. Between 1947-57 six ministries came into being. Five of them were Congress ministries. None of them could remain in office for the full term. Constitutional machinery in the State had broken down twice during this period; and the President's rule was imposed twice. Political instability in the State was brought about by the personal group and communal rivalries within the Congress. People wanted to get rid of the Congress regime which had earned notoriety for corruption, bribery and nepotism. The Communist Party stood out in the State with regard to strength, unity, discipline, resources, leadership and popularity. Then it changed its policies and tactics.[12] The change from orthodox revolution and armed struggle to a policy of conducting itself as an opposition party in parliamentary framework gained large popularity for the party. The Communist Party after complaining that "the constituent states of the Indian Union are denied power, resources and authority which they should have under a federal set up" goes on to declare that "the Communist

Party stands for wider powers and authority particularly in financial and economic matters being given to the states of the Indian Union. The Seventh Schedule of the Constitution must be revised and amended to enlarge the powers of the States and abridge those of the Central Government.[13] It is rather surprising that a party which believes in the doctrine of democratic centralism should take up the cause of the enlargement of the powers of the states.

Debacles rather than achievements can be seen in the electoral scene between 1947-56. The first mandate in the newly formed Kerala State in 1957 went in favour of the Communists. Though the Indian National Congress could reverse the trend in 1960, it did not last long as the Congress-P.S.P.-Muslim League coalition cracked and the Government was defeated subsequently. In 1965 Congress was reduced to the second position after the C.P.I. (M) and in 1967 the Congress was defeated by the C.P.I. (M) led coalition.

Period of Coalition

The 1967 elections were one of the most important events in Indian politics. It led to the replacement of the single-dominant party system by the multi-party system in which no particular party claimed absolute majority. "The model of intra-party coalition was replaced by the inter-party coalition system."[14] This period brought an end to the era of Congress domineering rule and opened the era of weakened Congress Government at the Centre and coalition governments in many states.

Inspite of the fact that Congress had been reduced to a minority in 1967, in U.P. it was still the largest party in the Assembly, Out of 425 seats the Congress Party won 195 seats in the 1967 elections. As no party got absolute majority, there was no option but to form a coalition government. The opposition parties joined together to form a United Front government and elected Ram Chandra Vikal as their leader. But C.B. Gupta formed a Congress

Government with the support of a few defectors. After only 18 days the government was toppled when Charan Singh and his faction defected to the opposition. Charan Singh became the Chief Minister. He resigned in 1968 and President rule was imposed.

None of the parties obtained a clear majority in the mid-term elections held in February 1969. The Congress formed the ministry with the help of independents and Swatantra members and with C.B. Gupta once again as Chief Minister. He quitted after the split in Congress in 1969. Again in 1970 coalition government was formed. Some differences developed between the B.K.D. and the Congress resulting in the dismissal of Charan Singh ministry in 1970. A new development in the Indian political process was that no important political party was willing to enter the election alone and began to think of entering with alliance or making adjustments with like-minded parties.

The break-down of the Congress monolith in 1967 led to an enhancement in the powers of individual legislators. This led many of them to sell their party label for money and other considerations. Defection from one party to another increased. There was intense political activity and restlessness in political parties as each of them tried to expand itself and fill up the power vacuum created by the reduction in the strength of the Congress Party after 1967. Earlier the politics revolved round the factional rivalry of Congress leaders. But after the fall of the Congress, political parties such as P.S.P. and C.P.I. gained prominence. The Samyukta Vidhayak Dal (S.V.D.)[15] in spite of the common minimum programmes, suffered from inner stresses and strains arising out of inter-party rivalry and divergent attitudes. But they could not emerge as an alternative to the Congress. Further during this period violent methods to secure political ends were on a larger scale than earlier.[16]

In Kerala the climate on the eve of Fourth General Elections was not favourable for the Congress. A.K. Gopalan in a statement at Delhi said that C.P.I.(M) was ready to form an alliance with any party to end Congress monopoly.[17]

A United Front government was forged in Kerala. E.M.S. Nampoodiripad became the Chief Minister of the seven party United Front.[18] The leaders of the United Front particularly the Marxists were trying to focus public attention on the alleged neglect by the Centre of the development of the State and to exert pressure on the Central Government to redefine Centre-State relationship in the changed circumstances. Namboodiripad himself admitted that his party wanted to use power to give the maximum trouble to the Centre for the realisation of this objective.[19] in the Assembly he stated that "his government was determined to deal with the Centre in the same way as the Centre was dealing with the State."[20]

Speaking at a reception arranged by the Malayalee Association in Delhi on 11th April 1967, E.M.S. Namboodiripad pointed out that the post of the Chief Minister of a State was an office without power and that the development of the States depended on the mercy of the Centre. "We have our office in the state capital, but New Delhi has the power".[21]

After 31 months of its tenure, the United Front government was torn by continuous conflict. Hanging on after the resignation of 7 of the 12 parties from the coalition government, Namboodiripad resigned in October 1969. C. Achyutha Menon, a C.P.I. Member of Parliament, placed responsibility for the government's collapse on the big party bossism of the C.P.M., its disruptive behaviour and sectarian policies.[22]

In November 1969, a new coalition ministry headed by C. Achyutha Menon (C.P.I.) was formed with the support of Congress. Very soon contradictions developed and as a result Achyutha Menon dissolved the Assembly in June 1970. Again in October 1970, Achyutha Menon formed a coalition government. Only this ministry enjoyed full five year term in the history of the State.

This period showed much political instability. Only two parties the Congress and the C.P.I. (M) have usually exercised power. The C.P.I. (M) has ideologically emerged as a more homogenous party compared to other parties. Political defection in Kerala has not been as rampant as in U.P.

This phase was characterised by the formation of the coalition ministries led by Congress as well as non-Congress parties. Non-Congress parties wanted to oust the Congress from power by any way. It was the period of fragmentation and instability in which political parties and groups united or deviated frequently with the primary aim of attaining or retaining political power.

In Kerala, the non-Congress parties either in a pre-electoral alliance or otherwise succeeded in keeping the Congress away from power and formed coalition governments on the basis of the existing pre-election alliance or the one forged after the election results were announced. In U.P. coalition governments were brought into being after the newly formed Congress governments fell prey to large scale defections and the leaders of the Congress breakaway groups headed those ministries. Single-party rule became an impossibility with the resignation of the Muslim League and the formation of Kerala Congress in mid sixties, which sowed the seeds for the growth of "permanent minority parties" in the State.

It is during this period that Regional Parties became active. Even earlier D.M.K. in Tamil Nadu, Akali Dal in Punjab, Muslim Conference in Jammu and Kashmir etc. did articulate the local issues to mobilise the people of their own regions in their support. But these parties challenged the Congress Party only after the break-up of uni-party rule in 1967. In Tamil Nadu D.M.K. came to power followed by Akali Dal's electoral success in 1969 mid-term polls. In Kerala Muslim League and Jan Sangh in U.P. gained strength.

Personalisation of Power

The period from 1971-77 and 1980-89 was the period of charismatic leadership. Opposition parties were decimated and influence and power of the Prime Minister were greatly magnified. These deeply affected the working of the Indian Federation. Congress legislative parties in the states have quite frequently left the choice of the Chief Minister to Prime Minister Indira Gandhi as well as to Rajiv Gandhi. During this period decisions regarding states were taken in New Delhi and there was an emasculation of the federal structure.

Since 1970s when the outcome of election gave Indira Gandhi a profound victory, the party changed its role and organisational design. It developed into an extremely centralised party. Both the institutions of cultural and informal federalism within the Congress collapsed and states became increasingly dependent upon the party's political Centre.[23]

During the tenure of Rajiv Gandhi, Chief Ministers were nominated in New Delhi and then elected unanimously by the Congress (I) State legislative parties. State Congress (I) Chiefs are being replaced by appointees. Former Karnataka Chief Minister, Ramakrishna Hedge said "As for the ruling party it remains a practorian guard of a single individual. Its programme reflects his changing whims. The Congress (I) simply does not exist as a political party. Chief Ministers are nominated in New Delhi. Of what avail are the constitutional provisions for federalism if the ruling state party itself is held in bondage by the centre?"[24]

The land slide victory of the Congress led by Indira Gandhi in the 1971 mid-term elections to the Lok Sabha from U.P. gave a new dimension to the state politics. Mass defections from the S.V.D. began to take place and the government was reduced to a minority. T.N. Singh resigned and K. Tripathi was appointed Chief Minister. But he was also compelled to resign and then H.N. Bahuguna became the next Chief Minister. Mr. T.N. Singh blamed the Centre for having accepted as Prime Minister people who were undeserving and for not giving U.P. the requisite finance.[25]

Mrs. Indira Gandhi's victory in 1971 strengthened her

faith in her personal charisma and brought into play the authoritarian streak in her personality. From 1971 onwards, she started concentrating power in her hands. During this period, state units had little freedom to take decisions on their own. For example, state committees took the first step in nominating candidates for election to state assemblies, and it was the Central Parliamentary Board which took final decisions on the matter. This gave to it a sort of control over the Congress members in the Assemblies. It was the Central Parliamentary Board (C.P.B.) that decided as to who should be the leader of the Congress Legislature Party in states. In some cases C.P.B. sent an outsider to become the Chief Minister of state irrespective of the wishes of the Congress legislatures of that state. In 1972, the appointment of H.N. Bahuguna as Chief Minister of U.P. by Indira Gandhi is an example.

H.N. Bahuguna was under constant attack from the dissident party members but continued in office as he enjoyed the confidence of the Party High Command. But on 29 November 1975, the High Command apparently wished him to step down and the same day he resigned. Then Congress Party elected its leader on January 21, 1976 and the President's rule was revoked. The position of a Congress Chief Minister in Mrs. Gandhi and Rajiv Gandhi era depended largely on the kind of relations he had with the High Command and the support he received from them. They had reduced themselves to the status of chief messengers of the party led by the Prime Minister.[26]

Unprecedented centralisation of power at the top of the pyramid and the attempt by Mrs. Gandhi during the Emergency, imposed in June 1975, to modify the federal character of the party by strengthening unitary features have contributed to the gradual erosion of the Congress base in U.P.[27] This sharply increased central intervention in U.P. politics as it led to transfer of power from state factions to the national party leadership, and decay of the party machine. The principle of representation was abandoned by Mrs. Gandhi and replaced by selection of personnel at every level of the party after 1972. In U.P. since 1977 there have been no elections of the party's 8,000 cooperative societies which form an essential links to local constituencies.

In Kerala the Achyutha Menon Ministry of 1970 provided a stable administration to the State. Its term was extended thrice following the imposition of Emergency in 1975. This was the largest tenure enjoyed by a ministry in the State's history. Inspite of the personalisation of power in the hands of Mrs. Gandhi, there was less interference in the politics of the state. In 1980, Kerala failed to elect a Congress government whereas most other states voted for Congress. In the May 1982 Assembly Elections, people of the State opted in favour of a non-Marxist-led coalition government. This ministry of Karunakaran (1982-1987) was infected by communalism and widely accused of venality. In 1984 Lok Sabha Elections, Kerala voted for the Congress-led coalition, but in the bye-elections that followed to Assembly seats the coalition suffered reverses in all seats. In Kerala, there is no demand of autonomy though the C.P.M. continues to harp on reducing the powers of the Centre.

Rajni Kothari remarked "Congress party in its centenary year has been close to being scrapped as an institution".[28]

Instead of being enemies at the national level, the Janata Party and the Congress (I) were allies in Kerala. Politics at the national level had little relevance to the Kerala scene.

The 1982 Assembly election marked the culmination of certain political developments in the State. The process of political fragmentation in the form of split in political parties reached its highest watermark at this time.[29]

Janata Party could not maintain itself for a long time and collapsed after two years. The constituent groups and their leaders had different political background and diverse social perspectives. They were involved in making alliances and coalitions to dominate the party and not to integrate it. Again in 1980 and 1984 Congress Party achieved success and once again dominance of the Centre in the form of charismatic personality of Mrs. Gandhi and Rajiv Gandhi started. This was an era of one party-one leader. Rajiv Gandhi ran the States like his personal fiefdoms, changed about 20 Chief Ministers within a span of five years.

Indira Gandhi was more powerful as an individual, but dominated a system which was less politically viable. According to Chandra Shekhar, the Janata Party President who while in Congress had sided with Indira Gandhi during the 1969 split, "there was no possibility of expressing a dissenting voice in the Congress" and Indira Gandhi has demolished the Congress Party as a political entity.[30]

Break From Single Party Dominance: Era of Janata Party Rule

The results of March 1977 election marked the end of the one party dominant system. The newly formed Janata Party assumed power at the Centre and a large number of regional parties emerged in the States. The change was towards competitive party system. Now it became difficult for the Central Government to impose its discretion on the states. States became conscious to maintain their constitutional status and demand for state autonomy also gained importance.

In U.P. also Janata Party assumed power in 1977. Ram Naresh Yadav became the Chief Minister (B.L.D.). Then Jan Sangh emerged as the 'Chief prop'of the B.L.D. After some time factional quarrel started within the Janata Party. Yadav lost his chief ministership and B.D. Gupta became the Chief Minister (Congress (O)).

This phase left no impact on Kerala politics as the same coalition maintained its majority and the Congress (I) emerged as the largest party in the Assembly. Due to party strains and differences the coalition government resigned. Then M. Koya (Muslim League) was installed as Chief Minister. After the resignation of Koya Ministry, the Kerala Assembly was dissolved and fresh elections were held in 1980.

The first act of Janata Government on coming to power

was the dissolution of nine state Assemblies under Congress rule. The Congress repaid in the same way when it returned to power in 1980 and imposed the President's rule under Article 356, dissolving the nine assemblies under the Janata rule.

Between 1977-1979, Kerala was anti-Congress and in the mid-term elections of 1980 the Janata-Congress (I) alliance materialised. The constant re-alignment of political forces drew Janata factions into periphery.

Janata Dal emerged as an alternative to the Congress in 1989. It formed the government in U.P. also. It was the major component of the anti-Congressism. The V.P. Singh government of 1989-90, was intolerant towards the Congress ruled state governments and all the Governors appointed by Rajiv Gandhi were ordered to quit by the V.P. Singh's government. Then Chandra Shekhar government dismissed the state governments of Assam and Tamil Nadu during his brief tenure. These dismissals had no exceptional reason resulting in the weakening of political federalism by such actions of Central Government. The 1989 polls left the U.P. Congress badly fractured.[31]

The working of the party system in Kerala reveals that only two political parties, the Congress and the C.P.I. (M) have usually exercised power. The C.P.I.(M) has ideologically emerged as a more homogenous party. Inspite of multi party system in Kerala, political defection has not been as rampant as in U.P. The Communist-Congress conflict has taken the form of a confrontation between the Centre and the States over relative spheres of dominance. In fact, in Kerala's politics political forces tend to gather around the Communists or Congress (I). No third force is possible. This has led to much political instability and frequent imposition of President's rule. No other state in India presents such a picture of political confusion.

The factional structure of the U.P. Congress party has affected the orientation of government leaders and the functioning of local administration. The constant struggle for power within tne Congress has caused most state ministers to be concerned primarily with the question of patronage and political support rather than policy. At all times, the Chief Ministers tried to Keep as much power and patronage as possible and his closest associates while giving as little as possible to less reliable members, when a prestigious portfolio must be given to a political rival. the patronage power is tafcen away to make the position less dangerous politically. The result is fragmentation of authority and responsibility and confusion in administration. Factionalism in the Congress and the aggressiveness of opposition parties both tend to make it difficult for the government to pass desired legislation and to administer efficiently programmes designed to accelerate economic development.

As U.P. has been a stronghold of the Congress from the very beginning the Communist party is among the weakest state units. It has made no significant progress. The main reasons for the low level of support enjoyed by the Congress Party in Kerala is that, it had become one of the most disgruntled states from an economic point of view. Profits from plantations were seldom ploughed back. The cashew industry has been in a state of crisis. Industrialisation is also less developed. Unemployment is also increasing continuously.

C.P.I. is the only serious political force in Kerala's history which had struggled within the nationalist movement against colonialism in Malabar and feudalism in the states of Travancore and Cochin where the Congress Party was basically the party of the landlords, industrialists and white collar workers.

From the perspective of the leadership of C.P.I. (M) the real enemy was the centre and not the anti-Communist partners in the U.L.F. coalition. In its view the manifesto of ULF represented a clear challenge to the central leadership which might be met either with refusal to allow the coalition to take power in the state or by starving U.L.F. government of resources to such an extent as to make it unviable. E.M.S.

Namboodiripad openly expressed his misgivings about the behaviour of the Central Government towards an U.L.F. government in Kerala.[32]

The multi party system in Kerala owed its emergence to the caste and communal forces.[33] The role of caste in the politics of Kerala has received a major set back owing to the confrontation of the Hindus with the Christians on the west coast and with the Muslims in the northern part of the State. With the merger of Travancore-Cochin states in 1956, Kerala became a bigger Malayali state with an overwhelming population of the Hindus divided into many castes like Brahmins (mainly Namboodiripads), Nairs, Ezhavas etc. Despite the sociological make up of the Hindus it looks that Kerala state politics is dominated more by religion than caste. For instance, many Christians who once supported the Indian National Congress parted company when they found that the state government wanted to control educational institutions managed by Christian missionaries. Rifts within the Congress widened when the Christian members of this party supported and voted a Christian candidate against the official Hindu nominee and in retaliation Hindu Congress members did likewise for the sake of Hindu independents against official Christian nominees. The politics of religion gave a rude setback to the politics of caste in Kerala. This State gave a different political picture where mutually antagonistic caste, communal and regional groups "have been concentrated in separate political parties unable to cooperate for long under any condition for fear that one particular group may gain disproportionately and the result has been continuous instability".[34] Here people are divided on the basis of religion. Castes within the religions prefer to be called communities. In fact they are the pillars of political life in Kerala and the slightest shift in their voting pattern has an impact upon the fortunes of political parties in the state. In Kerala ideology as the dominating factor and C.P.I.(M) has emerged as a more homogeneous party ideologically.

In U.P. ideology cannot come into prominence as its

system depends for its functioning on religion and caste as the two main social divisions and on appeal to independents and political entrepreneurs. The religion dominates politics very effectively. Religion is the technique here for political mobilisation. The latest example is the controversy on Ram Janambhoomi - Babri Masjid. Conflict and tension increased recently over this issue, Hindu-Muslim riots, often resulting in many deaths became a common occurrence in the life of the state. This bitterness which developed between the two communities in this period has continued to be an important element in U.P. politics.

Changes in the party system has profoundly altered the working of the Constitution. They have transformed the functioning of state institutions. In fact it is well recognised that the political process, which is principally animated by political parties, is a powerful instrument of constitutional change. There is a great impact of political institutions on political parties in the form of their mobilization strategies.

It is difficult to comprehend the extent to which regional identities, and by implication federalism, have taken root in contemporary political life through the operation of the party system. It is the strength of the ruling party at the centre and its distribution in the states, the quality of leadership, and the capacity of these ruling parties to mobilise public opinion that influence the federal dynamics.

The end of Congress party dominance and lack of a clear single party majority since the assassination of Indira Gandhi in 1984 ushered in an era of coalition politics in the context of a fragmented party system. The growth and increased prominence of state-based or regional parties introduced a new element in the working of the federal system. It has undergone a significant change from a one party dominant system, what has been termed the *Congress system*, to a multi-party regionalised system. This realignment was evident in the late 1980's with the decline of the Congress party and the rise of *backward caste based* and regional parties. Congress dominance was replaced by minority and multiparty coalitions at the Centre and the states reflecting the major changes that have occurred in political life since late 1980s. It confirms the tendency towards the regionalisation that has been apparent since the 1989 elections which propelled the National Front coalition government of V.P. Singh to power. The 1989 General Elections began an era of coalition governments coincided with the politics of accommodation and adjustments which has affected Centre-State relations seriously.

The National Front in its 71 points programme presented before 1989 elections, committed itself to decentralisation and autonomy of states. After coming to power, the National Front Government did set up the Inter-State Council and rejuvenated the National Development Council, but because of some internal problems and challenges, it could not devote much time for large scale reforms in the federal process.

The 1991 elections gave a very different scenario where no party could get a clear majority in the Lok Sabha and at the same time they could not even form a coalition government. Moreover people were now more conscious of their caste and class positions. Therefore, allegiance to parties, representing their interests, rather stability through one party or coalition was their concern, there was a major downflow of vote share of the Congress in these elections.

The 1996 Lok Sabha elections gave the way to coalition politics where no national party had emerged strong enough to take unilateral decisions at the Central level and regional parties had not only gained power in several states but also leverage in the Union, the Federal structure and its working is likely to be strengthened. The most striking feature of the 1996 elections was the spectacular rise of regional parties and the challenge posed by these alterations to the *nationalisation of politics* which had gained ascendancy in the previous two decades.[35] In July 2000, the Union Govt., while rejecting autonomy resolution passed by Jammu & Kashmir Assembly, expressed its willingness to devolve legislative and financial powers to states. In January 2003, efforts were also made to resolve the Naga issue by holding talks with National Socialist Council of Nagaland.[36] A commitment to state autonomy was further reassured in context of Bodo settlement in February 2003.[37] Still, because of coalition at all levels, centre-state issues are by and large resolved on the basis of pre- and post-electoral alliances. These types of demands will be more difficult to ignore as some combinations of regional parties are indispensable for any government in present scenario.

Further it is clear with the 2004 General Elections that the days of one party dominance are over and in future the *national politics would be the sum total of state politics.*[38] Today each state is a political system into itself with its own party system. There has been an emergence of various types of party systems at the state level. Some are one party dominant states e.g. West Bengal. Two party systems are found in Kerala, Maharashtra, Orissa, Rajasthan etc. while U.P., Bihar etc. shows a fragmented party system with Congress's insignificant role.

However if we analyse the verdict at the national level, it is the sum total of the state level verdict. The result is showing nation's diversity with a struggle for political space by numerous forces. Ironically regional parties have become critical for the survival of multiparty governing coalitions.[39] Although regionalism which was once portrayed as a potential threat to national unity, gradually national politics, with more or less equal electoral strength act as central pillars to the rival coalitions.[39] This competitive multi-party system is "bi-nodal" a mode being a centering[40] point of component parts. He sees in this process both the trends of federalization of party system and renewal of parties.

REFERENCES

1. William H. Riker, "Federalism: Origin, Operation, Significance" in *American Federalism in Perspective,* edited by A. Wildavsky, Little Brown and Co., 1967 p. 59.
2. *Ibid.,* p. 56.
3. Amal Ray, "Party Politics", *Seminar* (357) May 1989.
4. K. Santhanam, *Union-State Relations in India,* (Delhi: Asia Publishing House), 1960, p. 63.

5. Asok Chanda, *Federalism in India*, (London: George Allen and Unwin Ltd.), 1965, p. 132.
6. See Paul R. Brass, *Factional Politics in an Indian State: The Congress Party in U.P.* (Bombay; Oxford University Press), 1966.
7. For details see, Myron Weiner, *Party Politics in India: The Development of a Multi-party System*, (Princeton: Princeton University Press), 1957, Chapter IV.
8. *The Statesman*, December 20, 1962.
9. *Asian Recorder*, November 22-28, 1958, p. 2359.
10. *Ibid.*
11. The Statement of Policy of C.PI., Bombay, November, 1950.
12. R. Ramakrishnan Nair, *How Communists Came to Power in Kerala* (Trivandrum: The Kerala Academy of Political Science), 1965.
13. See Communist Party of India, *Election Manifestoes*, 1962, 1967, and 1971.
14. As B.L. Maheshwari explains: In an intra-party coalition, consensus tends to become the accepted method of conflict resolution and in the final analysis the call of party unity works. On the other hand, in an inter-party coalition, since the parties do not have common leadership, common programmes, and common memories, the bargaining process stresses the collateral relationship. Refer to his paper, "Politics of Coalition" in *E.P.W.* (Bombay) Annual No. 1970, p. 118.
15. At the initiative of the Jan Sangh, the opposition parties—the Congress (O), the Jan Sangh, the Samyukta Socialist Party (S.S.P.), the Swantantra and the Bhartiya Kranti Dal, (B.K.D.), formed Samyukta Vidhayak Dal (S.V.D.) on 5 March, 1967 with Ram Chandra Vikal as its leader.
16. There were several incidents of violence during the fifth Lok Sabha elections in the State. During the mid-term assembly elections also, there were many cases of violence especially in the western districts.
17. *Kerala Kaumudi*, 4 May, 1966.
18. Seven parties were—C.P.M., C.P.I., S.S.P., R.S.P., K.T.P., K.S.P. and the Muslim League.
19. *Indian Express*, January 9, 1969.
20. *Ibid.*, January 10, 1969.
21. *Janayugam*, April 13, 1967.
22. Myron Weiner, John Osgood Field (Eds.) *Electoral Politics in the Indian States* (Delhi: Manohar Book Service) 1975, pp. 177-209.

23. Amal Ray, "Party Politics", *op. cit.*, p. 24.
24. *Indian Express*, Bangalore, 30 November 1987.
25. *Asian Recorder*, May 7-13 (1971) p. 10138.
26. Johri, J.C. *Indian Government and Politics*. (New Delhi), 1974, p. 396.
27. Stanley A. Kochanek in *Indira Gandhi's India: A Political System Reappraised* (ed.) H.C. Hart, (Boulder, Colorado: West View Press), 1976, pp. 93-125.
28. Rajni Kothari, "The Next Generation", *Seminar*, New Delhi, December 1985.
29. N. Jose Chander, *Dynamics of State Politics: Kerala* (Delhi: Sterling Publishers Pvt. Ltd.), 1986, p. 187.
30. R.A. Sharma, *Indira Gandhi's Leadership*, (New Delhi: Raaj Prakashan), 1986, p. 26.
31. *Times of India*, "U.P. Congress Fractured", New Delhi, November 13, 1989.
32. T.V, Sathyamurthy, *India Since Independence*, (New Delhi: Ajanta Publications), 1985, p. 115.
33. R.M. Mammen, "The Multi-party System in Kerala", *Indian Journal of Political Science Review*, Vol. VIII, July 1974, pp. 170-185.
34. Stanley A. Kochanek, *The Congress Party of India*, (Princeton: Princeton University Press), 1968. pp. 443-44.
35. Yogendra Yadav, "How India Voted?", *India Today*, 31 May 1996.
36. *The Times of India*, January 7 & 11, 2003.
37. *The Hindu*, February 13, 2003.
38. Yogendra Yadav, "Radical Shift in the Social Basis of Political Power", *The Hindu*, Delhi, May 20, 2004.
39. Sridharan, E., "Electoral Coalitions in 2004 General Elections: Theory and Evidence", *Economic and Political Weekly* 39(51) December 18, 2004, 5418-25; 88; *Ibid.*; "The Fragmentation of the Indian Party System: 1989-99" in Zoya Hasan (ed.), *Parties and Party Politics in India*, New Delhi: Oxford University Press, 2002, pp. 475-503.
40. Balveer Arora, "Negotiating Differences: Federal Coalitions and National Cohesion", in Francine R. Frankel and Zoya Hasan (ed.) *Transforming India: Social and Political Dynamics of Democracy*, New Delhi: Oxford University Press, 2005, pp. 176-205.

5

Economic Dynamics of Centre-State Relations

A Federation consists of a combination of governing units which have to work with the Centre over a considerable field independently. Towards this objective, the States should be financially autonomous. In practice it is the strength of the financial resources that paves the way to the success of a government.

In a Federation, the sharing of financial resources has to be effected in such a way so that the balance is kept steady between the two units. It is also necessary that each layer of government has access to sufficient financial resources so that all obligations are fulfilled. However, "of all Federal problems, the financial relations between the Centre and the units are most difficult".[1] "The troubled history of federal finance in the older federations and frequent adjustments in relatively new federations amply prove the crucial position of federal finance".[2]

When the Constituent Assembly examined the financial relations between the Centre and the constituent units, it was apparent that the problems had to be considered anew. "For one thing, the Partition of India, by altering the boundaries, brought in its wake demands on the Centre for vast expenditure on rehabilitation of displaced people; for another,the divided provinces of West Bengal, Punjab, and Assam had to face the issue of keeping their economy on an even keel".[3] At the time of debate on the provisions relating to Centre-State financial relations, some members were in favour of state's autonomy in financial matters. "The provinces should not be beggars at the doors of the Centre."[4]

An Expert Finance Committee of the Constituent Assembly pointed out that "in normal circumstances, the Centre would be comparatively stable, but the functions assigned to Provincial Governments would necessitate growing expenditure. So the provinces should be assured of adequate resources. A division of revenues was needed to the units for carrying out their functions efficiently. The allocation of customs, income tax and excise duties to the Centre leads to an imbalance which increased the dependence of units. The income from these heads of revenue forms a higher proportion of total Government revenues than the expenditure of the Centre forms, to total Government expenditures. This makes the units short of money while the Centre has too much. The Committee affirmed that it would be impossible to avoid divided heads of revenue and that the aim should be to have a few divided heads "well balanced and high yielding and to arrange that the shares of the Centre and the provinces in their heads are adjusted automatically, without friction or mutual interference."[5] By the time it came up for discussion, political integration took place followed by financial integration.

There was near unanimity amongst the members of the Constituent Assembly, lending support voluntarily, that the Constitution for purposes of financial relationship, shall not be federal. Even among the members of the Drafting Committee there was near unanimity in this regard. A.K. Aiyar and Mohd. Sa'adulla, members of the Drafting Committee, who had supported the case for provincial autonomy, gave up their stand to espouse an unfederal stand in the matter of financial relations. They couched it in such a way that their intentions were obvious. Speaking on the motion regarding the Draft Constitution on 8th November 1948, A.K. Aiyar observed:

> "The financial provisions in the Draft constitution have also came in for strong comment ... while an independent course of sources of revenue are certainly necessary for the proper functioning of a federal government, there is a distinct tendency, however, in the several federations, for the central government to act as the taxing agency, taking care to make adequate provisions for the units sharing the proceeds as also the central or National Government granting subsidies."[6]

Syed Mohd. Sa'adulla, another member of the Drafting Committee, who was critical of the over-centralisation in the Centre and the emergency powers given to the President as constituting the 'utmost interference in provincial affairs', merely lamented the want of any provisions of financial help of the provinces/states instead of demanding state autonomy. While speaking on the motion regarding the Draft Constitution on 21 November 1948, he said:

> "Sir, the absence of any provision for financial help to the poor and needy provinces brings one to the question of the province from which I came, namely Assam.... It is very well said that the strength of a unit is the measure of the strength of the federation and, no doubt, we have tried to make the Centre strong in the Draft of the federal constitution of India ... Sir, I honestly beseech this house and through this house the authorities at the Centre to look to this whole State of affairs in Assam and come to its aid liberally and timely. They need not give anything from their own coffers for as I have pointed out earlier, two or three months ago, that as much as ten crores of rupees are being derived in various

> shapes from Assam as revenues of the Central Government. So, if one fourth or one third of this sum is given to Assam, if would not be a gift or any special concession, but only rendering Caesar what belongs to Caesar."[7]

As finance is the backbone of administration and development, financial dimensions of Centre-State relations acquire greater significance than the political and administrative. K. Santhanam, the former chairman of the Second Finance Commission, described financial relations as "the Achilles Heel" of every federation. No system of federation can be successful unless both the Union and the States have at their disposal adequate financial resources to enable them to discharge their respective responsibilities.

To achieve this object, there are provisions in the Constitution, relating to the distribution of the taxes as well as non-tax revenues and the power of borrowing, supplemented by provisions for grants-in-aid by the Union to the States. The aim was an equitable distribution of the financial resources between the two units of the federation, instead of dividing the resources into two watertight compartments, as under the usual federal system. A fitting introduction to this arrangement has been given by the Supreme Court in these words:

> "Sources of revenue which have been allocated to the union are not meant entirely for the purposes of the union but have to be distributed according to the principles laid down by parliamentary legislation. Thus all the taxes and duties levied by the union... do not form part of the Consolidated Fund of India but many of these taxes and duties are distributed amongst the States and form part of the Consolidated Fund of the States. Even those taxes and duties which constitute the Consolidated Fund of India may be used for the purposes of supplementing the revenues of the States in accordance with their needs. The

> question of distribution of the aforesaid taxes and duties amongst the States and the principles governing them, as also the principles governing grants-in-aid... are matters which have to be decided by a high powered Finance Commission which is a responsible body designated to determine those matters in an objective way.... The Constitution makers realised the fact that those sources of revenue allocated to the States may not be sufficient for their purposes and that the Government of India would have to subsidise their welfare activities. ... Realising the limitations on the financial resources of the States and the growing needs of the community in a welfare state, the constitution has made... specific provisions empowering parliament to set aside a portion of its revenues... for the benefit of the States, not in stated proportions but according to their needs.... The resources of the Union Government are not meant exclusively for the benefit of the Union activities.... In other words, the Union and the States together form an organic whole for the purposes of utilisation of the resources of the territories of India as a whole."[8]

The Constitution reflects a different picture, an overwhelming concern of its framers in favour of a strong Centre. The framers thought that only a strong Centre could preserve the unity of the nation in the face of regionalism and strong disruptive forces that could weaken the nation. So they have deliberately distributed the functions and sources of revenue between the Union and the States in such a manner that the Union has relatively more elastic sources of revenue and the States have expanding and expensive functions, but relatively less elastic sources of revenue. "The Centre has been given more resources, than it can digest."[7] Such an allocation, would lead to both vertical and horizontal federal fiscal imbalances. But at this stage there was no clear view of the kind of planning that might evolve in the future. For this reason, 'economic and social planning' was placed in the concurrent list. Under the scheme of the Constitution, it was apparent that there would be a growing gap between the resources ordinarily available to the States and the tasks they were expected to carry out. This gap could be reduced by periodic transfers of resources from the Centre to the States.

Financial provisions in the Constitution, divide resources between the Centre and the States by adopting a particular scheme of distribution of revenues and includes following features:

(i) exclusive of tax divisions between the Centre and States

(ii) sharing of certain tax proceeds

(iii) borrowing by the Centre and the States

(iv) and grants-in-aid by the Centre to the States.

The Constitution provided the Centre with sources of revenue which were likely to grow with the development of the industrial and commercial sectors of the economy, increase in exports and imports and growth of consumption. The most notable were taxes on income other than agricultural income, corporation tax, customs duties, and excise duties. The States were given resources which, barring sales tax and state excise duties, would grew as agriculture became more of an industry and the rural sector began to be taxed adequately. However, the scope of central taxes from which transfers have been made, has been limited on account of the exclusion of the corporation tax and of customs duties. Moreover, States have found it difficult politically and administratively to carry the taxation of land and water and other rural services for enough. While the yield of indirect taxes has increased proportionately both for the Centre and the States, direct taxes allotted to the States has grown far less compared to the yield of direct taxes available to the Centre. To be precise, despite the mitigating influence of Finance Commissions, States have became heavily dependent on the Centre for financing their plans. In the Indian Federation, the sources of taxes are divided between the Centre and the units. Under the Leviathan of Planning, the States have been burdened with a number of developmental activities which calls for a great deal of financial sources. The central policy affects the prosperity of the State as it has not only got more resources but there are several constitutional provisions of which it gets surplus revenues, loans and grants from international sources. These are non-statutory activities. Nevertheless, the Centre has a lot of discretion in the matter of helping the units. Grants are always made on conditions. It is here that the Centre is able to influence the policies of the State Governments. The Finance Minister of a State cannot hope to have discretion in putting forth a new policy especially when the State is poor in resources. Grants-in-aid and gifts by the Centre are the powerful means whereby strings can be attached by the Centre to influence the policies of the State and even bring pressure indirectly to carry through central directions.

In the Seventh Schedule, certain large taxing powers are vested in the Centre.[10] Article 275 gives the Centre power to make grants. All these are ways and means of entering into the financial structure of the State, For example: in matters of education the State introduced basic education, the Centre by its readiness to encourage it subsidises it more easily. So also the Central Welfare Board, the U.G.C. are other examples whereby the Centre is able to influence the policy of the State Government on subjects in the State List which are entirely the concern of the units. The States have no doubt, the right to borrow upon the security of the Consolidated Fund of India [Article 288(2)], but here also the sanction of the Government of India has to be obtained before hand while as for the borrowing power, the Union has got unlimited power,[11] the States have been placed under a number of limitations. For example in the matter of getting loans, its power is limited by the Union.[12] The States also have no power to borrow outside India (even with the consent of the Union) which was allowed under the Act of 1935. Further, the phrase 'outstanding-loan' may be interpreted by the Centre according to its own convenience. Moreover, while giving loans to the States, the Central Government functions as a money lender with a profit motive. For example,"the Centre obtained loans from international agencies at two percent interest and passed it to the States at ten percent interest".[13] Even more, "the Centre reduced the period of repayment from forty or fifty years to ten or fifteen years while passing on the funds to the States".[14]

The tax structure is complicated and highly centralised. Under the head 'Social and Economic Planning' and "National Interest[1] the Centre Government is given a predominant position. The productive and elastic resources are maintained by the Central Government. More than anything else, grants-in-aid is one of the main instruments whereby the Union Government can play cat and mouse with State Autonomy. The Reserve Bank is also another means of influencing the States policy in financial matters, for instance when there were overdrafts by States from the Reserve Bank, Morarji Desai, the then Union Finance Minister, replying to the debate on the General Budget in Rajya Sabha on March 28th, 1963 said: "The Government is taking steps to prevent the States from resorting to overdrafts on their grants with the Reserve Bank". Regarding an adhoc loan of Rs. 30 crores of four States to meet their overdrafts, Morarji Desai said that these States had been given loans on conditions that in future they would not be allowed to overdraw on their accounts with the Reserve Bank and the Reserve Bank can be instructed not to pay them the overdrafts. In planning therefore, the Centre is able to influence policies in the second list through the financial structure especially when the States are not in a position to meet their developmental expenditures.

Revenues of the State Governments in India are derived from three distinct sources: state taxes, non-tax revenues and transfer of funds from the Centre to the States. It appears that there is a problem of inelasticity of state revenues. The U.P. Chief Minister, Kalyan Singh (1991) had called for the redefining of Centre-State relations so as to give more financial powers and resources to the States. He said that "at present the States were like municipalities earning revenue from just three sources—excise, sales tax, and stamp duty."[15] This he said, "led to the State becoming entirely dependent on the Centre for funds for development. The Centre uses this fiscal power to dictate terms to the Chief Minister resulting in a situation where all powers get centered with the Central Government much against the ethics of democratic functioning of the States."[16]

There are two kinds of federal fiscal imbalances— vertical and horizontal. The former refers to a situation where division of revenue sources and expenditure functions between the federal government on the one hand and the States government on the other are not on equal footing. The latter refers to the prevailing inequalities among the States. All these imbalances between the Centre and the States and among the States are sought to be reduced by the Constitution mainly through the transfer of resources from the Centre to the States. Commenting on the overall situations of fiscal imbalances, D.T. Lakdawala (Deputy Chairman of the Fifth Planning Commission) said that, "with the increasing integration of nation economy, this implied that States own revenues would fall short of State expenditures necessary for the efficient discharge of functions assigned to them. For the purpose of bridging the gap as well as for horizontal transfer to the weaker States, the Constitution has provided for a finance commission to recommend distribution of income tax and central excises and grants-in-aid of revenue to weaker States in need of assistance".[17] in fact there has not been uniformity in the distribution of revenue between the Centre and the States and among the States by the finance commission. For instance "the divisible pool (excise revenue) had stagnated at the twenty percent level till 1977-78 when the Seventh Finance Commission recommended to raise the State's share to 40 percent. Successive Finance Commissions have recognised the fact that increasing participation of the States in the net proceeds of Union excise duties will alone bring about some degree of balance between their financial commitments in an era of planning and their resources".[18]

When Gujrat approached the Ninth Finance Commission for assistance as the State was losing income for having a firm prohibition policy, the Commission "had guts to tell, you scrap prohibition, we have nothing to do with your policy, we are not going to help you",[19] said Chimanbhai Patel, the Chief Minister of Gujrat few days before joining Congress (I) along with the entire Council of Ministers.

The Planning Commission has been distributing Central Assistance for state plan in accordance with the Gadgil formula since 1969-70. Starting with 1969-70, 70% of the central assistance is being given in the form of loans and 30% in the form of grants. Most of the States have also opposed the financial form of the transfer. They have pointed out that if the transfer is done on the basis of 70% loan and 30% grant, "the loan repayment burden on the States would go up tremendously and could even lead to a net withdraw of resources from the States to the Centre".[20] Shanta Kumar, the Chief Minister of Himachal Pradesh even went on to say that "Central assistance to special category States be transferred on a 100 percent grant basis, keeping in view the mounting debt burdens and massive increase in the interest liability".[21] However, the Kerala Chief Minister Mr, K. Karunakaran was little moderate about it. Referring to the proposal of Central assistance, he said, "the grant component should be raised from the present 30 to 50% so that loan-grant ratio became more balanced".[22]

The crux of the problem in Centre-State financial relations lies in the fact that the States do not have sufficient resources to discharge their responsibilities. Naturally they have to rely upon central assistance. The absence of any uniform policy regarding central assistance provides ample scope for the Centre to exercise its discretion and discriminate against the States especially those ruled by opposition parties. All these very often result in conflicts and tensions between the Centre and the States. Even the fathers of the constitution anticipated the possibility of the Indian federation facing both vertical and horizontal financial imbalances and conflicts between the federal financial system and quasi-federal nature of the political structure. There were several such instances when the Centre foisted on the State policies that were clearly in violation of the federal spirit. It was alleged that in the absence of equitable financial devolution, the States were no better than municipalities.

C.P.I.(M) especially contended that the Centre would not allow the States, more so the C.P.I.(M) led State of Kerala, to be independent and viable financially for fear of losing its grip on the politics of the State.

Kerala's stagnancy in overall economic growth is an enigma. This is because the State is having abundant natural resources and is possessing a vigilant and lettered array of human resources. To support growth, the State enjoys a fairly developed socio-economic infra-structure while many acclaim its 'quality of life' and call it a model for other developing nations, a fact remains overlooked—a dismaying proportion of its population lives in absolute poverty, an alarming number are in a search for employment for their subsistence. The State's inadequate growth and economic stagnation have been further aggravated recently by the slackening of 'gulf boom'. Within the State too, the problems are regionalised, the backward northern districts (the Malabar region) in the State have since long been striving for a way out. The formation of the present State in 1956 by merging two princely States (Cochin and Travancore) with the British ruled Malabar district did not bring about an integrated economic structure. It is true that the State has achieved rapid development in the field of social services and health. But the achievement towards economic development have been far from satisfactory as is evident from the lack of modern industries, low productivity of industrial sector, chronic food shortage etc.

Kerala has been described as a 'problem State' of India.

The difficulty of securing a sympathetic hearing in Delhi is heightened by the fact that Keraia is—in Indian terms—a small State. Its population of 29,032,828 (1991) entitled it to twenty seats in the Lok Sabha less than a quarter of U.P.'s representation and half of that of other States. Kerala has consistently claimed that it has been treated like a poor relation in the allocation of plan resources, the distribution of centrally collected taxes and in the supply of food grains. However, there is a case to answer in the Centre's failure to make good the State's food deficit which amounts to about half its grain consumption in the average year. Kerala makes a disproportionate contribution to India's foreign exchange earnings and savings through its plantation and cash crops. So, it expects the Centre to honour its off-repeated commitment to ensure an equitable supply of rice. That this has not been forthcoming is indisputable. The question is why? The logistic difficulties of guaranteeing that the grain is in the right place at the right time cannot be dismissed, nor the possibility that in the past, some interests at the Centre had played politics with food at the expense of marxist-led ministries. However the major factor had probably been the inability of the Centre to stand up to the forming lobby in the surplus States, Kerala has therefore been termed a 'problem-State' a factor discouraging inflow of private capital.[23] Further, the policies of the union government have also came in for same criticism, for either ignoring the development of the State or doing out irrational resources.[24]

The Malayalis are bitter about the neglect of their State by the Centre. They constitute only 4% of the country's population but contribute over 12% of its foreign exchange earnings. They manage to make this contribution by starving themselves by growing cash crops instead of rice. The least they expect from New Delhi is to make up the State's deficit in food. In asking the Centre for a more generous allocation of funds, Malayalis feel that they are not asking for charity but claiming their right to a share in the fruits of their labour. The central sector investment in the State formed only 2.27 percent of the total central sector investment aid the country. Kerala's share of central investment in fact declined from 2.44 percent on march 1979 to 2.33 percent on march 1980 and declined further in march 1981 to 2.27 percent.

The current expenditure pattern of Kerala leaves practically very little to be spent for economic development through augmented development expenditure. It has a weak tax base and yield from it is very inadequate and inelastic and functions to be carried out by the State is increasing year after year. The State is at the mercy of the Centre for its existence and it cannot think of setting up any development schemes independently without additional financial assistance from the Centre.

"Kerala's fiscal crisis and its economic crisis are reinforcing each other. Due to paucity of funds, there has been deceleration in the State's plan expenditure in recent years."[25] This has contributed to a slow expansion of the State's resource base. The absence of any surplus on non-plan account has led to the reduction in size of the State's plans. An Examination of State Plans has revealed that financial resources available to Kerala are highly inadequate to meet its needs of plan finances. "Kerala is facing serious financial crisis as the resources gap is yawning plan after plan. From Rs. 4.97 crores in the Second Plan the gap increased to Rs. 274.36 crores in the Fifth Plan. In the Sixth Plan it was Rs. 149.76 crores."[26] The financial crisis of the Kerala government is not of recent origin, though its frequency and magnitude have increased in recent years. "Even during the Fifth Five Year-Plan period, Kerala had budgetary crisis in two years. However, the amounts involved were small. During the Sixth Five Year Plan, Kerala had deficits in four years and the amounts involved became larger. During the Seventh Plan period, despite strict treasury controls and piling up of unpaid dues to the public, Kerala had deficits in four years. In 1986-87 the State had the biggest ever budgetary deficit of Rs. 193 crore which represented 2.5 percent of the State Domestic Product."[27]

The Central assistance played a relatively smaller part in meeting the State's expenditure. Except during one year (1974-75) the proportion of expenditure financed by central assistance was lower in Kerala than in all States. The reduced inflow of central assistance is one of the contributory causes for Kerala's recent fiscal crisis.

The First Finance Commission didn't consider the economic backwardness of the State while assigning the State's share in Central taxes and grants. It was population that came under their consideration, while determining about the division of resources. They didn't consider even tax performance of State or economy in expenditure. The appointment of the Second Finance Commission in 1956 coincided with formation of the Kerala State, This Commission did not favour the interest of the State. For instance, in those years, revenue from sales tax had been rapidly increasing. Yet there are practically no increase in the actual receipts of the Kerala on account of its share of additional excise duties. "Between 1957-58 and 1961-62, the revenue from sales tax was Rs.34.17 crores, but Kerala's share of additional excise duties was only to the extent of Rs. 4.58 crores (i.e. 13.40%)".[28] On the basis of recommendation of Second Finance Commission, the State of Kerala received Rs. 2945 lakhs which met 19.8% of the total revenue expenditure of the State. This was a meagre percent when compared with the revenue requirements of the State. This again worsened the situation as a result of the new activities, both developmental and non-developmental, which the newly formed State had to undertake. The Third and Fourth Finance Commissions with a weightage of 80 percent to population and 20 percent to collection did not make any improvements in their approach towards federal fiscal transfers. The Fourth Finance Commission did not take budgetary deficit as a criterion for distribution in the case of divisible taxes and duties. If the tax sharings are not related as closely as possible to budgetary needs, the total amount of financial transfers from the Centre will be much larger than the needs of some States and this will result in surplus. This method of operation of the Finance Commission was highly disadvantageous to States like Kerala, having specific needs of development. The recommendations of the Fifth Finance Commission was not favourable to Kerala. During the period between 1969-70 and 1973-74, Kerala received only Rs. 232.43 crores leaving an estimated gap, under the Revenue account of the State of Rs. 695.31 crores. Thus the unfilled gap was about Rs. 216.61 crores and was left to the State. The State was not in a position to meet this because of its special problems in those days.[29] The scarcity of funds has prevented the State Government from proper maintenance of public assets particularly roads and buildings which has led to damages and loss of public assets. On account of all these, the State Government had little scope for raising additional resources for meeting the additional expenditure. The Fifth Finance Commission ignored the special problems of the State and did not take into consideration the fact that committed non-developmental expenditure of the State had increased considerably. The share of Kerala has come down from 6.54 percent of the total divisible past in the Fourth Finance Commission award to 4.53% in the award of the Fifth Finance Commission. Increase in the share of Kerala as a result of the award of the Fifth Finance Commission was meagre as compared to 66.24 percent in respect of U.P. The Fifth Finance Commission has not succeeded in wiping out the disparities and inequalities among States as could be seen from the case of Kerala. The successive Finance Commissions also followed the footsteps of earlier commissions without giving any attention to the State's problems. In the Seventh Plan, the State Government proposed an outlay of Rs. 3300 crores. However in the discussions held in Planning Commission, the outlay was reduced to Rs. 2100 crores. Comparatively 10447.00 crores of U.P. The recommendations of the Eighth Finance Commission was disadvantageous to the State of Kerala from several view points. Under the Seventh Finance Commission award, Kerala's share of income tax was 3.95

percent. This share was reduced to 3.76% under Eighth Finance Commission. Kerala's share of union excise duties also came down to 3.8% of the divisible pool during the Eighth Finance Commission period. it was 4.03 percent during the Seventh Finance Commission period.

The award of Eighth Financial Commission is not favourable for Keralites, K. Karunakaran said that "Its recommendations are applicable for all States in the country. But when it calculated the quantum of assistance to us, its approach was very much detrimental to the State".[30] He wanted the Centre to adopt an overall impartial outlook and approach so that every State gets its due share on matters of aid, assistance or investments.[31]

It was also pointed out that when the same party was in power in Kerala the relations were harmonious, and financial assistance was also good comparatively during other parties rule. Mr. E.K. Nayanar said that "Kerala is receiving a step-motherly treatment. The Centre is not being fair to the Left Democratic Front Government".[32] In 1987 he submitted a memorandum to the Prime Minister explaining the crisis of the State and alleged that the Centre was discriminatory against the State Government; while it had adopted a very 'liberal attitude' towards the previous Government led by the Congress (I).[33] He also said that "when Karunakaran asked for plan advance, the Centre gave it but when Nayanar asked for it, the response was a treasury bandh. That is not fair."[34]

This clearly shows that when context changes, relation between the Centre and the State also changes.

"Eighth Finance Commission considered Kerala as a surplus State without having a look at its deficits. Consequently the State was excluded from entitlement to the revenue gap grant under Article 275 of the Constitution. The State's share of Central taxes went down in the context of maximum tax efforts."[35] In March 1988, E.K. Nayanar the Chief Minister, pointed out the partisan role of the Congress Party within the state. "The financial crisis is not exactly of the Left Democratic Front Governments making. The Karunakaran regime which had run up massive overdrafts got them converted into loans. The present Government is groaning under the burden of this debt and of making interest payments on the debt. The Centre's unhelpful attitude towards the State's financial woes is generating much resentment. During the Karunakaran rule the Centre agreed to convert Rs. 2477 crore overdraft into loans but when the L.D.F. Government ran up a Rs. 24 crore overdraft, the Centre cut-off payments to the State. Similarly with drought relief, Mr. Karunakaran could get a considerable amount of funds as relief but the L.D.F. could get only Rs. 29 crore despite a severe drought. This controversy has to be viewed in the context of the deteriorating relationship between the State and the Centre".[36] He listed several grievances of the State in the Assembly and said that "these were yet to be redressed as a result of neglect and discrimination by the Centre".[37] He further added that "various power projects were in cold storage because of the Centre's unsympathetic attitude".[38]

Kerala stands above national average regarding the commencement of primary schools, and its achievements in education and health care programmes. The Ninth Finance Commission disregarded the achievements of Kerala in these fields and did not give any share of the grant of Rs. 200 crores awarded to the States for constructing primary schools.

Table 1[39]

Five Year Plans: Per Capita Plan Outlays

Plans	*Kerala*	*All States (Rs.)*
1st	22	26
IInd	45	54
IIIrd	96	88
Annual Plan 1966-1969	66	63
IVth	121	128

Vth	588	683
VIth	588	683
VIIth	741	1054
Annual Plan 1985-1986	130	178
1986-1987	140	213
1987-1988	155	245

During Five Year Plans, the per capita plan outlays of all States and Kerala (Table-1) shows that Kerala's position was better till 1969, but after that its position worsened. The growth in plan outlays, both in absolute and per capita terms, has been grossly inadequate to ensure the required level of economic growth in line with most of the other regions of the country. "The concentration of all economic power in the hands of the Centre has made the State Governments a supplicant at the door of the Union Government. Their economic programme their agricultural programmes, all are at the mercy of the Centre...."[40]

The Uttar Pradesh is one of the most important States from the view point of population and area but economically it is a backward State of India. The progress in the various sectors of the economy has been so poor that it has remained more than one plan behind the all India progress. Even in the field of agriculture, in which it should have done better, its progress has been so slow that it depends upon other States for its food requirements. Industrially, the State is extremely backward. Similarly, the progress in the field of various social and economic overheaas has been so inadequate that it has failed in meeting even the barest infrastructure requirements of the economy. The inevitable result has, therefore, been that the per capita income of U.P. has increased relatively slowly and in some years for instance during 1.960-61 to 1963-64 the per capita income (at 1960-61 prices) of the State actually declined.

The State has fallen behind other States of comparable

size in economic development and modernisation. In 1950-51 the per capita income in U.P. at 1948-49 prices was Rs. 259.62 as against the national per capita income of Rs. 247.50. After a decade, the per capita income in U.P. at 1960-61 prices came down to Rs. 245.88 as against Rs. 310 for the country. In 1967-68, the per capita income in U.P. was Rs. 247 against the national level of Rs. 321. U.P is thus more than a decade behind the stage that has been reached by the country as a whole. "Within the State itself, different regions have different levels of economic development."[41]

U.P. has also been neglected in the allocation of Central projects. During the first seventeen years of planning, the Centre invested a sum of Rs. 2,450 crores in central projects out of which U.P.'s share was only 6% of the total investment in the third plan. No central project was allocated to U.P. during the first and the second plans. While public financial institutions like Industrial Finance Corporation, ICICI and Industrial Development Bank have generally neglected this State, the private entrepreneurs also have shown their reluctance to invest their money.

For long, the economy of U.P. where one sixth of the country's population lives, has moved at a snail's pace creating a general impression that the State has exercised a dragging influence on India's economic progress. In fact, in terms of money indicators of socio-economic development, U.P. is not only lagging behind the national economy, but its relative position is also worsening.

Table 2 shows that the level of per capita plan expenditure in U.P. has remained significantly behind the all-India level throughout the planning period, particularly so in the first and the second five year plans. It is estimated that the per capita plan expenditure in U.P. over the period 1951-52 to 1986-87 amounted to only Rs. 465 as compared to the figure of Rs. 590 for all States. In fact all States, except Bihar had a higher level of plan expenditure over the plan period as compared to Union Territory. This table

Table 2[42]

Per Capita Plan Expenditure and Central Assistance: U.P. and All States

Plan Period	*Plan Expenditure Per Capita (Rs.)*			*Central Assistance Per Capita (Rs.)*			*States's Own Plan Resources Per Capita (Rs.)*		
	UP	*All States*	*UP as % of all States*	*UP*	*All States*	*UP as % of all States*	*UP*	*All States*	*UP as % of all States*
Ist Plan 1951-56	25	38	65.8	13	24	54.2	12	14	85.7
IInd Plan 1956-61	32	51	62.7	17	26	65.4	15	25	80.0
IIIrd Plan 1961-66	72	92	78.3	46	55	83.6	26	37	70.3
Annual Plan 1968-69	53	61	86.9	30	36	83.3	23	25	92.0
IVth Plan 1969-74	132	142	93.0	58	65	89.2	74	77	96.1
Vth Plan 1974-80	329	417	78.9	144	147	98.0	185	270	68.5
VIth Plan 1980-85	559	704	79.4	218	258	84.5	341	446	76.5
VIIth Plan 1985-90	942	1156	85.1	375	438	85.6	567	718	79.0

also reveals that the levels of the per capita plan expenditure financed through own resources in U.P. has been considerably lower as compared to the average for all States.

The taxable capacity in U.P. is expected to be lower in view of the lower per capita income of the State. Nevertheless there is substantial scope for raising more resources in the State as the ratio of State taxes to State income is only around 5.0 percent much below the figure for most of the other States, As can be seen from the Table 2 central assistance to U.P. in per capita terms has also been of a lower level as compared to other States, The situation improved to some extent with the introduction of the Gadgil Formula, though it has not been fully rectified. Furthermore, the inflow of outside resources through other mechanisms too has been of a relatively lower order in U.P. The per capita investment under the central sector plan in U.P. between 1951 and 1985 amounted to Rs. 1348 as compared to the all State average of Rs. 1615.

In terms of the location of the Central Public Sector Projects too, U.P. continued to be neglected for long. In the first three five year plans not a single public sector project was located in U.P. Till the end of the fifth five year plan, cumulative investment in central public sector undertakings in U.P. amounted to Rs. 376.2 crores, which was only 3.3% of such investment amounting to Rs. 11451.2 crores in the country as a whole.

Between 1951-67 the per capita central assistance to U.P. was Rs. 106 only as against all State average of Rs. 141. The per capita central assistance in U,P, during the first and the second five year plans was the lowest among 16 States, "In the third plan U.P. has at the 13 th place, higher than only three States viz., Bihar, West Bengal, Maharashtra, The position during the three annual plans remained nearly the same"[43] and during the Fourth Plan also the State was no better off when it ranked third from the bottom among the 17 States. As a result, U.P. has been left behind in the path of national progress in many fields.

Ms. Sucheta Kripalani observed when she was the Chief Minister of U.P. that "Generally speaking also, the State is still one Plan behind other States."[44]

The State lags behind with regard to many social and developmental services such as education, medical and public health, transport power etc. According to the 1971 Census, the literacy percentage was 21.8 in U.P. as against 29.5 for the country as a whole. The per capita expenditure on education, art and culture, scientific services and research was Rs. 24.99 as against the average of Rs. 32.91 for all the States in that year.

An economically backward State poses a great threat to the integrity of a federal structure. The Centre must give greater attention to the development of U.P. by providing adequate assistance. The State must also make earnest efforts to mobilise resources by making suitable changes in its fiscal system. The fact that the State government has not mobilised adequately its own resources is evident from the fact that "in 1977-78 (Budget) the revenue from State taxes formed 5.78 percent of the State income whereas the States of Karnataka (11.31%) Kerala (9.62%), M.P. (7.50%) and Rajasthan (6.35%) raised relatively higher percentage of their income through State taxes",[45] although the per capita income of these States is lower than that of U.P. Similarly the per capita revenue from State taxes in U.P. in 1977-78 (Budget) was Rs, 71,60 for all the States during that year.

The slow development is often said to be caused by the insufficient outlays and investments in the plan period. In the initial stages of planning the developing countries need a push up in the levels of investment to raise the per capita income which further helps in moving up the rate of investment to a point where economy secures an adequate rate of growth of income. During the first three plan period (1951-69), U.P. received only 13.2% of the central assistance even though her population constituted 17% of the country's population.

The five year and Annual plans are a series of continuous efforts towards fulfilling the goal of economic and social development. Yet U.P. the most populous State has remained one of the most backward States in the country. Though the successive five year plans have fully recognised the importance of regional approach to national planning, they lack sufficient awareness of regional conditions and problems,

So, it is clear that the actual financial relations between the Centre and States have been very different from those postulated in the Constitution. The working of the Constitution in terms of the financial relations has revealed the fact that there are imbalances between Centre and States regarding finances. The main reason being the uneven distribution of powers between them. An economically backward State poses a great threat to the integrity of a federal structure. The leaders must think objectively about the appalling situations of State. The context of both these type of States shows that, if the situation not taken seriously, it can become a major problem for the integrity of our federal system.

Federalism is not just a structure but it is a process. The essence of federalism is the existence of independent political decision-making at different levels of government. Yet such decision-making cannot operate in isolation and inter-dependence in governance necessitates shared-governance. Federalism, as a process has acquired new dimensions, with the globalization of world economy and a new shape of arrangements of functions and finances at the sub-national levels.

There is a gradual transformation of the Indian party system of Congress dominance to multiparty system of polarised Federalism, specially since the 1989 Lok Sabha elections. Further the initiation of economic reforms by the Congress minority government led by P.V. Narsimha Rao since 1991 has reduced centre's role in controlling the economy and accelerated the process of federalisation of parliamentary system.

Since the beginning of economic liberalization and the parallel process of regional representation in national governments, states although enjoy considerable political and economic autonomy, but at the same time there is an intense pressure on their economies. Economic liberalisation policies in the 1990s prompted a change in federal relations from inter-governmental co-operation toward inter jurisdictional competition among the states.[46]

Lloyd and Susanne Rudolph[47] have characterised the changes in the following manner "A federal market economy is fast replacing a Nehruvian centralised command economy in the country's economic imagination and practice."

There is a change and continuity in centre-state financial relations in post liberalisation phase. A domination by the centre and cooperation with other states was noticed in pre-reform phase. After 1991 the competition has changed from centrally determined resources to a wider variety of resources. Now the number of competing states has increased, regional disparities has become more visible. In fact "economic liberalisation has aggravated regional imbalances and it has generated inter-state ruthless competition to attract foreign capital".[48]

Before 1991 Centre was controlling everything related to industrialization but economic liberalization abolished this control. This means the centre is no more working as a superior in setting up industries.

Before liberalisation, regional units were expected to implement central directives leading to Centre-state harmony rather than conflict. The competition among states was indirect and was controlled by the central government.

After 1991 the competition became wider and symmetric with Uttar Pradesh, West Bengal, Bihar, Andhra Pradesh trying their best to become attractive sites for investment.[49] Apart from the this, there was a commitment to become industry friendly states. Mayawati declared on May 14, 1997 that her government was "giving top priority to restoration of law and order in the state for providing an industry-friendly environment."[50]

Kerala has traditionally pursued extensive redistributive policies. In 1991, Kerala govt. announced an industrial policy that recognised that "under the changed atmosphere of liberalisation and opening up, the state has to re-orient its approach to revitalise the industrial sector. Many anti-reform regimes were forced to change policy discourse in favour of liberalisation.

However the impact of economic liberalisation has tended to be concentrated towards a few states. It has disproportionately affected middle income and high income states. It is important to note that four of India's most populous states (UP, MP, Rajasthan and Bihar) are also low income states with comparatively less foreign direct investment (FDI) inflow. Since August 1991, to Dec. 1998, the combined proposed FDI in these politically powerful Hindi-belt states (Rs. 5,058 Cr.) approximates the proposed FDI to the southern state of Tamil Nadu (Rs. 5,006 Cr.) (see SIA Newsletter, Ministry of Industry, Jan. 1999).

Further, political party alignment appears to have been a key factor in some states ability to attract foreign investment. Those states that are two party system (Kerala, Gujarat, Maharashtra, Andhra Pradesh) etc. have been more successful than states with unstable multi-party systems (U.P. & Bihar) etc. There is addition to high income, there appears to be a correlation between political stability and ability to attract foreign investment.

However, India's economic reforms have reordered Centre-state relations, displacing both power and responsibilities to the regional states. Change and continuity are coexisting in today's India.

REFERENCES

1. K. Santhanam, *Union-State Relations in India,* (Bombay: Asia Publishing House), 1960, p. 29.
2. R.L. Watts, *New Federations: Experiments in the Commonwealth* (Oxford: Oxford Clarenden Press), 1966, p. 192.
3. A. Krishnaswami, *Indian Union and the States,* (London: Pergamon Press Ltd.), 1965, p.30.
4. *C.A.D.* views of K. Santhanam, Vol. III, p. 55.
5. See for details, *Report of the Committee of Financial Experts,* 1947.
6. *C.A.D.*, Vol. VII, p. 336.
7. *C.A.D.*, Vol. XI, p. 734.
8. *Coffee Board vs. C.T.O., A.I.R.*, 1971, S.C. 870.
9. K.V. Rao, *Parliamentary Democracy of India* (Calcutta: World Press), 1965, p. 324.
10. For example Articles, 269, 270, Constitution of India.
11. Under Article, 292, *Ibid.*
12. Article 293 of the Constitution of India.
13. *The Times of India,* New Delhi, 24 July, 1978.
14. *The Hindustan Times,* New Delhi, 12 August, 1978.
15. *The Hindu,* New Delhi, 1 May, 1992.
16. *Ibid.*
17. D.T. Lakdawala "Planning and Centre-State Relations", Seminar Paper, (Bangalore: Economic and Planning Council, Government of Karnataka), 1983, p. 2.
18. D.D. Panigrahi, *Centre-State Financial Relations in India,* (Delhi: Vikas Publishing House), 1985, p. 45.
19. *The Hindu,* New Delhi, 1 June, 1992.
20. *Ibid.*, 24 December, 1991.
21. *Ibid.*
22. *Ibid.*
23. Woodcock, *Kerala: A Portrait of the Malabar Coast,* (London: Faber and Faber), 1967, pp. 299-302.

24. For details see: S.S. Madalgi, "Hunger in Rural India: 1960-61 to 1964-65", *E.P.W*, III (1&2) Annual Number, January 1968, pp. 61-68.
25. K.K., George, "Kerala's Fiscal Crisis: A Diagnosis", *E.P.W.*, September 15, 1990.
26. See: State Plans, *Kerala - State Planning Board,* Government of Kerala, Trivandrum.
27. See: *Reserve Bank of India Bulletin,* State Finances from 1974-88.
28. Government of Kerala, Memorandum Submitted to the Third Finance Commission, 1960.
29. Government of Kerala, Memorandum Submitted to the Fifth Finance Commission, 1965.
30. In an interview with *Blitz,* 1 June, 1985.
31. *Ibid.*
32. E.K. Nayanar in an interview with Mr. Nair for *Hindu*, 1987.
33. *Financial Express,* 30 June, 1987,
34. *The Hindustan Times,* (New Delhi), 25 March, 1988.
35. (i) Nayanar, E.K. "Kerala's Financial Position", *Kerala Calling,* Vol. 8, February, 1988.
    (ii) Nayanar, E.K. "Prejudicial Report of the Ninth Finance Commission", *Kerala Calling,* Vol. 9, November, 1988.
    (iii) Viswanathan Menon, V. "Fiscal Position of Kerala", *Kerala Calling,* Vol. 8 May, 1988.
36. *Deccan Herald* (Bangalore) 29 March, 1988.
37. *The Statesman* (New Delhi) 22 December, 1988
38. *Ibid.*
39. *Source: Kerala Economy in Figures 1987,* State Planning Board.
40. C.P.M. Manifesto, *Seminar,* February 1971, (138) p. 37.
41. *Techno-Economic Survey of U.P.,* National Council of Applied Economic Research, New Delhi, p. 14.
42. *Source:* Based on Plan Documents of U.P.
43. *Draft Fifth Five Year Plan. U.P.* Vol. I, Government of U.P. Planning Department, May 1973, p. 76.
44. Development in U.P: A Supplement to the *Times of India,* September 8, 1965.

45. The percentages for different States have been calculated on the basis of state's income for 1975-76.
46. Lawrence Saez, *Federalism without a Centre: The Impact of Political and Economic Reform in India's Federal System*, New Delhi, Sage, 2002, p. 135.
47. Lloyd I. Rudolph & Susanne H. Rudolph, "The Iconization of Chandrababu: Sharing Sovereignty in India's Federal Market Economy", *Economic and Political Weekly*, May 5, 2001, p. 1546.
48. C.P. Bhambhri, *The Indian State: Fifty Years* (New Delhi: Shipra Publications), 1997, p. 221.
49. P. Jacob, "First Among Equals", *Business Standard*, March 19, 1997.
50. "Mayawati Promises Industry Friendly U.P.", *The Statesman*, May 14, 1997.

Conclusion

Federalism is a necessity for the union of a number of independent States which are not strong enough individually to protect themselves from outside danger and whose union is requisite for their safety and promotion of economic interests, but which are not prepared to surrender their independence completely. India was not an exception to it. In fact, to build a political institution, context play an important role in terms of structure and functioning of an institution.

Federation reflects the nature and extent of relationship between the Centre and States. It is a device for territorial decentralisation and a method of dividing powers so that the Centre and the State Governments operate within their respective spheres sanctioned by the Constitution. In fact, a federation is conceived mainly to maintain a balance between over-centralization and autonomy of states. The identity of States is sanctioned by the supreme law of the land.

India adopted this model with necessary modifications and a tilt towards central hegemony over States, but with a commitment of allowing states to retain and develop their identity as a member of union of States.

On functional level, although the powers are divided between Centre and states, but the pre-dominance of the Centre, indicated by the increasing concentration of power at the central level, and the shrinking base of the States, has led to strains as well as conflicts.

India became independent with the emergence of forces causing threats to its unity and integrity. The Constituent Assembly was preoccupied with the idea of making provisions for a strong Centre. Till 1947, the States were strong with residuary powers, but just after partition, the whole model was changed and Centre was given more powers including residuary powers.

The idea of a federal set up for the whole of India was suggested for the first time by the Simon Commission in 1927. It recommended for strong provinces but not the establishment of an All-India Federation including the Indian states. The provinces were not interested about the federal idea but they agreed for the sake of unity of India. These provinces wanted to maintain their identity and were not ready to compromise on federal finance. Gradually some limitations were imposed on the autonomy of provinces and Centre was made strong, Governor-General was equipped with special responsibilities which could enable him to dominate the provinces. But the princely provinces were willing to accede only limited powers to the Centre. During debates in the Constituent Assembly, before Partition, the Centre had only three powers of Defence, Foreign Affairs and Communications, but just after Partition it was pointed out that now Centre should be strong enough to maintain unity and integrity of the country. So, the outcome of the Constitution was just opposite.

Independent India faced the problem of finding a suitable constitution, and opted for federal arrangement as a feasible mechanism. The pattern introduced by the 1935 Government of India Act continued to remain as the basic framework of the new Constitution.

In a federal political system, Union-State relations are

a significant pointer to the pattern of political processes. This has to be viewed in the context of Parliamentary Democracy wherein ruling parties, at the Centre and in the States are likely to be different. There are evidently two dominant models of Union-State relations in Indian Federal System. First, different parties in power in the Centre and in the States, e.g. Kerala; second, same parties in power at both levels, e.g. Uttar Pradesh. In these two models there is clear understanding of political institutions and behaviour of political actors.

The Congress party was in power at both the levels till 1967 (barring Kerala) due to which there was a tilt towards centralisation. There is a change in the relationship of Centre and States and the Constitution has been worked in a manner contrary to the intentions of the framers. Various conflicts emerged regarding some provisions of the Constitution. For example, the use of Article 356, the role of Governor etc. An analysis of the functioning of Constitution reveals the fact that States are dependent on the Centre in various ways. The Congress has always played an active role in the internal affairs of the same party State. Because of same party rule, there has been a central intervention. All political decisions at the State level are determined by decisions made at the central level. In fact, national party organs had always considered a matter from the national angle and not from the view point of the interest of the concerned State.

While in the case of Kerala, the Centre being geographically remote, also became politically distant and the situation in Kerala is viewed as if from the Himalayan heights removed from the realities of the present.

Actually the framers had viewed the federation in legal and constitutional than in ethnic, linguistic or cultural terms. They relied heavily on the Act of 1935 and thought that problems could be satisfactorily solved within that framework. But in reality, Centre-State relations got under strains on account of not only there being different parties in power but also because of the great deal of infighting and different policy preferences within the major parties. The working of Federation resulted in the growth of centrifugal tendencies, some of which are prominent in all States while some are linked with a particular state only. Again, these trends are assessed within two models i.e. U.P. and Kerala. Although there is a difference in models along with their context, the trends do not show difference in kind but only in degree. The most important and conflicting trend which has been present in India since independence is of centralization. The Centre is grabbing more and more powers at the expense of States. Due to uni-party rule, States had no hesitation in accepting the directions, leadership and authority of the central government. There was a tendency to abdicate even their constitutional authority in favour of the Union. The power of declaring failure of constitutional machinery has been misused by the President on the report of the Governors, who have been giving priority to the interest of the ruling party at the Centre, whenever the ruling party at the Centre felt that it would be in a position to form an alternative ministry either by manoeuvaring defections or otherwise, the Assemblies were suspended, or dissolved.

The Constitution vests complete power with the President for the selection and appointment of Governor, making him a nominee of the central government.

The role of Governor is viewed as a device for an authoritarian Centre to curtail the autonomy of the States, Instead of balancing the pulls and tensions of a federal policy, he is identified as an agent of the Centre, It is a practice that Central Government consults the Chief Minister of the state before announcing the appointment of the Governor. This convention created problems after 1967, when different parties came to power in States. The Centre refused to accept the names given by chief ministers. In states where different party is in power, the Centre control and interfere in State's jurisdiction through governor. The process of consultation was not there in States (e.g. U.P.) ruled by the same party. Another way of controlling the State's affairs is through appointing chief ministers, who were having patronage for the congress leaders at the Centre, Almost all the chief ministers in U.P. since 1950 are nominees of the Centre. These tendencies were not available in states, having different environment.

The balance of federal finance is also tilted in favour of the Centre. The Constitution provides that the Centre can levy taxes on State heads of revenue as well as a surcharge for its own benefit. Even in the obligatory shareable income tax receipts, the actual proportion to be made is left unspecified, leaving it to the Finance Commission to recommend and Parliament to accept while the excise revenue is available to the States only at the discretion of the Centre. These are some of the ways and means through which Centre can enter into the financial structure of the state. This trend is continuing. Kerala has demanded a number of times for redistribution of finances between Centre and states. It has pointed out a step-motherly treatment and said that Centre is not fair to the Left Democratic Front Government. The demand for revision of financial resources from UP. came up after 1967.

The most important is the role of Planning Commission, as extra-constitutional body in the hands of Centre to control State's finances, has also strengthened the trend of centralisation. President Sanjiva Reddy, while delivering the G.B. Pant Memorial Lecture on 7 March 1978, said: "A considerable devolution of authority from the Centre to the States within the Constitutional framework and without endangering the fundamental unity of the country would be necessary if the common man is to play an effective role in national development. Only this policy would put an end to the present centralised system where fewer people tend to take basic decisions and the common man is alienated, and marginalised."

Another trend that has become more perceptible is the

growth of regionalism. It is a product of imbalances in development-social, economic and political. The states reorganisation in 1956 made the states compact and homogenous entities. This naturally led to the growth of a strong sentiment in favour of the rights of the States, the self-consciousness and self-assertion of the regions. Over the years, the sense of regional assertion is noticeable due to a variety of factors. Most important is the unbalanced economic growth of States. Secondly, due to personal and selfish ends of the politicians, regional tendencies are gaining strength. Thirdly, creation of linguistic states has also reinforced regionalism. The trend of regionalism is more manifest in Kerala than in U.P. Kerala was formed as a result of the linguistic assertion, which is a major factor of regionalism. Further due to economic disparity and backwardness, Keralites have become more conscious about their state. It has repeatedly complained about the partisan role of the Finance Commission and the negligence of Centre.

The trend of regionalism in the form of separatist statehood is there in the hill areas of U.P. However this trend is more prevalent in other states despite difference in context.

The trend of regionalism is becoming critical to the future of the country. There is a demand for greater powers on the one hand and growing lawlessness and communal ism on the other. Due to economic imbalances and demand for distributive justice, regional and sub-regional movements have become more manifest.

The trend of communal ism has emerged in both the States. In Kerala, despite being a communist stronghold, communalism has continued to be a major factor in political conflicts. Mobilisation along religious lines became a legitimate part of social and political movements. People are organised on communal lines to protect their interests collectively. An important feature of the Kerala's social structure is that all the major communities have their own powerful organisations to safeguard their interests. We may mention here for example the Nair Service Society, the Sree Narayana Dharma Paripalana Yogam and the Christian Churches. As a result, political party leaders are more loyal to their community. While in U.P. system depends for its functioning on religion and caste. Religion dominates politics very effectively in the State. Hindu-Muslim riots have become a common feature of the State. The controversy over Ram-Janambhurai - Babri Masjid took an ugly turn in December 1992. This bitterness between two communities has continued to be an important trend in U.P. politics.

Besides these factors, the functioning of the federal system in India depends on a number of other factors affecting national political processes. The working of the party system in Kerala reveals that only two political parties, the Congress and the C.P.I. (M) have usually exercised power and C.P.I. (M) has ideologically emerged a more homogenous party. Inspite of multi-party system in Kerala, political defection has not been as rampant as in U.P. The Communist-Congress conflict has taken the form of conflicting relationship between Kerala and the Centre. This has led to much political instability and frequent imposition of President's rule. No other State in India presents such a picture of political confus ion.

U.P. has been a stronghold of the Congress from the very beginning. The constant struggle for power within the Congress has made most state government ministers to be concerned primarily with the question of patronage and political support rather than policy. Most of the times Chief Ministers tried to keep as much power as possible while giving as little as possible to less reliable members. If any prestigious portfolio must be given to a political power, the patronage power is taken away to make the position less dangerous politically. The result is the fragmentation of authority and responsibility and confusion in administration. Factionalism in the Congress and the aggressiveness of opposition parties, both tend to make it difficult for the government to pass desired legislation and to administer efficiently, programmes designed to accelerate economic development.

Communist Party of India is the only serious political force in Kerala inspite of a multi-party system emerged out of the prevailing caste and communal forces. This State presents a different political picture where mutually antagonistic caste, communal and regional groups have been concentrated in separate political parties which are unable to co-operate for long under any condition owing to the fear that one particular group may gain an upper hand and the result is political instability.

No doubt these all factors do effect the political system but it is the strength of the financial resources that paves the way to the success of a government in practice. As finance is the backbone of administration and development, financial dimensions of Centre-State relations acquire integrity of the nation in the face of regionalism and strong disruptive forces that could weaken the nation. So they have deliberately distributed the functions and sources of revenue between the Union and States, in a manner that the Centre has more than it can digest. An analysis of the economic dynamics shows the dependence of the states, giving them a sense of weakness, subservience and subordination. Under the existing constitutional arrangements, there are imbalances and inadequacies giving rise to a sense of demoralisation and frustration among the states. The state governments of non-Congress (I)-ruled parties (Kerala) are particularly seething with discontent. The political leaders of the state are vociferously manifesting their feelings. Further the existing arrangement for the devolution of funds from the Centre to the States is imperfect, ineffective and inadequate.

An economically backward state is a threat to the integrity of a federal structure. The regional assertions asking for more autonomy have been the result of inequitable distribution of economic gains. This is the reason that many of the demands for constituting new States are primarily based on the alleged unfair distribution of developmental benefits and expenditures in the existing states.

Further due to the increasing role of Planning Commission in the allocation of funds, there is a demand to re-define Centre-State relations. The working of Planning Commission has led to the concentration of powers in the Centre far beyond what was envisaged in the Constitution. The Finance Commission was expected to counter-balance the centralising tendencies of the Planning Commission in taking decisions about plan priorities and giving conditional, discretionary and even discriminatory assistance to the States. But the increasing role of planning has reduced the importance of Finance Commission which was considered to be a safeguard against state's economic dependence on the Centre. It has been pointed out many times that Finance Commission's awards are not favourable to Kerala because of the different party rule. While during same party rule, the economic condition is better. However, in U.P. inspite of same party rule since independence, economic condition is deteriorating. The absence of any uniform policy regarding central assistance gives way for central interference. It was also pointed out that Centre would not allow the states (ruled by different parties) to be financially independent for fear of losing its grip on the politics of the State. So a step should be taken to reduce the dependence of States on Centre, and for this adequate finances should be provided to backward states. Financial autonomy of the States is as essential and vital to the preservation of the federation as the maintenance of unity and integrity of the country.

The character of Centre-State relations till 1967 was cooperative. After that it changed into a confrontationist and bargaining model. Now it has become a conflicting model which needs immediate redressals.

This all shows that India's federal polity on the threshold of the final decade of this century, is confronted with problems and challenges which has deep roots and vide ranging implications.

An analysis of functioning in two different dominant models in India reveals the need for proper assessment of context of Indian federation. With each passing year, since India's emergence as an independent sovereign State, the problem of Centre-State relationship has been getting more and more complicated. The socio-economic and political changes in the context that have taken place during the past decades demand that the problem be considered 'de novo' and no longer within the framework of a traditional federal model, as it has ceased to be merely a constitutional problem but has become a political one. Now mere amendments in the Constitution are not required. A proper improvement in the context is needed to avoid frictions and conflicts. We, in this country have been toying for years with ideas on the nature of Centre-State relations and autonomy in political and economic matters inconclusively and without due seriousness, simply drifting along. On the issue of autonomy, it is worthwhile to take the cue from K. Santhanam who said that "the main purpose of the federal system is that when the conditions, the traditions, the circumstances, the climate, the geography differ, there should be state autonomy."

As India is a heterogenous country with so many diversities in culture, language religion etc, a tolerant attitude should be there to accept the problems of the States. Now a prescriptive approach is not needed to solve these various problems, but an accommodative approach is called for an improvement in the context. Actually the States view the Centre as an "alien" power means something which is perceived to be foreign in terms of ethnic and cultural composition. States' culture is being neglected by the Centre which gives them a feeling of not a part of India. For this communication media should be used.

Secondly, economic grievances of the states should be taken seriously and adequate financial assistance should be provided to them. The failure on this front is one of the basic reasons for the development of the trend of regionalism in the country.

Further there should be a drastic reduction in the bloated central bureaucracy coupled with a total shedding of power by the Centre in domains, which belong to the states. The states suffer from the present situation in two ways. First, their initiative is curbed, and in the final analysis they have to pay for the Centre's expenses.

The context of government since the last decade of 20th century has changed not only within India but outside India also and the global changes have a direct impact on the arrangement for governance of the country.

Political institutions are contrived by human beings for certain specific purposes. But they tend to change over time. The change may occur with or without knowledge of the people concerned directly within those institutions. Federalism is one of those political institutions which has fallen prey to those uncertainties, curiosities and idiosyncracies engrossing scholars, statesmen and activists. It is not only undergoing massive transformation but also is currently being made to meet the ends which are usually regarded reverse to its origin growth and sustenance. It started its career to realise democracy freedom and unity with diversity on a larger scale, but now surprisingly almost everywhere it has become a mechanism to constrain them in an increasing manner and trample over the rights of constituent units, even to the extent of posing a threat to individuals, groups and nation. However, there has been a fundamental transformation in the operative principles of Federalism, particularly during the last decade or so. The rhythm and the beat of the political system, and of the federal system within it, has changed on account of a variety of socio-economic and political factors, but primarily because of a disarray of the party system, neo-liberal economic policies and judicial decisions.

To conclude a sincere effort for more participation in the decision-making process should be taken. Over and above, a political will is required, to make the Federation a reality in India.

Select Bibliography

Constituent Assembly Debates, 1946-50, 11 volumes (Government of India Press, New Delhi).

Government of India Act, 1935, (Government of India Press, New Delhi, 1936).

Government of Kerala: *A Statistical Hand Book on Finances of States,* State Planning Board, Trivandrum, 1980.

Government of Kerala: *Economic Review,* various issues, State Planning Board, Trivandrum.

Government of Kerala: *Kerala Calling,* Department of Public Relations, various issues.

Government of Tamil Nadu, *Report of the Centre-State Enquiry Committee,* 1971.

Lok Sabha Debates (Lok Sabha Secretariat; New Delhi).

Memoranda Submitted by Provincial Governments to the Indian Statutory Commission, 1928.

Proceedings of Federal Structure Committee and Minorities Committee, Indian Round Table Conference (Second Session) 1932, 3 volumes.

Proceedings of the Indian Parliamentary Symposium on the Role and Position of Governors and Centre-State Relations, 2-3 May, 1970 (Parliament House, New Delhi, 1970).

Proceedings of Indian Round Table Conference, 12 November 1930-19 January 1931 (1931).

Proceedings of the Plenary Sessions, Indian Round Table Conference (Second Session) 7 September 1931-1 December 1931,

Rajya Sabha Debates (Rajya Sabha Secretariat, New Delhi)

Report on Centre-State Relations, June 1969, Administrative Reforms Commission, (Manager of Publications, New Delhi, 1969).

Report of the Commission on Centre-State Relations, Part I and II (Government of India Press, New Delhi, 1987).

Report of the First Finance Commission, Government of India Press, 1952.

*Report of the Second Finance Com*mission, Government of India Press, 1957.

Report of the Third Finance Commission, Government of India Press, 1962.

Report of the Fourth Finance Commission, Government of India Press, 1965.

Report of the Fifth Finance Commission, Government of India Press, 1969.

Report of the Sixth Finance Commission, Government of India Press, 1973.

Report of the Seventh Finance Commission, Government of India Press, 1979.

Report of the Eighth Finance Commission, Government of India Press, 1984.

Report of the Ninth Finance Commission, Government of India Press, 1989.

Report on Indian Constitutional Reforms (Delhi, 1918).

Report of the Indian States Committee (Delhi, 1929).

Report of the Indian Statutory Commission (Delhi, 1930).

Report of the Nehru Committee (All Parties Conference) (Delhi, 1948).

Report of the Linguistic Provinces Commission (Delhi, 1948).

Report of the States Reorganisation Commission (Delhi, 1955).

Reserve Bank of India, *Reserve Bank of India Bulletins,* Issues from 1956 to 1990.

Sir Maurice Gwyer and Appadorai, A., (Eds.) *Speeches and Documents on the Indian Constitution, 1921-47,* London, 1957.

The First Five Year Plan, Planning Commission (1951).

The Second Five Year Plan, Planning Commission (1956).

The Third Five Year Plan, Planning Commission (1961).

Annual Plans, 1966-67, 1967-68, 1966-69, Planning Commission.

The Fourth Five Year Plan, Planning Commission (1969).

The Fifth Five Year Plan, Planning Commission (1974).

The Sixth Five Year Plan, (1980-85), Planning Commission (1981).

The Seventh Five Year Plan, (1985-90), Planning Commission, (1985).

The White Paper on Indian States (New Delhi: 1950).

Uttar Pradesh, Report on General Administration, 1967-72, 1974 and 1978, (Lucknow): Department of Information.

Views of Indian States on the Government of India Bill (1935) Cmd 4843.

Aiyar, S.P., (1961) *Federalism and Social Change* (Bombay: Asia Publishing House).

________, and Mehta, Usha (eds.), (1965) *Essays on Indian Federalism* (Bombay: Allied Publishers).

Alexandrowicz, C.H., (1951), *Constitutional Development in India* (Bombay: Oxford University Press).

Ambedkar, B.R., (1939), *Federation vs. Freedom* (Bombay: Shree Laxmi Narayan Press).

Austin, Granville, (1966), *The Indian Constitution: Cornerstone of a Nation* (Oxford: Clarendon Press).

Bagchi, A., J.L. Bajaj, William A., Byrd (Eds.) (1992), *State Finances in India* (New Delhi: Vikas Publishing House Pvt. Ltd.),

Bajaj, J.L., K.S. Sinha and O.P. Aggarwal, (1985), *Finance Commission and Backward States* (Lucknow: Print House).

Bakhru, Mira, (1988) *Dynamics of Federal Bargaining*, (New Delhi: Intellectual Publishing House).

Banerjee, Anil Chandra, (1977-78), *The Constitutional History of India: 1919-1977*, Vol. III, (Delhi: Macmillan).

Basu, D.D., (1992) *Introduction to the Constitution of India* (Delhi: Prentice Hall of India).

Bhargava, Madhuri (1976) *Inter-Governmental Financial Relations in India since Independence* (Allahabad: Chaitanya Publishing House).

Bhargava, P.K., (1982) *Centre-State Resource Transfer in India* (Gurgaon: Academic Press).

Bhatnagar, Sudha, (1979) *Union-State Financial Relations and Finance Commissions* (Allahabad: Chugh Publications),

Bombwall, K.R., (1967) *The Foundations of Indian Federalism* (Delhi: Asia Publishing House).

________, (1977) *National Power and State Autonomy* (Meerut: Meenakshi Prakashan).

Bose, T.C., (1987) *Indian Federalism: Problems and Issues* (Calcutta: K.P. Bagchi).

Brass, Paul R., (1984) *Caste Faction and Party in Indian Politics*, vol. 1, (Delhi: Chanakya).

________, (1966) *Factional Politics in an Indian State: The Congress Party in U.P.* (Bombay: Oxford Press).

________, (1975) *Language, Religion and Politics in North India* (Delhi: Vikas Publishing House Pvt. Ltd.).

Chabra, Harinder, K., (1977) *State Politics in India: Study of Centre-State Relations* (Delhi: Surjeet Publications).

Chakraborty, Bidyut (ed.) (1990) *Centre-State Relations in India* (Delhi: Segment Book Distributors).

Chand, Phul, (ed.) (1974) *Federal Financial Relations in India* (New Delhi: The Institute of Constitutional and Parliamentary Studies).

Chanda, Asok, (1965) *Federalism in India: A Study of Union-State Relations* (London: George Allen and Unwin).

Chandra, R.J., (1962) *Fiscal Policies in Underdeveloped Countries* (London: George Allen and Unwin).

Chandra Shekhar, S., (1988) *Indian Federalism and Autonomy* (Delhi: B.R. Publishing Corporation).

Chaturvedi, J.P. (1970) *States of Our Union* (Delhi: Government of India, Ministry of Information and Broadcasting, Publication Division).

Coondoo, R., (1964) *The Division of Powers in the Indian Constitution* (Calcutta: Book Land).

Dahiya, M.S., (1979) *Office of the Governor in India: Critical Commentary* (Delhi: Sundeep Prakashan).

Dar, R.K., (1981) *Recent Developments in Federal Financial Re lations in India,* (Canberra: Centre for Federal Financial Relations, ANU).

Desai, A.R., (1973) *Recent Trends in Indian Nationalism* (Bombay: Popular Prakashan).

Diwan, Paras, (1981) *Union-State Fiscal Relations: An Overview* (New Delhi: Light and Life Publishers).

Dua, B.D. and M.P. Singh (eds) *Indian Federalism in the New Millennium,* New Delhi, Manohar, 2003.

Eldersveld, S.J. (1971) *Political Parties: A Behavioural Analysis,* (Bombay: Vora and Company Publishers).

Fie, Victor M., (1970) *Kerala: Yenan of India,* (Bombay: Nachiketa Publications Ltd.).

Frankel, Francine R., and Zoya Hasan (eds.) *Transforming India: Social and Political Dynamics of Democracy,* New Delhi, Oxford University Press, 2005.

Gadgil, D.R., (1947) *The Federal Problem of India* (Poona: Gokhle Institute of Politics and Economics).

Gehlot, N.S., (1977) *The Indian Office of the Governor—Its Constitutional Image and Reality* (Allahabad: Chugh Publications).

George K.K., (1988) *Centre-State Financial Flows and Inter-state Disparities* (Delhi: Criterion Books).

Grewal, B.S., (1974) *Fiscal Federalism in India* (Canberra: Centre for Research on Federal Financial Relations. The Australian National University).

Ghosh, B.N., (1985) *Political Economy of Neocolonialism in Third World Countries,* (Delhi: Sterling Publishers Pvt. Ltd.),

Gopa Kumar G., (1984) *The Congress Party and State Politics* (New Delhi: Deep and Deep Publications).

Gopalan, A.K., (1959) *Kerala: Past and Present* (London: Lawrence and Wishart).

Govindan Nair, M.N., (1957) *Challenge of Kerala* (Delhi).

Gupta, U.N. (ed.) (1988) *Indian Federalism and Unity of Nation; A Review of Indian Constitutional Experience* (Allahabad: Vohra Publishers).

Haksar, K.M., and Panikkar, K.M., (1930) *Federal India* (London: Martin Hopkinson).

Haqqi, S.A.H. (ed.) (1967): *Union-State Relations in India,* (Meerut, Meenakshi Prakashan).

______, (ed.) (1984) *Democracy, Pluralism and Nation-Building,* (Delhi: N.B.O.).

Hardgrave, R.L. (Jr.) (1979) *Essays in the Political Sociology of South India* (New Delhi: Usha Publications).

Hartmann, Horst, (1971) *Political Parties in India* (Meerut: Meenakshi Prakashan).

Hussain, M.A. (1989) *Socio-Legal Perspective of Centre-State Relations in India* (New Delhi: Deep and Deep Publications).

Jain, R.B., (1976) *The Indian Parliament: Innovations, Reform and Development* (Calcutta: Minerva Associates).

Jain, S.N. and other (eds.) (1972) *The Union and the States* (Delhi: National).

Jennings, Sir Ivor (1953) *Some Characteristics of the Indian Constitution* (London: Oxford University Press).

John P. John, (1983) *Coalition Government in Kerala* (Trivandrum: Institute for the Study of Public Policy and Management).

Johari, J.C. (1977) *Indian Government and Politics* (Delhi: Vishal).

Jose Chander, N., (1981) *The Legislative Process in Kerala* (Trivandrum).

______, (1986) *Dynamics of State Politics: Kerala* (Delhi: Sterling Publishers Pvt. Ltd.).

Kashyap, Subhash C., (ed.) (1972) *Indian Parties and Politics* (New Delhi: Institute of Constitutional and Parliamentary Studies).

______, (ed.) (1969) *Union-State Relations in India* (New Delhi: Institute of Constitutional and Parliamentary Studies).

______, (1971) *Indian Politicl Parties* (Delhi: Research).

Khan, Shafa'at Ahmad (1937) *Indian Federation: An Exposition and Critical Review* (London).

Khan, Rasheeduddin, *Bewildered India: Identity, Pluralism, Discord,* New Delhi: Har Anand Publications, 1994.

Kochanek, S.A. (1968) *The Congress Party of India: The Dynamics of One Party Democracy,* (Princeton: New Jersey).

Koshy, M.J. (1972) *Genesis of Political Consciousness in Kerala* (Trivendrum: Kerala Historical Society).

Kothari, Rajni (ed.) (1967) *Party, System and Election Studies* (Bombay: Allied Publishers).

______, (1972) *Politics in India* (Bombay: Orient Longman).

______, (1989) *Politics and the People: In Search of a Humane India,* (Vol. I & II, New Delhi: Ajanta Publications).

______, (1988) *State Against Democracy: In Search of Humane Governance* (New Delhi: Ajanta Publications).

Krishnamurthy, K.G. and Lakshmana Rao, G., (1968) *Political Preferences in Kerala: An Electoral Analysis of Kerala General Elections, 1957, 1960, 1965 and 1967* (New Delhi: Radha Krishna Prakashan).

Krishnaswami, A., (1965) *The Indian Union and the States: A Study in Anatomy and Integration,* (London: Pergamon Press).

Kumar Pradeep, (1988) *Studies in Indian Federalism,* (New Delhi: Deep and Deep Publications).

Lakdawala, D.T., (1967) *Union-State Financial Relations* (Bombay: Lalwani Publishing House).

Lal, Mukut Behari, (1958) *Indictment of U.P. Government-Praja Socialist Party* (Lucknow: Sardar Press).

Livingston, W.S., (1956) Federalism and the Constitutional Change, (Oxford: Clarendon Press).

Maheshwari, B.L. (ed.) (1973) *Centre-State Relations in the Seventies* (Calcutta: Minerva Associates).

Maheshwari, S.R., (1977) *Presidents' Rule in India* (New Delhi: Macmillan).

______, (1979) *State Government in India* (New Delhi: Macmillan).

______, (1981) *Indian Parliamentary System* (Agra: Lakshmi Narain Aggarwal).

Majeed, Akhtar (ed.) (1984) *Regionalism: Developmental Tensions in India.* (New Delhi: Cosmo Publications).

Mathur, P.L., (1988) *Role of Governor in Non-Congress States* (Jaipur: Rawat Publications).

Mitra, Subrata Kumar, (1978) *Governmental Instability in Indian States* (Ajanta Publications, Delhi).

Mogi, Sobei, (1931) *The Problem of Federalism*, Vol. 1, (London: George Allen and Unwin).

Morris-Jones, W.H., (1974) *Government and Politics in India* (New Delhi: B.I. Publications).

______, (1978) *Politics Mainly Indian* (Bombay: Orient Longman).

Mukharjee, A.B., (1967) *Parliamentary Procedure in India* (Calcutta: O.U.P.).

Namboodiripad, E.M.S., (1968) 2nd edn. *Kerala: Yesterday, Today and Tomorrow* (Calcutta: National Book Agency).

Narain, Iqbal (ed.) (1976) *State Politics in India* (Meerut: Meenakshi Prakashan).

Noorani, A.G., (ed.) (1972) *Centre-State Relations in India* (Bombay: Orient House).

Nossiter, T.J., (1982) *Communism in Kerala* (Delhi: Oxford University Press).

Pal, Chandra (1983) *Centre-State Relations and Cooperative Federalism* (New Delhi: Deep and Deep Publications).

Palmer, Norman D., (1971) *The Indian Political System* (Boston: Houghton Mifflin Co.).

______, (1976) *Elections and Political Development* (New Delhi: Vikas Publishing House).

Pandey, Jawahar Lal, (1982) *State Politics in India* (New Delhi: Uppal Publishing House).

Panvar, R.D., (1980) *Economic Federation* (Delhi: Pragati Publications).

Park, Richard L., and Tinker, Irene (ed.) (1960) *Leadership and Political institutions in India* (Madras: Oxford University Press).

Prakash, Karat, (1973) *Language and Nationality Politics in India* (Bombay: Orient Longman).

Prasad, Anirudh (1981) *Presidential Government or Parliamentary Democracy* (New Delhi: Deep and Deep Publications).

______, (1985) *Centre-State Relations in India: Consti tutional Provisions, Judicial Reviews, Recent Trends* (New Delhi: Deep and Deep Publications).

Pye, Lucian W., and Verba Sidney (ed.) (1965) *Political Culture and Political Development* (New Jersey: Princeton).

Pylee, M.V., (1977) *Constitutional Government in India* (Bombay: Asia Publishing House).

Rajendran, G. , (1974) *The Ezhava Community and Kerala Politics* (Trivandrum: Kerala Academy of Political Science).

Ramakrishnan Nair, (1964) *Constitutional Experiments in Kerala* (Trivandrum: Kerala Academy of Political Science).

______, (1965) *How Communists Came to Power in Kerala* (Trivandrum: Kerala Academy of Political Science).

Rao. , K.V., (1961) *Parliamentary Democracy of India* (Calcutta: The World Press Pvt. Ltd.).

Rao, N.R, (1972) *Union-State Financial Relations in India* (Karnataka University, Dharwar).

Rath, Sharda, (1984) *Federalism Today* (New Delhi: Sterling Publishers).

Ravindran, T.K., (1978) *Institutions and Movements in Kerala History* (Trivandrum).

Ray, Amal, (1979) *Federal Politics and Government* (New Delhi: The Macmillan Company of India Ltd.).

______,(1966) *Inter Governmental Relations in India* (Bombay: Asia Publishing House.

______, (1970), *Tension Areas in India's Federal System* (Calcutta; World Press).

Ray, Bharati, (1967) *Evolution of Federalism in India* (Calcutta: Progressive Publishers).

Reagon, Michael D., (1972) *The New Federalism* (New York: Oxford Press).

Riker, William, H., (1964) *Federalism* (Boston: Little Brown).

Rosen, George, (1966) *Democracy and Economic Change in India* (Bombay: Vora and Co. Publishers Pvt Ltd.).

Roy, N.C. (1962) *Federalism and the Linguistic States* (Calcutta: Firma K.L. Mukhopadhyay).

Roy, Ramashray, (1973) *Uncertain Verdict: A Study of the 1969 Elections in Four States* (New Delhi: Orient Longman).

Sadasivan, Nair, Dr. K., (1984) *Congress and Kerala Politics* (Trivandrum).

Saez Lawrence, *Federalism Without a Centre,* New Delhi, Sage Publication, 2002.

Sahni, N.C. (ed.) (1971) *Coalition Politics in India* (Jullunder: New Academic Publishing House).

Sahni, Sati, (ed.) (1984) *Centre-State Relations* (New Delhi: Vikas Publishing House).

Sampurnanand, (1962) *Memories and Reflections* (Bombay: Asia Publishing House).

Santhanam, K. (1960) *Union-State Relations In India* (Bombay: Asia Publishing House).

Sastry, M.L. and Reddy, G.R., (1988) *Centre-State Financial Relations: A Study in Levels of Development of States* (New Delhi: Concept Publications).

Saxena, K.S., (1985) *Indian Democracy: Recent Trends and Issues* (New Delhi: Anmol Publications).

Sen, Ashok K., (1975) *Role of Governor in the Emerging Pattern of Centre-State Relations in India* (New Delhi: National).

Shankhdher, M.M., (ed.) (1983) *Framework of Indian Politics* (New Delhi: Gitanjali).

Sharma, P.K., (1969) *Political Aspects of States Reorganisation in India* (New Delhi: Mohini Publications).

Sharma, T.R., (ed.) (1986) *New Challenges of Politics in Indian States* (New Delhi: Uppal Publications).

Singhvi, L.M., (ed.) (1972) *Parliament and Administration in India* (New Delhi: Institute of Constitutional and Parliamentary Studies).

Siwach, J.R., (1977) *The Office of the Governor: A Critical Analysis - 1950-73* (New Delhi: Sterling Publishers).

Spann, R.N., (ed.) (1963) *Constitutionalism in India* (Bombay: Asia Publishing House).

Spratt, P. (1970) *D.M.K. in Power* (Bombay: Nachiketa Publications).

Srivastava, Meera, (1980) *Constitutional Crisis in the States in India,* (New Delhi: Concept Publishing Co.).

Subba Rao, K. (1972) *The Indian Federal System* (Madras: Institute for Techno-Economic Studies).

Sukumaran Nayar, Dr. V.K., (ed.) (1969) *Kerala Society and Politics* (Trivandrum).

Suresh, C.P., (1983) *Political Behaviour in Kerala* (Trivandrum: Institute for the Study of Policy and Management).

Thimmaiah,G., (1985) *Burning Issues in Centre-State Financial Relations* (New Delhi: Ashish Publishing House).

Tiwari, Umakant, (1967) *The Making of the Indian Constitution* (Allahabad: Central Book Depot).

Tripathy, R.N. (1982) *Federal Finance and Economic Development in India* (New Delhi: Sterling Publishers).

Veeravaghavachar, S.M., (1969) *Union-State Financial Relations* (New Delhi: Sterling Publishers).

Venkatarangaiya, M. and Shiviah M., (1975) *Indian Federalism* (New Delhi: Arnold-Hinemann).

Verma, Ganeshi Lal (1978) Party Politics in U.P. (Delhi : Sandeep).

Verma, S.L. (1987) *Federal Authority in the Indian Political System* (Jaipur: R.B.S.A. Publishers).

Wallace, Paul (ed.) (1985) *Region and Nation in India* (New Delhi: American Institute).

Weiner, Myron (1957) *Party Politics in India: The Development of a Multiparty System* (New Jeresy: Princeton).

______, (1963) *Political Change in South Asia* (Calcutta: Firma K.L. Mukhopadhyaya).

______, (1963) *The Politics of Scarcity* (Bombay Asia Publishing House).

______, (ed.) (1968) *State Politics in India* (Princeton: Princeton University Press).

Wheare, K.C. (1953) *Federal Government* (London: Oxford University Press).

______, (1971) *Modern Constitutions* (London: Oxford University Press).

Woodcock, (1967) *A Portrait of the Malabar Coast* (London: Faber and Faber).

ARTICLES

Ahmad, Bashirudddin, "Communist and Congress Prospects in Kerala", *Asian Survey,* 6, July, 1966.

______, "Trends and options", *Seminar,* April 1980.

______, "Process of Integration", *Seminar,* August, 1979.

Alexander, K.C., "Emergence of Peasant Organisations in South India", *Economic and Political Weekly,* 28 June 1980.

Ansari, M.M. "A Critique of the developments in Indian Fiscal Federalism", *Margin* 17 (1) October 1984.

______, "At New Delhi's Mercy", *Economic and Political Weekly* 8 (31-33); August 1973.

Azam, Kouser J., "The Indian Muslims: A Quest For Identity", *Indian Journal of Political Science,* July-September 1976.

Bagchi, A.T.K., Sen and V.B. Tulasidhar "Issues before the Ninth Finance Commission", *Economic and Political Weekly,* May 1988.

Bahl, A.K., "Post War Developments in Federalism", *Indian Journal of Political Science,* October-December 1960.

Banerjee, B.K., "Centre-State Relations: A Critique of West Bengal Memorandum", *Mainstream,* 11 March 1978.

Benegal, Sen, "Search For Alternative to Parliamentary Democracy", *Mainstream,* July 1980.

Bhambhri, C.P., "The Limits", *Seminar,* April 1973.

______, "Political Parties and Centre-State Relations in India", in Subhash C. Kashyap (ed.) *Union-State Relations in India* (New Delhi: Institute of Constitutional and Parliamentary Studies) 1969.

______, "Profile of Janata Party leadership in Lok Sabha", *Mainstream,* March 25, 1978.

______, and Verma, P.S., "Social Background of Seventh Lok Sabha" (1980), *Mainstream* 4 July 1981.

______, and ______, "Social Background of Eighth Lok Sabha", (1984), *Mainstream,* August 2, 1986.

Bhaskar, M. "Social Economic and Political Forces of Communalism in Kerala", *Social Action,* July-September, 1987.

Bhattacharya, S., "Federalism and Indian Unity", *Mainstream,* October 20, 1984.

Biju, M.R. and J.N. Pandya, "Democratic Indian Decentralisation in an Indian State: Kerala", *Indian Journal of Political JournalScience,* 52 (3); July-September 1991.

Bombwall, K.R., "The Finance Commission and Union-State Relations in India", *Indian Journal of Public Administration,* April-June, 1964.

Brass, Paul, R., "National Power and Local Politics in India: A twenty Year Perspective", *Modern Asian Studies,* February 18 (i), 1984.

Burman, P.C., "Centre-State Relations", *Janata,* December 15, 1985.

Chandrasekharan, K. "Co-operative Federalism", *Popular Jurist* 5(4) July-August 1988.

Chaube, S.K., "Analysis of the Social Basis of Federalism" *Indian Journal of Political Science,* October-December 1978.

______, "Cultural Frame and the dynamics of Federalism in India", *Social Science Probings,* 1(2), June 1984.

Chelliah, R. "Towards a Decentalised Polity: Outlines of a Proposal", *Mainstream* 29(31) 25 May 1991.

Chopra, Pran, "Political Re-alignment in India", *Pacific Affairs,* Winter 1971-72.

Chopra, S.P. "U.P. Miles to Go", *Eastern Economist,* August 18, 1972.

Chowdhary, D.G., "Non-Congress (I) Chief Minister's Demand more Resources", *New Age* 37(6) February 1989.

______, "Communal Stereotypes in Kerala", *Indian Psychological Review* 34 (3-4) March-April 1989.

______, "Cry of Neglect by the Centre", *Illustrated Weekly of India* 94 (49); December 1973, 94(50)

Dang, S. "Centre and States-Learning From Experience", *Mainstream,* October 22, 1983.

Dange, S.A. 20+5 = ? *Mainstream,* November 20, 1976.

Dharamvira, "Cooperative Federalism", *Seminar,* June 1978.

Douglas, M., "Solid Congress Support in 1967: A Statistical Enquiry", *Asian Survey,* November 1970.

Dua, B.D. and McCormick, P., "The Politics of Federalism: Canada and India" Paper presented at India-Canada Workshop on Federalism, held at Hyderabad, August 1-7, 1981.

Dua, B.D. "Federalism or Patrimonialsm: The Making and unmaking of Chief ministers in India", *Asian Survey* 25 (8); August 1985.

Dutta, Ratna, "The Party Representative in Fourth Lok Sabha", *Economic and Political Weekly,* Annual Number 1969.

Elazar, Daniel J,, "The Ends of Federalism: Noted Towards a Theory of Federal Political Arrangements", Inaugural Address at a seminar held at Chandigarh, January 29-31, 1976.

______, "Economic Backwardness of U.P.", *Indian Journal of Economics* 57, 207, April 1972.

Fadia, B.L., "Selection Of State Governors: An Exploratory Study of the Sarkaria Commission's Recommendations", *Journal of Constitutional and Parliamentary Studies* (1-4) January-December 1988.

______, "Federalism: A Symposium of the Need for a Genuine Federal Polity", *Seminar* (357); May 1989.

Fickett, Lewis P.Jr., "The Politics of Regionalism in India" *Pacific Affairs,* Summer 1971.

Forrester, Duncan B. , "Indian State Ministers and Their Roles", *Asian Survey,* June 1970.

Gann, N., "Conceptualising Indian Federalism: A Matrix of Dynamics of Power: Omnipotence of Centre a myth?" *Indian Journal of Political Science,* 52 (1) January-March, 1991.

George, K.K. and I.S. Gulati "Centre-State Resource Transfers, 1951-84 An appraisal", *Economic and Political Weekly* 20 (7) 16 February 1985.

______ and ______, "Central In-Roads into State: An analysis of Economic Subjects: Services", *Economic and Political Weekly* 20(14) 6 April 1985.

Ghosal, A.K., "Need For a New Look at Centre-State Relations in India after 1967", *Indian Journal of Political Science,* July-September 1969.

______, "Forum: The Role of the State Governors in India" *The Indian Political Science Review,* Vol II, No. 1-2 October 1967.

Ghosh, Arun "Centre-State Economic Relations: A Study", *Monthly Commentary on Indian Economic Conditions,* 30 (4) (352) November 1988.

Goel, M.L., "Social Basis of Party Support and Political Participation in India", *Political Science Review,* January-December 1974.

Gopalkrishnan, P.K., "Centre-State Relations in Finance and Planning" *Mainstream,* 22(46); July 14, 1984.

Gough, Kathleen, "Village Politics in Kerala" I & II, *Economic Weekly* 20 and 27 February 1965.

______, "Kerala Politics and the 1965 Elections", *Journal of Comparative Sociology* 8(1); 1967.

Graham, B.D., "A Report on Some Trends in Indian Elections: The Case of Uttar Pradesh", *Journal of Commonwealth Political Studies,* Vol. 5, No 3, November 1967.

Guhan, S. "Devolution Criteria: From Gamble to Policy", *Economic and Political Weekly* 19 (48) 1 December 1984.

Gulati, I.S., "Indian Federal Fiscal Model: A Case of Increasing Centralisation", *Social Scientist* 16(2) February 1988.

Gupta, U.P. and Misra, S., "Quest For Regional Political Party Structure in Uttar Pradesh", *Indian Journal of Political Science* 49(1) January-March 1988.

Hardgrave, Robert L., Jr. "Caste in Kerala Elections", *Economic Weekly* 17 April, 1965.

______, "Caste in Kerala: A Preface to the Elections", *Economic Weekly,* 21 November, 1964.

Hegde, Ramakrishna "Plea For a United States of India", *Mainstream* 29(32) 1 June, 1991.

______, "State Autonomy", *Seminar* (357) May 1989.

Hill P., "Kerala is Different", *Modern Asian Studies* 20(4); October 1986.

Jain, R.B., "The Federal Polity in India: Some Emerging Concerns" Paper presented at India-Canada workshop on Federalism held at Hyderabad, August 1-7, 1981.

Jain, S.K. "Centre-State Relations: Prospect and Retrospect" *Mainstream* 27(28) 8 April 1989.

John, P. John, "Challenge of Religious Pressure Groups to Indian Political System—A Study with Reference to Kerala", *Indian Journal of Political Science,* 38: 54-63 January-March 1977.

Jose Chander, N., "Factionalism in Kerala Politics", *Journal of Kerala Politics,* 1982.

______, "Agitation cum Administration: The Theory and its Application in Kerala", *Research Review,* 3(1) 86-93, 1984.

Joseph, Benny, "Politics of Communalism: Lessons From Kerala", *Mainstream* 30 (51) 17 October 1992.

Joshi, Ram, and Desai, K.D., "Towards a more Competitive Party System in India", *Asian Survey,* November 1978.

Karunakaran, G.P, "Why Should States Overdraw?", *Yojana* 29(16) 1 September, 1985.

Kashyap, Subhash, C. , "The Politics of Defection: The Changing Contours of the Political Power Structure in State Politics in India", *Asian Survey,* March 1970.

Kaushik, B.K., "Nature of Federal Polity in India", *Kurukshetra University Journal,* (23) 1989.

Kaviraj, Sudipta, "Indira Gandhi and Indian Politics", *Economic and Political Weekly,* Vol. XXI, No. 38 and 39, September 20-27, 1986.

———, "Kerala Economy: A Survey", *Southern Economist* 24 (1) July 1, 1985.

Khan, Rasheeduddin, "Checking the Draft", *Seminar,* September 1969.

———, "National Integration", *Seminar,* April 1970.

———, "Political and Socio-cultural Determinant of Federalism in India", in K.R. Bombwall (ed.) *National Power and State Autonomy* (Meerut: Meenakshi Prakashan), 1978.

———, "Regional Dimension", *Seminar,* April, 1973.

———, "Territorial Reorganisation", *Seminar,* January 1971.

Klatt, Werner, "Caste, Class and Communism in Kerala", *Asian Affairs,* October 1972.

Kochanek, Stanley A., "Political Recruitment in the I.N.C: The Fourth General Elections", *Asian Survey,* May 1967.

Kothari, Rajni, "The Call of the Eighties", *Seminar,* January 1980.

———, "The Congress System in India" in Rajni Kothari (ed.) *Party System and Election Studies* (1967) (Bombay: Allied Publishers).

———, "Democracy without Consensus", *Seminar,* January 1979.

———, "Historic Necessity", *Seminar,* June 1978.

———, "India: The Congress System on Trial", *Asian Survey* February, 1967.

———, "Re-building the State", *Seminar,* January 1981.

———, "Retrospect and Prospect", *Seminar,* April, 1977.

———, "The Non-Party Political Process", *Economic and Political Weekly,* February 4, 1984.

———, "Will the State wither Away", *The Illustrated Weekly of India,* July 8, 1984.

Kumar, Pradeep, "Demand For State Autonomy: A Case Study of West Bengal and Kashmir", *Social Sciences Research Journal,* March 1978.

———, "How a National Party Coalesces with a Regional Party: A Study of Akali-Janata Relations in the 1977-79 Period", *Indian Journal of Politics,* August-December 1980.

———, "Growing Regionalism", *Asian Profile,* August, 1984.

———, "Why is our Constitution Centre-Oriented?", *Journal of Constitutional and Parliamentary Studies,* July-December 1983.

——— and Manas Chakraborty, "People's Participation, Voter's Preference and Electoral Politics—A Study of Kerala, 1957-1980", *Constitutional and Parliamentary Studies* 21 (3-4) July-December, 1987.

Kurup, K.K.N., "Kayyur riot and Communist leadership", *Journal of Kerala Studies,* 9(1-4); March-June, September and December 1982.

Lal, Jai Narain, "Factionalism in the Congress Party: Causes and Consequences", *Indian Journal of Politics,* June 1975.

Lal, M., "India's Heartland—Uttar Pradesh", *Indian and Foreign Review,* volume 9, No 4, 1 December 1971.

Livingston, W.S, "A Note on the nature of Federalism", *Political Science Quarterly,* Volume 67, 1952.

Maheswari, S.R., "Indian Federal System: Distortions and Correctives", Indian Journal of Public Administration, 29 (4), October-December 1983.

Majeed, Akhtar, "Mal-Development and Sub-Regional Tensions", *Indian Journal of Politics,* December 1978.

Mathur, A.B., "State Politics in India: The shape of things to come", *Indian Journal of Political Science,* 48(4); October 1987.

Mathur, G.B., "State Government and Politics of Agitation", *Political Science Review* (1969).

Misra, "New beginnings in U.P. Politics", *Economic and Political Weekly,* 27(3) 18 January 1992.

Mishra, G., "Centre-State Relations and Polls", *Link* 27(19) 16 December 1984.

Morris Jones, W.H. "From Monopoly to Competition in India's Politics", *Asian Review,* November 1967.

"India—More Questions than Answers", *Asian Survey,* 1984.

Mukharji, N., "Democratic Decentralization and System of Governance", *Mainstream,* 27 (33) 13 May 1989.

M.Y. Ghorpade, "A Total Approach to Centre State Financial Relations", *Man and Development,* 7 (1) March 1985.

Namboodiripad, E.M.S., "Centre-State Relations over the Years", *Marxist* 5 (2-3); April-September 1987.

Narain, Iqbal, "Cultural Pluralism, National Integration and Democracy in India", *Asian Survey,* October 1976.

Nayanar, E.K., "One Year of Centre-State Relations", *New Age,* 29 (5) 1 February 1981.

Nigam, "Caste Politics U.P.", *Indian Journal of Politics,* 21 (1-2) March-June, 1987.

Nossiter, T.J., "State-level Politics in India, 1975-77, The Emergency and its Aftermath in Kerala", *Journal of Commonwealth and Comparative Politics,* 16 (1), 1978.

Pal, Chandra, "Union—State Fiscal Relations", *Journal of Comparative and Political Studies,* July-December 1983.

———, "Greater Fiscal Autonomy : A Justified demand of States, Cochin University", *Law Review,* 7 (3) September 1983.

Pande, G.C., "U.P. : A Profile of Economic Retardation", *Radical Humanist* 38(7); October 1974.

Paranjape, H.K., "Planning Commission As a Constitutional Body", *Economic and Political Weekly,* November 10, 1990.

———, "A note on Centre-State Relations", *Mainstream,* January 11, 1986.

Pillai, K.R., "Politics of Kerala", *Indian Journal of Political Science* 48(4); October-December 1987.

Pinto, M.R., "Sharing the Financial Cake", *Freedom First* (389) April 1986.

Pylee, M.V., "Centre-State Financial Relations in India", Paper Presented at India-Canada Workshop on Federalism held at Hyderabad, August 1-7, 1981.

Quraishi, Z.M., "Socio-Economic Determinants of Federalism", Paper Presented at a Seminar held at Chandigarh, January 29-31, 1976.

Radhakrishnan, V., "Centre-State Relations: Constitutional Amendment Needed", *Popular Jurist,* 5(4) July-August, 1988.

Raipura, Kalyan, "Financial Transfers to States: Issues and Outlook", *Economic and Political Weekly* 27(49-50); 5-12 December, 1992.

Raj, K.N., "Centre-State Relations: Kerala's Problems in the National Context", *Mainstream*, 23 (46) 13 July 1985.

Rao, K.V., "Centre-State Relations in Theory and Practice", *Indian Journal of Political Science*, Vol. XIV, No. 4, October-December, 1953.

Rao, M.G., and R.J., Chelliah, "Survey of Research on Fiscal Federalism in India", *NIPFP*, New Delhi, 1991.

——— and Vandana Aggarwal, "Central Transfers to Offset Fiscal Disadvantages of the States: Measurement of Cost Disabilities and Expenditure Needs", *Indian Economic Review*, Vol. XXVI, No. 1, 1991.

Rath, Sharda, "Federalism: A Conceptual Analysis", *Indian Journal of Political Science*, October-December 1978.

Ray, Amal, "Party Politics", *Seminar*, (357) May 1989.

———, "New Economic Policy and Indian Federalism", *Economic and Political Weekly*, 27 (4); 25 January 1992.

Ray, Rabi "Towards a Responsive Centre-State Relations", *Link*, March 15, 1992,

Ray, S.R., "Nature and Working of the Federalising Process in India 1947-1970", *Socialist Perspective*, 14(1-2) July-September 1986.

Retzlaff, Ralph H., "The Problem of Communal Minorities in the Drafting of the Indian Constitution", in R.N. Spann (ed.) *Constitutionalism in India* (1963) (Bombay: Asia Publishing House).

Sandilya, T.K., "Centre-State Financial Relations in India", *Southern Economist*, 30 (17); January 1992.

Sankhder, M.M., and Permanand, "Lok Sabha Election: 1980—A Case Study of U.P.", *Indian Political Science Review*, Vol. XIV, No. 2, July 1980.

Sarkaria Commission's "Recommendations: A Critical Evaluation", *Man and Development*, 10 (4); December 1988.

Sathyamurthy, T.V., "Impact of Centre-State Relations on Indian Politics", *Economic and Political Weekly,* September 23, 1989.

Sen, R.N., "Heartland and Borderland", *Economic and Political Weekly,* 26(20), 18 May 1991.

Sharma, P.N., "Regional Planning in U.P.", *Eastern Economist,* 60(5) February 2, 1973.

Singh, "Decentralised Planning in U.P.", *Indian Journal of Regional Science,* 19(1), 1987.

Singh L.S. and Nand Kumar, U.K., "Restructuring Indian Federalism with Special Reference to Article 356", *U.P. Journal of Political Science,* 2 (2); July-December 1990.

Singh L.R. and R.P. Srivastava "Centre-State Relations in India: A Geopolitical Perspective", *Natural Geographer* 24(1) July 1989.

Singh, M.P., "Social Structure Processes and Party System in India", *Indian Political Science Review,* July 1980,

Siwach, J.R., "Financial Autonomy: A Justified Demand of States", *Indian Journal of Political Studies,* January 1980.

Srinivasan, G., "Yes, This abolition was overdue", *Yojana* 29(16) 1 September, 1985.

Srinivasan, R., "Tamil Regionalism", *Seminar,* April, 1978.

Srinivasavaradan, T.C.A., "Federal Management", *Journal of the Indian Law Institute,* 28(2), April-June 1986.

Srivastava, M., "Transfer of Resources from the Centre to the States and Correction of Regional imbalance in India", *BHU Journal of Social Sciences* 3(4), 1982-83,

Sukumaran Nayar, V.K., "Communal Interest Groups in Kerala", Donald Eugene Smith (ed.) (1966) *South Asian Politics and Religion,* Princeton University Press, Princeton.

Swarup, S., "Political Mobilisation and Pressures on Federalism", Paper Presented at India-Canada Workshop on Federalism held at Hyderabad, August,

1-7, 1981,

"U.P.: Mobilisation of Resources and Development," *Socialist India*, December 28, 1974,

Valacherry, J., "Communal Conflict between Christians and Muslims in Kerala", *Social Action* 33(4) October-December 1983.

Verney, D.V., "Resisting Federalism", *Seminar*, (357) May 1989.

Visalakshi, N.R., "President's Rule in Kerala", *Indian Journal of Political Science*, 27 (1-2): 1966.

Vithal, B.P.R. and Shastri, M.L., "Terms of Reference of Ninth Finance Commission: Some Preliminary Comments", *Economic and Political Weekly*, July 25, 1987.

Weiner, Myron, "The 1971 Elections and the Indian Party System", *Asian Survey*, December 1971.

NEWSPAPERS

Indian Express (New Delhi)

National Herald (Lucknow)

Pioneer (Lucknow)

The Hindu (Madras)

The Hindustan Times (New Delhi)

The Statesman (Calcutta)

The Times of India (Bombay)

PERIODICALS

Asian Profile

Asian Recorder

Asian Survey

Commerce

Economic and Political Weekly

Indian Journal of Politics

Indian Journal of Political Science
Indian Journal of Political Studies
Indian Journal of Public Administration
Journal of Commonwealth and Comparative Politics
Journal of Constitutional and Parliamentary Studies
Keesings Contemporary Archives
Link
Mainstream
Man and Development
Marxist
Modern Asian Studies
Pacific Affairs
Political Science Quarterly
Political Science Review
Radical Humanist
Seminar
Social Action
Socialist India
Southern Economist
The Illustrated Weekly of India
Yojana

Index